GCSE DESIGN AND TECHNOLOGY

Textiles Technology

Alison Bartle & Bernie O'Connor

CPL

Bernie and Alison would like to thank friends and family for all their support and encouragement during the writing and production of this book. Bernie and Alison are both Design and Technology teachers who work at Park High School in Harrow.

Cover and page design   Caroline Waring-Collins (Waring Collins Partnership)
Cover photograph   Eye of Science/Science Photo Library

The cover photograph shows an electron micrograph of nylon hooks and loops in Velcro material. Magnification: x15 at 6x6cm size.

Original graphics   Elaine Sumner (Waring Collins Partnership)
Original artwork (Unit 3)   Norrie Beswick-Calvert
Original photographs   Steve Lancaster
Educational consultant   Alan Mawson
Reader   Annemarie Work
Editor   Steve Lancaster

Acknowledgements
The authors and publishers would like to thank the following for their help in the production of this book: Albright and Wilson Ltd; Anti-Slavery International; James Bailey (Engineers) Ltd; Berghaus; Bernina; Biotex; Bonas Machine Company Ltd; Brintons Ltd; British Wool Marketing Board (BWMB); J.B. Broadley; Emma Broster; Brother; Camber International Ltd; Carrington Career and Workwear; Chicco; Christian Aid; Coats Viyella; Cobra Seats; Courtaulds Fibres; Craghoppers; Creda; Debenhams; Chris Dee & family; Crombie; DuPont; Dylon International; Jo Edwards; Ethical Consumer; David Evans; Fairchild Company; Fashion Services for People with Disabilities; Judith Goldson; Greenwoods (Mens Wear) Ltd, Ormskirk; Harris Tweed Authority; Claire Heyes; Hotpoint; International Institute for Cotton (IIC); International Wool Secretariat (IWS); Irish Linen Guild; Paul Jones, The Standish Company; Debbie Knight, Dukes Theatre; Lands' End Direct Merchants UK; Macpherson Ltd; Maureen's Fabrics, Ormskirk; Monk Cotton Group; Readicut International; Oasis; Oxfam; Philips; Riccar; Selectus Ltd; Neville Shulton, Classic Lace; Simplicity Ltd; Speedo; Testrite; Tomy; Trumeter Co Ltd; Vango; Zanussi.

Picture credits
Albright and Wilson Ltd 125; James Bailey (Engineers) Ltd 101; Bartle/O'Connor 46; Berghaus 44, 115; Bernina 92br; Biotex 48; Norrie Beswick-Calvert 10t & bl, 11t & l, 12tl & tr; Bonas 109b; Brintons Ltd 130, 131; J.B. Broadley 63; Emma Broster 78, 79; BWMB 38b, 96; Brother 92t, 93t, 140; Camber 96b, 98t, 108; Christian Aid 141; Coats Viyella 54b; Cobra Seats 106b; Courtaulds Fibres 3t, 4br; Craghoppers 118; Creda 103bm, 116br; Crombie 126br; Debenhams 21l & b, 107t; DuPont 36, 37; Dylon International 68, 69; Jo Edwards 51; Fairchild Company 107b; Harris Tweed Authority 50; IIC 31t; 32, 41mr, 70tl & b, 132b, 137bl; Hotpoint 116bl; Image Bank 4t, 6t, 14t, 30t, 42, 43, 56br, 74bl, 121t, 122; Irish Linen Guild 31b; Irish Linen Guild/CELC 31m; IWS 28; Loughborough University (Dept of Design & Technology) 12; Macpherson Ltd 99; Monk Cotton Group 97, 103t; Oasis 128 b; Oxfam 134; Philips 90tl; Readicut International 126t; Rex Features 10br, 15tl & b, 22, 24b & t2&3; 25; 26t, bl & bm, 113; Riccar 92bl; Science Photo Library 34, 61b, 62; Selectus Ltd 57; Simplicity 41ml, 56bl, 75blmr, 84br, 88, 119; Singer 92bm; Speedo 16; Tefal 90tr, 94; Testrite 14, 117; Tomy 22tl; Trumeter Co Ltd 98; Vango 53bl & br, 56bm, 60tm; Mary Walton 41b, 106; Webb Ivory 20; Zanussi 116bm

Every effort has been made to locate the copyright owners of material used in this book. Any errors or omissions brought to our attention are regretted and will be credited in subsequent printings.

Causeway Press Limited
PO Box 13, Ormskirk, L39 5HP

© Alison Bartle and Bernie O'Connor, 1997
1st impression 1997
Reprinted 1998

British Library Cataloguing in Publication Data
A catalogue record for this book is available from the British Library

ISBN 1-873929-65-X

Origination and layout by John Collins, Caroline Waring-Collins and Elaine Sumner (Waring Collins Partnership), Ormskirk, Lancashire

Printed and bound by Jarrold Book Printing Limited, Thetford, Norfolk

Contents

1 What are textiles?

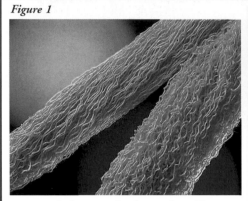

Figure 1

A magnified image of polypropylene fibres used for carpets

A woven piece of fabric

What are textiles?

The word TEXTILES comes from the Latin word 'texere' which means 'to weave'. Textiles are made from FIBRES (fine, hair-like structures). Fibres can be made into fabrics in a variety of ways, not just weaving. Fibres can be spun into yarn, then woven or knitted into fabrics, or the fibres can be made into fabrics without being first spun.

Textiles in various forms have been used for many hundreds of years. The development of technology over the past 100 years, however, has meant that the type of fibres used and the way in which they are joined together has changed significantly.

Most textile items can be broken down into three elements:

● fibres - the raw materials used in textiles

● YARNS- the threads that fibres are twisted or spun into

● FABRIC - the material which is made by joining together pieces of yarn.

Fabrics are generally pieces of two-dimensional, flexible material. Some textile items, however, are not two-dimensional. For example, the felt used on piano hammers or for a hat is made in a three-dimensional form.

Most textile items are made from fabric.

The fibres used to make the fabric and the methods used to construct it affect the properties of the fabric and therefore affect what it can be used for (see Unit 8). The appearance, texture and density of fabrics vary a great deal. Indeed, different fabrics have few characteristics in common.

Textiles have a very wide range of applications. Within minutes of being born, our skin comes into contact with textiles and for the rest of our lives there are few occasions when it is not. Textiles play an important part in life at home. Not only is the textiles industry an important industry in its own right, textile items are also used in many other industries.

Clothing

When people think of textiles, the most obvious starting point is to think of clothing. People have worn clothing since prehistoric times. As a result, the range of styles of clothing and the techniques used to make it are immense. Clothing has many functions. For example:

● it keeps people warm

● it provides protection

● it adds comfort.

Clothing can also serve less practical purposes:

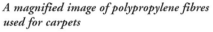

activities

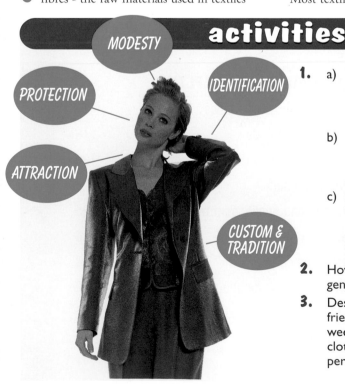

MODESTY

PROTECTION

IDENTIFICATION

ATTRACTION

CUSTOM & TRADITION

1. a) Give TWO different examples of clothing that is worn for each of the reasons suggested left.

b) For each of your examples, explain how the piece of clothing achieves that particular purpose.

c) Are there any other functions that each of your chosen items of clothing performs? Explain what the functions are and how they are performed.

2. How do culture, religion and gender affect what people wear?

3. Describe the clothing that a friend or relative wears at the weekend and explain what the clothing tells you about their personality.

- it can be used to tell us something about people's personalities or their jobs
- it may be used to make people look attractive
- it may tell us something about a custom or a tradition.

Throughout history, the reasons for wearing particular types of clothes have changed. For example, in the 19th century modesty was considered to be a very important function of clothing for middle and upper class women. As a result, middle class women wore clothing which covered up their bodies with not even their ankles being visible. Today, however, in the Western world modesty is less important and it is common for middle class women to wear skirts which reveal their legs and ankles.

Fashion

Fashion has a strong influence over what people wear. In the past, only the rich could afford to be fashionable. Now, however, almost everyone has access to fashionable clothing because of cheaper

Figure 2 The denim above is made from Tencel fibre. Tencel is a new fibre. The first range of fashion garments in Tencel was launched in 1992.

fabrics, faster and cheaper production techniques and a highly developed communication system. Since most people have leisure time, they have time to keep up with fashions and wear what is fashionable, if they so choose. Today, the fashion industry is a vast, highly competitive industry which employs many people - from people who work on the production of fibres to people who sell the finished garments.

Workwear

There are some jobs which require people to wear a uniform - for example,

working as a nurse or a police officer. A uniform is worn for safety, health and identity. Members of the armed forces, police and emergency services and people working in hazardous environments require clothing which protects them but does not impede movement. There are also some jobs which do not have a set uniform but which still require certain types of clothing to be worn - for example, a car mechanic might be required to wear tough overalls whilst somebody working in a shop will be required to look neat and tidy.

Textiles used in the home

Textiles are widely used in the home. They have two main functions:
- decoration
- protection.

Very often textiles in the home are used for both decoration and protection.

Soft furnishings

The term used to describe textiles which make our homes more attractive and comfortable is SOFT FURNISHINGS. Soft furnishings often provide both decoration and protection. Soft furnishings include:
- curtains
- carpets
- cushions
- upholstery.

Like clothing, soft furnishings are chosen for a number of reasons. The way in which a house is decorated says a great deal about the people who live in it. Soft furnishings, therefore, reflect people's personalities, opinions and taste. Often, homes reflect current fashions. For example, the soft furnishings in one house might reflect current fashion and style with less emphasis on comfort, whilst the soft furnishings in another might place an emphasis on comfort and durability and make few concessions to current fashions.

Soft furnishings are not just important in

activities

1. Make a list of all the textile items in the photo above, saying whether each item is decorative, functional or both.
2. How might the use of textiles reflect the personality of the person who decorated the room?
3. Textiles are used extensively in the home. Give TWO examples of: (i) protective textile items; (ii) decorative textile items; (iii) textile items used for comfort; (iv) textile items used for insulation.

homes. They are important in any building and most modes of transport. For example, public buildings, the workplace, aeroplanes, trains and cars are places where consideration is given to how fabrics can be used to make the environment more comfortable and pleasant.

Functional textiles

Some textile items used in the home are acquired primarily because they have a functional purpose. For example, towels and tea-towels may have a decorative function, but their main purpose is to absorb water. Oven gloves may be decorated, but their main purpose is to allow people to pick up hot pans and dishes. Around pipes and hot water tanks and in the roof, lagging (often made of fibres) is used as insulation to reduce heat loss. As well as being decorative, curtains shut out the light and help to reduce heat loss through windows.

Other uses of textiles

Textiles are not just used for clothing and in the home, they are also used in less obvious ways.

The industrial use of textiles

Textiles are used as components in machinery and engines. They are used as filters, ropes, nets, supports, insulating material and for strengthening other materials (eg car tyres). In the building industry, textiles are made into tarpaulins and roofing felt. The use of dangerous chemicals in some industries necessitates highly specialised protective clothing - which is made from textiles. In civil engineering, textiles are used for railway track, road, dam and embankment reinforcement. In the aircraft industry, textile fibres are used as components for aircraft machinery, as soft furnishings in the interior of aircraft and for aircraft escape shutes.

The medical use of textiles

Textiles play an important part in the work done in hospitals and GPs' surgeries. Textiles are used as orthopaedic supports. They can be found in First Aid kits - they are used as dressings, bandages and wipes. Textiles are also used in surgery and as components for replacement joints and arteries. They are used

Figure 3 A hot air balloon

for sutures (stitches), surgical gowns, sanitary products, stretchers, dialysis and filter units.

Transport

Fabrics are used to make seat belts and air bags in cars. Car seats are covered in fabric and the floors of cars are carpeted. Air and oil filters are made of textiles. Fabric is used to

Figure 4

Netting and ropes are textile items.

This car hood is made from acrylic. The tyres are reinforced with fabric inside the rubber.

make sails for boats and hang gliders. Hot air balloons and parachutes are made of fabric.

Leisure

Increased leisure time means that people have more time to spend on travel and sport. Textile technology ensures that luggage is lightweight and lacks bulk. It also ensures that clothing appropriate for different weather conditions is available and that specialised clothing can be made. Also, equipment for sporting activities, synthetic turf, snooker table cloth, strings for musical instruments, bouncy castles and artificial ski slopes are all made of textiles.

Agriculture

Farmers and market gardeners have long used twine and netting. In recent years, however, other textiles have been used in new ways. For example, rockwool (mineral fibre) is used as a growing medium for some vegetable crops which are cultivated in glasshouses.

Figure 5   Computers play an increasingly important part in the textiles industry.

Rockwool reduces the risk of infection that is present when soil is used. Also, mats are sometimes used instead of straw for cattle kept indoors. This ensures that higher standards of hygiene are possible. Textiles are also used to make fences and wind-breaks.

New technology

Technological developments mean that the uses and applications of textiles are constantly changing. Over the last 30 years, synthetic fibre, have been discovered and developed. As a result, many new fabrics with new properties have become available. Technological developments also mean that textiles can be used in new areas, often replacing other materials. In addition, technology has ensured that the equipment used to make fibres, yarns and fabrics has been improved.

The creative use of textiles

Fibres, yarns and fabrics have long been used to make purely decorative items. For example, a popular method of decorating the homes of the aristocracy in the 18th century was to hang large tapestries (pieces of cloth upon which a scene or pattern is sewn using embroidery stitches). Some people still hang textiles on their walls today. Like other artists' materials, textiles can be used creatively in many ways. Fabric can be printed, painted or dyed (see Unit 13). It can be embroidered, sewn into patchwork or made into a collage. Some artists work entirely with textiles. Many people spend their leisure time using textiles creatively.

activities

1. a) Make a list of all the textile items in the photo above, saying whether each item is decorative, functional or both.
    b) What other textile items might you find in a car?
2. Draw a spider diagram which shows all the different ways that textile items can be used. Place 'TEXTILES' in a box at the centre of the page and draw branches and sub-branches showing the different applications.
3. 'The textile industry is huge and very important.' Explain this statement using the information in this unit.

Key Terms

Textiles - objects made of material which contains fibres.
Fibres - fine, hair-like structures.
Yarns - the threads that fibres are twisted or spun into.
Fabric - the material which is made by joining together pieces of yarn.
Soft furnishings - textiles which are used to make a home more attractive and comfortable.

Identifying a problem

Every day we come into contact with and use a wide variety of textile items. For example, the bed we sleep in, the clothes we wear and even the transport we use - all contain or are made of textile products. Every year thousands of new textile products come onto the market. Some are brand new ideas. Others are existing products which have been redesigned. So, where do the ideas for new products come from? And, what criteria do companies use when redesigning products?

An idea for a textile product may develop in a number of ways. Results from experiments and research in a research and development laboratory may, for example, lead to the design of a new fibre or fabric (see Figure 1). Research into consumer need may result in a new design for a swimsuit that reduces water resistance. Occasionally, a designer's flash of inspiration may be the start of a new or re-designed product - as was the case with Velcro (a means of fastening fabric).

Much of the time, a design idea is a solution to a particular problem (see Figure 2). It is the problem that is the real starting point. The problem must therefore be identified. For example, mountain climbers need to carry specific equipment and supplies and yet they also need to be able to keep their hands free to climb. A rucksack designed to allow easy access to the equipment and supplies may solve this problem. Similarly, skiers need outfits which keep the body warm and yet allow them easy movement. Designing a ski suit in a warm but flexible fabric may solve this problem.

Figure 1 A gymnast wearing a leotard which contains a new fibre - LYCRA®

Solving problems like these will satisfy people's NEEDS. Situations occur that provide OPPORTUNITIES to design new products. Often, a range of products already on the market does not satisfy the needs of all customers. For example, snowboarders need clothing which not only combats low temperatures (like ski outfits), but also offers protection against frequent snow abrasion. To meet this need, two design opportunities present themselves. First, it may be necessary to design a completely new product (clothing specially designed for snowboarders). And second, an existing product could be redesigned to meet a new need (kneepads and elbow pads might be added

Children find long journeys boring and need a variety of games and activities to keep them occupied. These items need to be easily accessible. Halfords produce a range of car accessories. They have designed a range of products which enable a variety of items to be stored in a neat and safe way. The car holdall is designed to hang on the back of the seat and has a variety of pockets and compartments.
Source: Halfords, 1996

1. What is a car holdall?
2. What problems were identified which this design was created to solve?
3. Write a short design brief for the car holdall.
4. Suggest TWO other situations in which a similar design would be useful.

Figure 2 Products designed to be a solution to a problem

1. Oven gloves designed to protect hands when handling hot food containers.

2. A jewellery roll designed to hold jewellery safely in a light portable container.

3. A mobile phone case designed to protect the phone from damage and allow it to be clipped to a belt.

to an existing snow suit, for example).

As new materials are developed, opportunities are created that allow designers to look at the problem in a different way. For example, new fabrics such as LYCRA® allow clothing designs that stretch over the contours of the body and allow the garment to be stretched but then to return to its original shape (see Figure 1).

The design brief

When a problem has been identified and discussed in detail, it is then presented as a DESIGN BRIEF. Research and development can then begin. The brief is written as a short statement of intent (see Figure 3). Each aspect of the brief can be researched in detail. The purpose of research is to gather as much information about the problem as possible. This includes information about similar products, consumer or expert opinion, the working properties of material and current trends and fashions.

Information can be collected in a number of ways and from a variety of sources including:

● surveys/questionnaires given to consumers or experts
● research of similar products
● letters to/interviews with experts
● investigations of materials or products using models and prototypes
● photographs/video evidence
● written research from books, magazines or journals
● observation of events
● information from the World Wide Web on the Internet.

Having collected all this information, analysis must take place. Summaries need to be made of interviews to show opinions. Conclusions can be drawn from specific investigations. Surveys and questionnaires may reveal the most popular solutions. The information and data can then be presented in a variety of ways:

● graphs (including computer-aided examples)
● spreadsheets

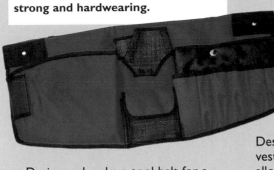

Figure 3 Examples of design briefs

Carpenters need to carry the tools they use regularly. A belt with separate sections would enable them to carry and use their tools safely and easily. The material used to make the belt would have to be strong and hardwearing.

Design and make a tool belt for a carpenter which is hardwearing.

Babies need clothing that is comfortable, can be easily washed and allows easy access for changing.

Design and make a vest for babies which allows easy changing and which can cope with frequent washing.

● tables
● charts
● written paragraphs
● pictures and photographs.

The design specification

Having collected and analysed a variety of information, a decision can then be made about whether the problem is worth pursuing to a final solution.

Collectively, the research should point to exactly what is needed for many of the component parts of the product. This is called the SPECIFICATION. The specification is likely to show the manufacturer:

● what types of materials are preferred
● the function of the product
● maximum/minimum dimensions
● general shape/form of the product
● special considerations or constraints required by the customer
● likely costs.

activities

1. Write a letter to a playgroup leader asking what activities children aged three should take part in and what toys made of textiles children aged three like to play with.

2. Devise a questionnaire for parents which is designed to find out what factors they consider when buying a toy.

3. Write (i) a design brief and (ii) a design specification which might have been drawn up when the educational toy (right) was being designed.

Generating ideas

The design brief and specification provide the information needed to begin designing. Some designers specialise in designing one particular product or system. For example, Philip Treacy is a millinery (hat) designer. He only designs hats. Other designers use their skills on a range of products. For example, Wayne Hemmingway of Red or Dead creates a whole range of clothing known as 'street fashion'.

Large firms may employ a number of designers on a full-time basis or they may call in a freelance or product designer when they need help with a particular project or product.

Designers come to the table with more than one idea in mind. It is important to present different ideas in order to consider as many solutions as possible. A designer may come up with totally new designs, interesting variations or INNOVATIONS on an original design. A number of strategies can be used to help generate ideas.

ATTRIBUTE ANALYSIS is a technique often used by designers to produce new designs for familiar objects. The designer examines an existing product and lists its attributes. These are then changed in keeping with the design brief or specification (see activities on page 9).

History and culture

By studying how similar design problems were tackled in the past or are dealt with by different cultures, design ideas can be generated - for example, ideas about how natural products were used to create dyes for clothes.

Lateral thinking

To come up with completely original ideas is very difficult. Completely new ideas are

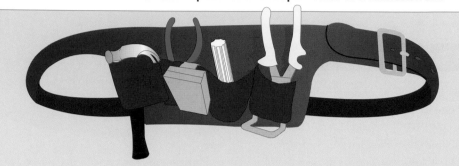

Figure 4 Part of a design specification for a tool belt

Materials - Nylon, Velcro, nylon thread, metal rivets.

Function - To hold safely a hammer, chisel, measuring tape and craft knife. To fit around the waist comfortably. To provide easy access to tools.

Dimensions - To fit waist sizes 76-102cm. Tape measure pouch - 10cm x 10cm. Hammer loop - 7cm. Chisel pouch - 16cm x 6cm. Craft knife pouch - 16cm x 7cm.

Other considerations - Position of pouches and loops. Points of weakness/wear.

activities

Moore's Interiors is a family run business based in Harrow, near London. The business produces customised home furnishings. It specialises in the upholstery of chairs and sofas. The showroom boasts a huge range of fabric sample books from fabric designers and manufacturers. The store also has photos and catalogues which help the customer to decide on style and fabric. Alternatively, a visit from an interior designer can be arranged. Trained fitters are then dispatched to the customer's home to take measurements and to complete a detailed specification sheet (see right). This sheet is then passed to the factory and the product is made accordingly.

Source: Interview with staff at Moore's Interiors, November 1996

1. Explain how the staff at Moore's Interiors obtain information about:
   a) new designs
   b) customers' requirements.

2. The specification sheet (right) was drawn up for a customer who wanted a two seater sofa to be reupholstered. Using the same format as that in Figure 4, draw up a design specification.

3. Suppose you had designed an article of clothing you are wearing today. Draw up a design specification for this article of clothing.

MOORE'S INTERIORS Specification Sheet   ESTIMATE NO. 2503

TO REMOVE EXISTING FABRIC	✓ SUPPLY PLATFORM LINING UNDER CUSHIONS
TO STYLE AS NEAR TO EXISTING	✓ SUPPLY ARM COVERS FULL LENGTH (PIPED)
SUPPLY HR 40 FR SEAT CUSHIONS	BOOST UP CUSHIONS
DACRON WRAPPED AND MUSLIN LINED	SUPPLY NEW CASTORS
CHECK FRAMES, PADDING, SPRINGING	✓ MAKE BACK CUSHIONS REVERSABLE
REPAIR FRAMES, PADDING, SPRINGING	MAKE SEAT CUSHIONS REVERSABLE
SUPPLY NEW WEBBING TO SEATS/BACKS	SUPPLY ARM CAPS (PIPED) ✓
SUPPLY FRINGE TO MATCH	PAD UP HARD EDGES ON ARMS
SUPPLY BRAID TO MATCH	✓ STAIN WOODWORK NOT POLISHING NO CHARGE
SUPPLY RUCHE TO MATCH	SUPPLY SKIRT BUCKRUM STIFFENED
SUPPLY NEW BUTTONS	✓ SCOTCHGUARD FABRIC 5 YEAR WARRANTY ✓
SUPPLY ZIPS TO CUSHIONS	EXISTING FABRIC CANNOT BE MATCHED
PIPE ARMS, CUSHIONS, BACKS	✓ PATTERN MATCH CUSHIONS ONLY
ALL EXTRA PADDING USED WILL BE FIRE	AND FRONT BORDERS
RETARDANT. PLEATING ETC. MAY COME UP	FABRIC ON BASES AS ORIGINALLY DESIGNED WILL
SLIGHTLY BIGGER DUE TO THICKER FABRIC	BE RANDOM CUT
FABRIC	COLLECTION DATE
METREAGE	COLLECTION TO BE ARRANGED ✓
ORDER MATERIAL	CAROL BOOK IN
CUTTING	

FURNITURE *2 Seater Sofa*
NAME *Ms. J. Hardy*
ADDRESS *122 Willow Tree Road Harrow*
TELEPHONE NUMBER *0181 9071569*

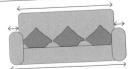

called INVENTIONS. One way of looking for new products is to examine existing problems or products from a different perspective. For example, clothing is usually designed for humans, but what if it was designed for animals? This way of looking at things from peculiar angles is called 'lateral thinking' and was developed by an American called Edward De Bono.

Considering all features

Designs have many different features. Each feature can be identified by making a list or labelling a sketch. Then, one or more of the features can be changed to suit a specific consumer. Changing a design to suit different needs is called 'adapting'. For example, a collection of clothes may be adapted to fit very small or very tall people.

Many products are designed for a particular use. But existing products can have alternative uses. For example, a rug might be used as a wall hanging. Using a product in a new way can lead to the development of a whole new range of products, designed specifically to be used in this alternative way.

Role play

Designs can be generated by putting yourself in different situations. For example, when designing clothes for extremely cold

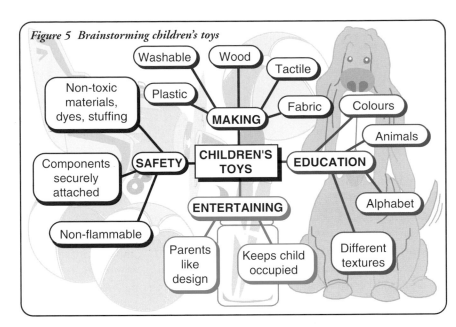

Figure 5 Brainstorming children's toys

weather, designers might expose themselves to low temperatures to determine which parts of their body need protection.

Brainstorming

Brainstorming allows all ideas and thoughts to be considered. Often a team will meet to pool ideas. There are no right or wrong ideas. It is simply a way of expressing all potential solutions. Preliminary design ideas, stages of planning and potential problems may all be discussed. Often the ideas are then set out in a spider diagram (see Figure 5).

Key Terms

Needs - people's requirements and desires.
Opportunities - situations that give the chance of new designs.
Design brief - a short statement explaining what is to be designed and made.
Specification - a list itemising features of a design with a reason for each.
Innovations - changes made to existing designs to adapt and improve them.
Attribute analysis - a technique used to produce new designs for familiar objects. The attributes of a familiar object are listed and then changed to make a new design.
Inventions - completely new designs, created after research and study.

activities

A team of designers has been asked to design a new strap for a Swatch pop watch. First they examine an existing watchstrap and record the words they use to describe the strap. They then draw up a table with headings appropriate to the descriptions. Other options are then added under each heading with an arrow showing the characteristics of the existing strap. This table can then be used to create a number of options for new designs.

Read the passage below and look at the table.

1. Which words are used to describe the existing watchstrap?
2. Use the attribute analysis for the pop watchstrap to design a new watchstrap.
3. Explain why you chose this design.
4. Devise an attribute analysis for a range of shirts and design THREE shirts.

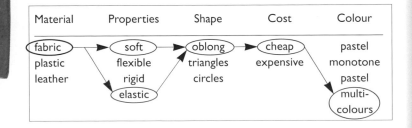

Material	Properties	Shape	Cost	Colour
fabric	soft	oblong	cheap	pastel
plastic	flexible	triangles	expensive	monotone
leather	rigid	circles		pastel
	elastic			multi-colours

Drawing

Because textile products have shape and form, the generation of ideas and development work before manufacture often takes the form of pictures, drawings and sketches. Drawings and sketches are used to:

● generate design ideas
● develop and improve designs
● present ideas to others
● evaluate designs.

It is very important to keep hold of all sketches - no matter how rough they are. They are useful for looking back to see how ideas have developed or for development work at a later stage.

Drawings can be very accurate or they may be just rough sketches so that designers can see their thoughts on paper. Rough sketches are called THUMBNAIL SKETCHES or 'concept sketches'. These sketches are usually simple and show the essence of the idea (see Figure 1).

Refining ideas

Concept sketches are rejected or accepted as possible ideas that meet the brief and design specification. They are then developed by adding detail (see Figure 2) and alternative colours, textures and materials. These alternative ideas are usually presented to a client in the form of a PRESENTATION

Figure 1 A thumbnail sketch - a hat

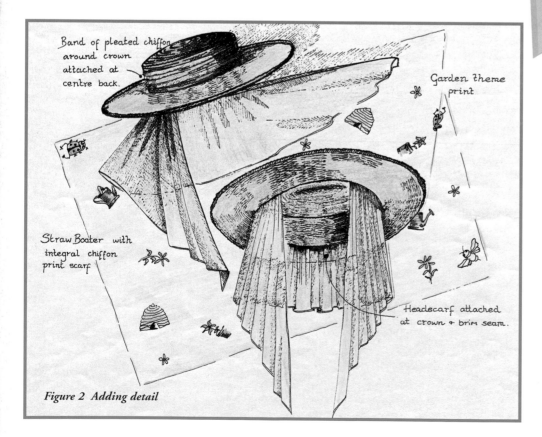

Band of pleated chiffon around crown attached at centre back.

Garden theme print

Straw Boater with integral chiffon print scarf

Headscarf attached at crown & brim seam.

Figure 2 Adding detail

activities

An all boys school and an all girls school are being amalgamated to create a new mixed school. A designer has been asked to create a new, unisex uniform to be worn by all students.

1. What is a thumbnail sketch?
2. Why might the designer use thumbnail sketches in the initial stages of a design?
3. Draw THREE thumbnail sketches of possible unisex school uniforms. Which of your sketches is most appropriate? Why?

DRAWING which visualises the possible solution.

Fashion drawings

Textile designs often involve clothing and their accessories. Usually, the clothing and accessories are presented as if in use - to convey size and proportion. The designs may also suggest the image and effect that the designer hopes to create. Fashion designers deliberately distort and exaggerate their illustrations in order to give the impression of the product being worn or used. Usually, the body on a fashion drawing is between 8 and 8.5 times longer than the head (the

Figure 3 A fashion drawing

average body is between 7 and 7.5 times longer than the head). The leg length is always exaggerated and so are the lines of the garment so that the style is immediately obvious. A 3-D effect is created, showing the way in which a garment will fit. The body is shown in a posed stance or movement position, giving a sense of realism. Figure 3 shows an example of a fashion drawing.

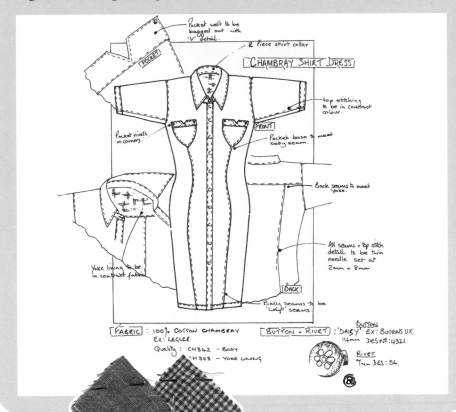

Figure 4 A working drawing

Working drawings

Before making a design, a WORKING DRAWING is needed. This shows the exact details of the design. It contains information about the fabric, components, sizes and construction techniques to be used. Often samples of material (SWATCHES) and components such as fastenings are attached to the working drawing. These give a more detailed picture of the final design (see Figure 4).

activities

Look at the photo of fabric toys.

1. What sort of drawings would have been made of these toys at the design stage?

2. What would be the advantage of producing a sectional drawing of one of these toys?

3. Produce a working drawing of any one of the toys.

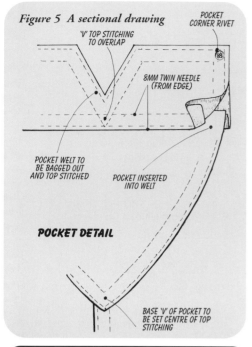

Figure 5 A sectional drawing

'V' TOP STITCHING TO OVERLAP

POCKET CORNER RIVET

8MM TWIN NEEDLE (FROM EDGE)

POCKET WELT TO BE BAGGED OUT AND TOP STITCHED

POCKET INSERTED INTO WELT

POCKET DETAIL

BASE 'V' OF POCKET TO BE SET CENTRE OF TOP STITCHING

jacket) SECTIONAL DIAGRAMS may be useful. They enable the designer to show more information especially about how parts of the design are assembled. A sectional drawing is a drawing which assumes there is an imaginary line that cuts through the product (see Figure 5). SEQUENTIAL DIAGRAMS, or step by step instructions, are drawings used to show how to make something (see Figure 6). Commercial sewing patterns, for example, usually contain a making up sheet which uses drawings or photographs to show how to construct a garment.

Using grids

Grid paper is useful for mapping and planning the arrangement of shapes. In textile designs, grids can be used to develop patterns - for example, when designing a knitted jumper. With a grid, the pattern can be reproduced accurately. Woven fabrics can also be designed using a grid.

Hidden detail

To show the detail inside a product (for example, the lining features or pockets of a

Figure 6 A sequential diagram

POCKET WELT - 'V' DETAIL

FIG 1. A) WITH WRONG SIDES TOGETHER, MATCH LARGE DOTS EITHER SIDE OF 'V'
        B) MACHINE STITCH 1.5CM IN FROM EDGE; FOLLOWING SHAPE OF TOP EDGE.

FIG 1.

FIG 2. A) CUT AWAY CORNERS AT TOP OF 'V' TO 2MM FROM STITCH LINE.
        B) CUT VERTICALLY FROM BASE OF 'V' TO STITCH LINE.

FIG 2

FIG 3. A) TURN POCKET WELT THROUGH TO RIGHT SIDE AND PRESS. ENSURE THAT 'V' IS CRISP AT CORNERS AND BASE.

FIG 3

activities

At Loughborough University students have taken on a design brief to develop a new baby carrier. Although the concepts were well established, the students decided to make up a number of alternative carriers for holding the baby in different positions. These prototypes were fairly crudely made, but were sufficiently strong for parents and representatives of companies to wear them while undertaking activities such as shopping. The testers were then asked to describe their experiences. In this way, the prototypes allowed greater understanding of the problems and added to the brief provided by the company. The prototypes also helped the designers in their discussions with manufacturers since they could use the data to illustrate their comments.
Source: New Designer, January 1996

1. What is meant by a prototype?
2. What benefits do a prototype provide to a manufacturer before production?
3. Suggest TWO features you might add to the baby carrier and explain how they might improve the design.

4. Make TWO concept drawings for the prototype of a portable carrier for a lap top computer. Annotate your drawings to highlight the differences between the designs and how they would affect its use.

Using the right materials

When drawing a textile product, it is important to capture the nature of the fabric in the drawing. There are many different graphic media and designers need to use those which are most appropriate for the the design. Table 1 shows a number of graphic media and their properties.

Modelling and testing

Having generated a number of possible design ideas for a product, each idea or part of an idea must be examined in detail. This is called PRODUCT DEVELOPMENT. Product development involves testing and trialling to find the most suitable design - the design which will be carried through to manufacture.

When designing garments, soft furnishings, accessories or artefacts, experimental modelling is important as it develops new skills and allows the imagination of the designer to expand. It also allows the designer to build up a store of knowledge about materials, equipment, methods and processes. The models show how textiles handle and how they can be manipulated and changed. They also provide information about how the product is to be constructed and how practical and versatile the product is.

Models or trials are crucial. Sometimes, a 3-D sketch can look good, but when the 3-D model is made, it quickly becomes clear that the design needs major adjustments. The information gained from modelling, therefore, is essential in deciding whether a design will be useful or successful.

Models or trials can be used at many stages in the design process. They may be used in research, prior to drawing up a specification. They may be used to help develop ideas or as part of presentational work. Rough models that are used in early stages of design are called MOCK-UPS. More detailed models that are used in development work are called PROTOTYPES. Mock-ups or prototypes can be made to the same size as the actual product. They can also be made to scale. Each part can be made smaller ('scaled down') or larger ('scaled up') by the same amounts so that all aspects of the design stay in proportion. A scaled down model of a parachute, for example, might be made and tested for strength. Similarly, a scaled up model of the seam of a waterproof jacket might be made and tested to see how it functions under very wet conditions. These types of tests, using models to gather evidence, are called SIMULATIONS. Some can be performed using computer software. Models or trials are only used when a drawing cannot convey an overall effect or provide the information needed.

Computer aided design

Designers are making more and more use of technological developments when drawing and developing their designs. Computer aided design (CAD) involves the use of computer software packages when designing products. There is a huge variety of software packages available to help designers design textile items such as clothing, soft furnishing and fabric finishes. Using these packages, designers are able to draw accurately, visualise the product in three dimensions and rotate the design to see it from a variety of angles. Changes and modifications can easily be made to the design before a model or prototype is made and before testing takes place. This saves time and reduces cost. Some software packages even allow designs to be tested on the computer. Simulations can be set up to test the properties of the design. For example, using a software package, it is possible to test the strength and durability of a tent on the computer. This means that only designs which pass the computer test go on to the next stage. CAD can be used in the design of one-off items, batches or mass produced products (see Unit 19).

Table 1 Graphic media

Watercolour paints - for colour washes

Acrylic paints - for strong flat colour

Pencil crayons - for hinting at detail and texture on top of colour washes

Pastels - to give a soft matt effect

Brush pens - to give strong, flowing outlines to clothes

Felt tip markers - for bold outlines

Lead pencils - for faint outlining and adding detail

Charcoal - for a rough look

Fine line pens - for outlining and giving detail

activities

Carrington Career and Workwear has for many years been the largest UK producer of high performance fabrics for both the workwear and careerwear markets. Key to its success in the careerwear market is an in-house design facility using state-of-the-art CAD equipment. This enables new print or colour-woven designs to be originated, or existing designs to be re-coloured, to meet customers' precise requirements. For example, the patterns and colours of fabric used for dresses and overalls can be adapted to produce an individual style for a particular company.
Source: IPT Group 1997

1. What is meant by the abbreviation 'CAD'?
2. Suggest THREE functions that may be carried out by a textile designer using CAD.
3. What advantages does the use of CAD bring Carrington Career and Workwear?

Modelling in the clothing industry

In industry, when a garment has been through the initial stages of design development, the final drawings are given to a pattern designer. Pattern designing is very creative work. The pattern maker needs great skill to translate the drawing into flat, two-dimensional pattern pieces. Computers may be used at this stage.

As the design process continues, more complex and realistic models of the product are made using fabric. Often, these models are called TOILES. Toiles are usually made using a cheap fabric (calico). In clothing design, MANNEQUINS (plastic or wooden dummies in the shape of the human body - see Figure 7) are used to see how the product fits and shapes to the body. Changes can easily be made at this stage. The designer and toile maker need to work closely together as adjustments to the original design may well be needed. At the next stage, the designer makes a toile that can be tested on a person (who is also, rather confusingly, called a 'model') - to make sure that the fitting is accurate. Again, a cheap fabric is used to make the toile. When the toile has been corrected to the designer's satisfaction, a sample garment can be made in the chosen fabric. At this stage, a costing analysis may be made. Even after the sample garment has been assembled, it may still be altered. Once the sample garment has been tested and altered, it is then shown to the manufacturer or to retailers before full-scale production commences. In the fashion world, designers produce a COLLECTION (a series of models of their products). Retailers use fashion shows to view designers' products (see Figure 8) and to place orders for the completed products. The trial garments or models produced for these occasions need to be of high quality. For a summary of the various stages which clothes pass through, see Figure 9.

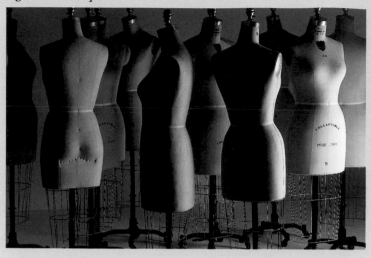

Figure 7 Mannequins

Grading

For the mass production of garments, the next step is GRADING. This is where a variety of sizes of patterns is produced from the single design. Like many aspects of the textiles industry, grading and pattern making

activities

The Testrite Mk V Shrinkage and Force tester has been designed to work out the shrinkage of tyre cord yarns at closely controlled temperatures. This is important because if they shrink too much at a certain temperature the tyre might blow out. When designing a new tyre, therefore, the tester helps to ensure that it will perform well in difficult conditions. Other artificial yarns can also be tested using this machine. The tester works out how they will perform when washed. If a yarn shrinks too much at 60°C, for example, it will be necasasry to wash items made from it at a lower temperature. Items made from the yarn can then be labelled accordingly. The Heater and Hardware unit is separate from the control module to allow ease of service and repair. The control module has a 20 key touch pad to programme test requirements. The temperature range that can be tested is 20°C to 250°C. The shrinkage range is -5% to +32.5%. A built-in miniature printer produces an accurate graph of the result.

Source: Testrite, 1997

1. a) What does the Testrite Mk V Shrinkage and Force tester test?
   b) What design features have been included to make the tester easy to use?
2. Describe THREE textile designs which might benefit from using this tester.
3. Why is it important to carry out tests at the design stage?

Figure 8 Modelling clothes at a fashion show

are increasingly being completed using computers. Computer software has been developed which allows a designer to use the computer to translate designs into pattern pieces from basic pattern blocks. The basic shapes are stored in the computer and the operator uses the stylus or mouse to make the pattern pieces. Having been designed in one size, the pattern pieces are then graded by the computer to the number of different sizes required.

A design proposal

Once all the research and specification work has been completed, a designer puts together all the successful ideas and discards the unsuccessful ones. Decisions are based on the information gained through research and development compared to the specification. From this, a finalised design proposal is then drafted.

Figure 9 Modelling and testing clothes

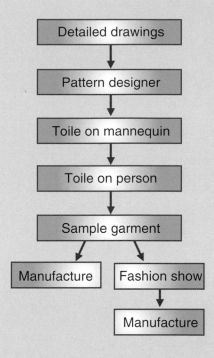

Detailed drawings → Pattern designer → Toile on mannequin → Toile on person → Sample garment → Manufacture / Fashion show → Manufacture

Key Terms

Thumbnail sketches - quick, freehand, basic sketches of ideas.
Presentation drawings - more detailed drawings showing design ideas.
Working drawing - a very detailed design drawing.
Swatches - samples of fabric.
Sectional diagram - a drawing made. of a product as if an imaginary line has cut through it.
Sequential diagrams - drawings which show step by step instructions.
Product development - examining the aspects and features of a design.
Mock-ups - rough models used at an early stage in the design process.
Prototypes - more detailed models.
Simulations - tests using models to gather evidence.
Toiles - accurate models of clothing using fabric.
Mannequins - plastic or wooden dummies in the shape of the human body.
A collection - a series of sample garments, often the creation of a single designer.
Grading - producing a variety of sizes of patterns from a single design.

activities

Dr Dee Dawson, who runs a clinic for children with eating disorders, said that media images of excessively thin models such as Kate Moss or Tanya Court added to the pressure on young girls. 'If you hear enough about jogging, about doing aerobic classes, about not eating fat and looking like Kate Moss, it is going to rub off on these kids', she said.
Source: Adapted from the Guardian, 22 April 95

Top models have always been stars. Models have also always been thin - 'adenoid Annies, rattling bundles of skin and bone' as one early agent, Harry Conover, described them. Carmen dell'Orefice, signed up at 14 on an American Vogue contract in 1946, was so thin that all her dresses had to be pinned in at the back. Embarassed, the magazine arranged for injections to bring on puberty, only to lose interest in her once the curves appeared.
Source: Adapted from the Guardian, 8 September 95

1. Why do designers use models to show their clothes?

2. What are designers looking for when they choose people to model their clothes?

3. a) Why is the shape of models important?
   b) Why is there concern about the shape of some models?
   c) How does the shape of models affect design?

The first national competitive swimming competition in Britain was held in 1837 after the founding of the National Swimming Society. In 1896, when the first modern Olympic Games were held, swimming was one of the sports to be included. Since 1896, swimming has grown in popularity and in competitiveness. Today, the top swimmers rely on top class swimwear to aid their performance. The design of this swimwear is of great importance since, in a sport were a hundreth of a second counts, it can make the difference between winning and coming second.

Swimwear can affect the performance of swimmers in a number of ways:

- it can create drag resistance in the water
- it can absorb water and therefore increase in weight, slowing the swimmer down
- if it is ill-fitting, air pockets might form, slowing the swimmer down
- it can inhibit movement.

Speedo set out to create a swimsuit that overcame these problems. Its aim for the 1996 Olympic Games at Atlanta was to produce the 'fastest performance suit in the world'. The result was the Aquablade suit (see left) which was specially designed for the Atlanta Games. When this suit was produced, the British Amateur Swimming Association argued that the British team would be placed at a disadvantage if swimmers were not allowed to compete in Aquablade suits. At the Games, 76% of all swimming medals were won by competitors wearing Speedo Aquablade suits.

The reason for the success of Aquablade suits is their design. The designers had identified the problems faced by Olympic swimmers and found ways to meet their needs. How they did this is explored in Table 1.

The Speedo Aquablade suit that was used in the 1996 Olympic Games

One of Speedo's earliest swimsuits from 1928

Table 1 - The characteristics of Speedo Aquablade suits

The fabric

The S2000 fabric has a 15% reduction in water drag resistance, absorbs less water so remains lighter and dries 20% quicker than conventional fabrics. The fabric is striped and coated with a water repellent resin, giving a smooth surface. The fabric has smooth and rough stripes which produce two currents - one slow and the other fast. When the fast water flows into slower water, spirals of water are created. As a result, the speed of the water flow increases and it stays closer to the body longer, allowing the swimmer to 'blade' through the water.

The fit

The S2000 fabric has superior stretch and strength characteristics. The fit is the closest possible, preventing air and water entering the suit.

Silhouettes/shape

As Aquablade is faster than human skin, swimmers should cover as much of their body as possible. The legsuit covers all leg muscles above the knee. Also, the zip is on the shoulder rather than the back, allowing a closer back fit and a high neckline. This prevents air and water entering via the neck. Five silhouettes cater for the different strokes - backstroke, butterfly stroke and so on.

Activities

1. Identify the problems that needed to be tackled when designing a swimsuit to be used by top-class swimmers.
2. How did the Speedo Aquablade suit meet Olympic swimmers' needs?
3. Write a design brief that may have been given to Speedo by the Olympic swimming team.
4. Write a specification for Aquablade suits.
5. What types of research do you think Speedo would have carried out before starting to design the Aquablade?

WEDDING DRESS DESIGNS - CLAIRE HEYES

CLAIRE Heyes is a wedding dress designer who trained at the City of Liverpool Community College. In October 1995 she opened a bridal shop in Burscough Street, Ormskirk which sells off-the-peg bridal gowns and evening wear. Claire also designs and makes individual dresses to order.

Claire gathers her ideas for dresses from a variety of sources. Books (particularly those portraying 18th century bridal dress designs), bridal magazines and pattern books all provide stimulus for her original creations. Claire works closely with the bride, interpreting her ideas and wishes. Brides often come to the initial consultation with photographs or pictures from magazines. Alternatively, they might try on ready-to-wear gowns and describe what they like or dislike about them. All this information gives Claire ideas to work from. These ideas are expressed as a series of thumbnail sketches. A concept sketch is drawn up to enable the bride to visualise and agree on the design of the dress. A second detailed drawing is then produced, taking into account any changes that the bride has decided upon or Claire has advised. From this detailed sketch, Claire is able to produce a working drawing that includes specific details such as measurements and notes about the making up of the garment.

Pattern pieces are produced using detailed measurements and information provided in the working drawing. A toile (a calico mock-up) of the bodice is made up and, after several fittings (during which alterations may be made), the bodice is made up using the bride's chosen fabric. Usually, brides choose silk, sateen, taffeta or damask. The rest of the dress is constructed and a final fitting held. The whole process usually takes around six months. An originally designed and hand-made dress costs around £900.

Claire's shop in Ormskirk

Drawings for the dress pictured left

The finished dress

Activities

1. How does Claire Heyes decide on the design for a hand-made wedding dress?
2. Suppose Claire Heyes needed an assistant who will design and make wedding dresses. What skills should this assistant have?
3. Produce a flow chart to show the process involved in the making of a wedding dress - from initial idea to final product.
4. You have been asked to design your ideal wedding dress. Draw (i) a thumbnail sketch and (ii) a working drawing illustrating your design.

4 Planning

Figure 1 Materials and components list - a tent

Item	Nº.	Description	Dimensions
zip	1	blue	115
zip	2	blue	80
base	1	blue nylon	200 x 300
sides	2	red nylon	105 x 300
ends	2	red nylon	150 x 200
thread		blue nylon	50 m
cord		blue	10 m
pegs	8	aluminium	20 x 2
pole	1	aluminium	150 x 1
poles	4	aluminium	105 x 1

All figures in cm unless otherwise stated.

The need for planning

When a design has been finalised, the manufacture of the product has to be planned in great detail. Such planning provides the manufacturer with the following information:

● whether the design can be realistically made or not
● what type of materials and components are needed
● how much material is needed
● how long the product will take to make
● how much the product will cost to make and whether it is commercially viable
● whether one, a few or many products can be made (see Unit 19)
● any foreseeable problems.

Material and components lists

Producing a MATERIAL AND COMPONENTS LIST (see Figure 1) is an important part of planning. This tells the manufacturer what types of material and components will be needed and how much of each is required. Fabrics come in specific widths. Zips and threads come in standard lengths. Buttons come in standard sizes.

Wastage needs to be kept to a minimum in order to reduce costs. Careful planning will help to ensure this. Costs can also be kept to a minimum by shopping around for the cheapest available materials. However, a manufacturer must be careful not to use materials that are so cheap that they affect the quality of the product.

Production schedules

Once the types of material and components have been identified, a PRODUCTION SCHEDULE can be devised. This describes the sequence of the tasks needed to make the product. The first step is to identify each major step in the schedule. Each stage can then be broken down into sub-stages. Most production schedules for the manufacture of products include:

● measuring and marking out the materials
● cutting the materials to size
● shaping and forming the material
● assembling and joining the parts
● finishing the product
● tidying/clearing away tools, equipment and waste
● storing the product safely at each stage.

A production schedule can be illustrated in a number of ways - for example, as a FLOW CHART or as a STORY BOARD.

Flow charts

A flow chart is a shorthand diagram which sets out tasks in a logical order. Different shapes are used to symbolise different stages in the process (see Figure 2). Flow charts can be used to simplify the plan of action (see Figure 3).

Story boards

A story board is another method of planning. A series of sketches, diagrams or photographs shows how a design has developed or the various stages of processing

activities

Materials & components
1 ball four ply red knitting wool
Red cotton thread 100cm
zip 15cm
12 buttons

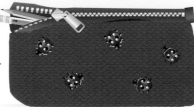

Instructions
1. Knit two pieces 15cm x 8cm.
2. Sew together one long side and both short sides.
3. Stitch zip onto opening.
4. Sew 6 buttons onto each side for decoration.

1. What is a flow chart?
2. Why might manufacturers produce a flow chart?

3. Using the information above, draw up a production schedule for the pencil case in the form of a flow chart.

Figure 2 Symbols used in flow charts

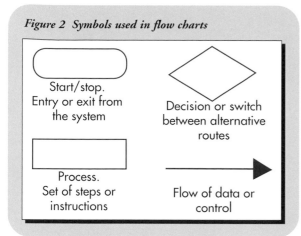

Start/stop.
Entry or exit from
the system

Decision or switch
between alternative
routes

Process.
Set of steps or
instructions

Flow of data or
control

and manufacture. The equipment for each stage of the manufacturing process must be identified to ensure availability.

Time plans

Every stage in the production schedule

Figure 3 Flow chart - tent

Develop a tent

Analyse the task using information given and then specify its requirements

Decide on specification

Investigate

Fabrics/yarns with suitable qualities

Best format, shape & size

Possible designs

Investigate construction processes and time

Decide final designs

No

Plan production

Make prototype (model of tent)

Does it satisfy the specification?

Yes

Begin production

STOP

must be given an allotted time. This builds into a TIME PLAN (see Figure 4). A manufacturer usually works to a deadline (the final date by which the product must be completed and delivered). A time plan must be organised to meet the deadline.

It is important that time plans are realistic and make allowances for foreseeable problems. For example, suppose a workshop which has won an order to

Figure 4 Time plan

Time	Activity
March 1-5	Analyse brief
March 8-13	Investigate ideas
March 16-21	Complete specification
March 24-29	Produce designs
April 1-5	Evaluate designs/choose final design
April 9-14	Construct final design
April 17-22	Construction
April 25-30	Test and evaluate final product

make jumpers has three knitting machines (for making the pieces of fabric) but only one sewing machine (for assembling the garments). The sewing machine would not be able cope with the amount of fabric produced and there would be a bottleneck,

activities

1. What type of presentation is being shown below?

2. Draw a flow chart to explain what is happening at each stage.

3. Suggest THREE reasons why a time plan for the manufacture and assembly of the pairs of shorts shown below would be useful.

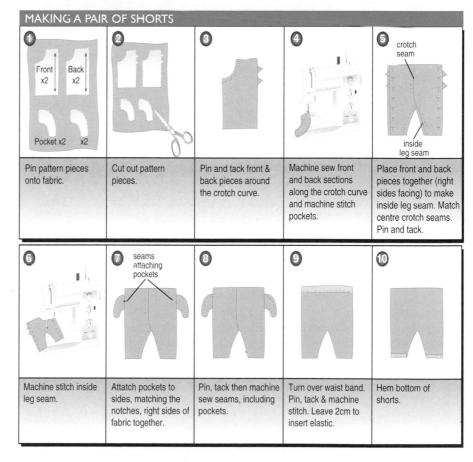

MAKING A PAIR OF SHORTS

❶ Front x2 Back x2 Pocket x2 x2	❷	❸	❹	❺ crotch seam / inside leg seam
Pin pattern pieces onto fabric.	Cut out pattern pieces.	Pin and tack front & back pieces around the crotch curve.	Machine sew front and back sections along the crotch curve and machine stitch pockets.	Place front and back pieces together (right sides facing) to make inside leg seam. Match centre crotch seams. Pin and tack.
❻	❼ seams attaching pockets	❽	❾	❿
Machine stitch inside leg seam.	Attatch pockets to sides, matching the notches, right sides of fabric together.	Pin, tack then machine sew seams, including pockets.	Turn over waist band. Pin, tack & machine stitch. Leave 2cm to insert elastic.	Hem bottom of shorts.

holding up production. Where bottlenecks are likely, alternatives should be suggested in order to keep on target to meet the deadline. This could involve changing the organisation of production or using other workers or equipment. In this case, extra sewing machines could be hired or bought and possibly extra workers hired to use them - so that the assembly of the jumpers could keep pace with the production of the pieces of knitted fabric. It is important to be aware of how any suggested alternative will affect the quality of the product.

Unexpected problems must also be allowed for if possible. For example, a machine might break down, holding up production. Any production schedule should include a 'slippage' section. This identifies tasks which have not been completed in the set time plan and will have to be fitted in at a later stage.

The stages in production and how problems were resolved should be recorded to help solve similar problems in the future.

Figure 5 A gantt chart used to plan a school play

Week 1	Week 2	Week 3	Week 4	Week 5	Week 6
Write script					
	Design costumes				
		Make costumes			
			Design and make scenery		
				Rehearsal	
					Performance

Gantt charts

GANTT CHARTS are useful when planning a number of activities that are to take place simultaneously within a set time. They show the start date for each task and when each task should be completed. By keeping to the dates in the chart, it is possible to meet the deadline. Figure 5 shows an example of a gantt chart which was used for the planning of a school play.

Working as a team

At the beginning of a project, it is worthwhile spending time deciding what tasks need to be done and allocating tasks to specific people. The group should work as a team, using the particular strengths of each person. Allowing time for reviewing and evaluating work as it progresses helps to keep the team working well. It allows for any changes which may need to be made to an ongoing plan. And, it helps to ensure a quality product.

activities

This advent calendar was advertised in the Imperial Cancer Research Christmas catalogue which was sent out in early August. The design was first generated in November of the previous year and finalised by January. A prototype was made in January and photographed for the catalogue in early April. The materials were ordered in February and delivered in early March. Production began in late March. The catalogue went to the printers in early June. The deadline for delivery of the final product to the warehouse was mid-June. The advent calendar is made of cotton with embroidered silk pockets. The pockets and decorations are machine stitched onto the cotton.
Source: Imperial Cancer Research 1996

1. Using the information above:
   a) draw (i) a time plan and (ii) a gantt chart showing the production schedule of the advent calendar
   b) explain why careful planning is so important.
2. Describe TWO foreseeable and TWO unexpected problems that could have affected the production schedule. How could these problems be overcome?

3. Suppose you worked for a company which had decided to produce and sell a new collection of textile Christmas tree ornaments. If you were in charge of planning, how would you proceed? Draw up a production schedule which would make sure that the products were available early enough for Christmas shoppers to buy them.

Key Terms

Material and components list - a list telling the manufacturer what types of material and components are needed and what quantities are needed.
Production schedule - a sequence of tasks undertaken to design and make a product.
Flow chart - a shorthand diagram which sets out tasks in a logical order.
Story board - diagrams or photos that show how a task is to be carried out.
Time plans - a schedule showing what tasks must be done within what time to meet the deadline.
Gantt charts - a chart used to plan activities which take place simultaneously within a set time.

case study JASPER CONRAN

FOR top designers, planning a collection means meeting tight deadlines. Take Jasper Conran for example. Between 8 January and 27 February 1997 (less than two months), he came up with 80 outfits. These were designed, drawn, sent off and turned into samples, rejected or redrawn and turned into still more samples until the look, feel and mix of the collection was up to its creator's standards.

By 22 January, the drawings had been completed. The aim of the show was to produce a set of outfits which were

Jasper Conran at his 1997 show

'very English'. But the show was not just about costumes. A complicated set had to be built and a complicated lighting system installed. Conran insisted that photographers should be contacted and informed that this was to be no ordinary catwalk presentation as the lighting would be changing. By 5 February, the toiles had been made. Each outfit is drawn and then made into a toile (a gauzy white creation) before being sent off to be sampled in the final, more expensive fabric. At the toile stage, Conran uses one model, Amanda Verdon. 'I do all my preliminary fittings on Amanda', he says, 'I don't wear the clothes but I do need to know what it feels like to wear them. If she thinks it makes her look fat or ugly, we won't put it in.'

By 24 February, the rails are filled with beautiful clothes. At this point each garment has to be tried with others and accessorised to become a complete outfit. Any item Conran does not like, he throws out.

Time after time, the model tries clothes on and then takes them off again. Each time the clothes are tried with something else. Each time a combination is tried on, a Polaroid photo is taken and pinned on the wall. The result is rows and rows of Polaroids of finished outfits. Only once this has been done can the outfits be fitted on the 20-odd models booked for the show. They are booked two days before the show is due. On the day itself, there is one dresser back-stage to every two models. Whilst the fitting is going on, the order of the show is worked out and the soundtrack is edited to fit the clothes perfectly. To meet the deadline, it is crucial that everybody in the team works together.

Source: Adapted from the Guardian, 26 February 1997

Jasper Conran was commissioned to produce the 'J. line', a special collection of clothes for Debenhams, (see also below right).

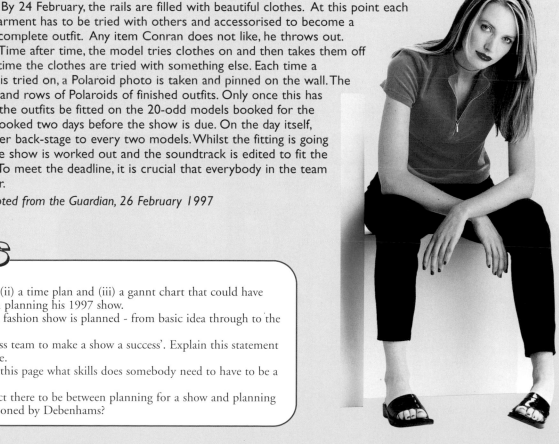

Activities

1. Devise (i) a production schedule, (ii) a time plan and (iii) a gannt chart that could have been used by Jasper Conran when planning his 1997 show.
2. Draw a flow chart showing how a fashion show is planned - from basic idea through to the show itself.
3. 'A top designer relies on a first class team to make a show a success'. Explain this statement using the information on this page.
4. Judging from the information on this page what skills does somebody need to have to be a successful designer?
5. What differences would you expect there to be between planning for a show and planning for a collection like that commissioned by Debenhams?

5 Influences on design

What influences design?

Over the last 100 years there have been dramatic changes in lifestyle. Technology has led to the development of thousands of new designs and innovations. There have been astonishing changes in clothing, transport and architecture.

Many factors influence design. This unit describes some of these factors and provides ideas that can be used when starting to design. Influences on design include:

- nature
- history
- changing society
- trends
- music
- art
- technological development
- role models
- television and film
- the purpose for which an item is required.

Influences can be brought to designers'

attention through a range of media and activities including:

- music
- theatre
- radio
- television
- films
- paintings and drawings
- adverts
- magazines
- newspapers
- books
- computer games
- dance
- environmental issues
- influential people
- sport
- travel.

Learning to look and see is a designer's first job. Most people think that they are observant, but seeing detail is a difficult skill to learn. It is a necessary skill for designers, however, since it is a way of finding inspiration.

Figure 1 Nature and design

Nature

Nature is full of details that can provide inspiration for design. Take, for example, the patterns and lines on a piece of drift wood. These could inspire an idea for a piece of embroidery. Similarly, the rich and varied colours of fruit and vegetables might provide the starting point for the colours to be used on a collection of clothes.

Aspects of nature can provide the ideas and inspiration for a wealth of textile items. The sort of ideas inspired by nature might include ideas about:

- texture
- colour
- shape
- form.

Designers might copy, adapt or accentuate ideas from nature. For example, observing the way in which animals carry their young might inspire a designer to create a new style of baby carrier (see Figure 1).

activities

1. Nature is a great starting point for designers. Make a list of SIX natural objects saying what designs for textile items they might inspire.

2. Using nature as your inspiration, create a concept sketch for the design that might be used on one of the following textile items: (i) a beach towel (ii) a neck tie or (iii) a hat.

3. Suppose you had been asked to design a tent. What ideas from nature might help you to choose your design?

History

History has shaped and influenced many aspects of textile design. Designers often use ideas from the past to help create new ideas and images. For example, the design of the frock coats worn by TEDDY BOYS in the 1950s was inspired by the style of coats popular amongst the upper classes in the early 1900s (see Figure 3). Similarly, the New Romantic style of the early 1980s was inspired by clothing worn in the 18th century.

Changing society

Since the Second World War, Britain has become a multicultural society. In part, this is the result of ruling a huge Empire in the 19th and early 20th century. When the Empire began to collapse in the 1940s, immigration from colonies and former colonies began to grow. In the 1950s, many British employers recruited workers from the West Indies, Africa, India and Pakistan. These immigrants and their children have brought their own culture and their own designs. Many designs now reflect the multicultural nature of British society.

Figure 2 Long lasting trends

The pictures above show a design by William Morris (left) and an art nouveau block print. Designs like these remain popular today.

Society has also changed in other ways. Clothing, for example, used to reflect social status (a cloth cap for a worker and a top hat for a member of the upper classes). Today, there is more diversity than there used to be. This is partly due to the fact that values have changed. It is also partly due to the fact that mass production means that clothes are relatively cheap and people have more choice than they used to have.

Art

Throughout the centuries, famous artists have been a great source of inspiration for textile designers. Ideas may be triggered by a particular painting or the painting itself might be used as the design.

activities

1. How might a designer use a painting as the starting point for a design?
2. You have been asked to design (i) a print for a T-shirt (ii) a repeated pattern for wallpaper and (iii) a silk scarf. Which of the paintings above would best suit which design? Explain your answer.
3. Draw a concept sketch for each of your three designs.

Figure 3 The evolution of street style 1950-80

The montage above shows (1) a Teddy Boy (2) the mini skirt (3) glam rockers (4) hippies and (5) punks.

After the Second World War, the emergence of STREET STYLE began. This is a term used to refer to the style of clothing worn by groups of people (usually young people) who wish to make a particular statement. Their style of clothing usually attempted to portray a particular message about their attitudes, musical taste or political beliefs. Street style often starts as a trend amongst a small group and is then gradually adopted more widely. The evolution of street styles is summarised below.

The 1950s

The 1950s saw a great deal of change in the clothing industry. For example, nylon (invented in 1938) was produced for the clothing industry on a large scale for the first time. In Britain, the 1950s were a time of economic growth and, for most people, living standards rose. The designs from haute couture (the high-class designers and dressmakers) were converted into wearable fashion clothing which was accessible to all levels of society. The emergence of youth culture in this decade brought with it youth fashion. This was the first time that young people developed their own style in clothes, rather than wearing the same sort of clothes

Trends

Designers and craftspeople have been influenced by a long succession of movements or TRENDS. Some of the most significant before the Second World War were:

● **The Art and Craft movement** - begun by William Morris in the late 19th century. His aim was to revive handcrafting techniques which had almost been lost as a result of industrialisation (see Figure 2).

● **Art nouveau** - a decorative art movement lasting from the 1880s to 1914. This richly ornamental, fluid and organic style had a great influence on furniture and jewellery (see Figure 2).

● **Bauhaus** - a design school set up in Germany in 1919. Members of the Bauhaus experimented with new materials and aimed to transform nature rather than to imitate it.

● **Cubism** - an art movement lasting from 1907 to the 1920s in which three-dimensional objects were fragmented and redefined from several points of view at once. The most famous Cubist was the artist Pablo Picasso.

● **Art deco** - a decorative art movement which dominated the late 1920s and 1930s. Its main characteristics were

individuality, skilled work and expensive materials. The style was consciously modern and streamlined. The name came from the 1925 Paris Exposition Internationale des Arts Décoratifs et Industriels Modernes.

activities

Did the Spice Girls (above) set the trends in the late 1990s or follow them?

Three main trends characterise the 1990s. First, a concern for the environment has led to a greater use of natural fabrics such as linen, silk and cotton or of recycled fabrics such as Polartec. Second, brand names and logos now play an important part in clothing design. And third, there has been a tendency to revisit the style of the 1970s - flared trousers and platform shoes are making a come-back for example.

Your task is to find out what have been the major influences on design in the 1990s.
1. Write down what you think have been the major trends in the 1990s.
2. Devise a questionnaire to find out what your friends and relatives think have been the major trends in the 1990s and ask them to fill it in.
3. Write down the results of your survey. Do the results of your survey agree with your own assessment?
4. What is in fashion at the time you are writing? How do you think current fashions will influence design?

as their parents. The 1950s also saw the development of seasonal fashion changes in women's clothing.

The 1960s

For many people, the 1960s was a time of liberation. Young people began to wear unconventional clothing and 'youth' became the key theme for designers. The mini skirt made its first appearance (see Figure 3) and jeans, sweaters and T-shirts became the standard dress for young people. Men's clothing designers in particular challenged the old strict gender definitions by producing colourful and casual clothes. Space travel and abstract art also influenced the fashion scene. Bright colours and new plastic-coated material began to be used by designers. Towards the end of the 1960s came an anti-fashion movement. 'Nostalgic' style looked back to the past with affection. Hippy style (see Figure 3) reflected the protests against the consumer society that were widespread at the end of the decade.

The 1970s

The 1970s saw a wide spectrum of fashion. Glam rock took the trends in the late 1960s to an extreme. Followers of disco music wore shiny new materials and loud colours whilst the non-conformists created their own fashion with the Punk style (see Figure 3).

The 1980s

For some people, the 1980s brought a higher standard of living and this was reflected by the development of a huge range of clothing made from good quality fabrics and high-grade garment-making techniques, showing a great deal of attention to detail. Major trends included:
- the professional look
- glamour
- body consciousness.

The introduction of LYCRA® into many forms of clothing led to body-hugging designs.

Music

Throughout the 20th century musical

Figure 4 Music and fashion

The montage above shows (1) The Beatles (2) David Bowie (3) The Sex Pistols and (4) Oasis.

trends have influenced style and fashion. In the 1920s, jazz music shocked the older generation and inspired the flapper style of dress. In the 1950s, rock and roll emerged, bringing with it Teds, Mods and Rockers. The clothes worn by the Beatles made a huge impact on menswear in the 1960s. Glam rock and disco music dominated the early 1970s. Punk and the New Romantics made an impact in the late 1970s and early 1980s. Since then, House music, Rap and Hip Hop have all provided inspiration to designers as they have to musicians. The point is that music and fashion have become intertwined with each feeding off the other (see Figure 4).

Technological developments

Scientists, designers and engineers are constantly striving to push back the boundaries of science and invention. Many people working in these areas hope to come up with an idea for a product or a system that nobody else has thought of. Often, they use existing discoveries to create a new product, system or material. Most notably, the discovery of synthetic fibres enabled cheap new fabrics to be produced. This revolutionised the textile industry.

activities

The band Slade posing in the early 1970s.

1. What does the photo above tell us about fashion in the early 1970s? Suppose Slade was a new band today. What would you expect its members to wear?
2. What are the links between music and fashion?.
3. How might a designer use (i) a band and (ii) music as the starting point for a design?
4. Design an accessory which might be worn or carried by one of your favourite musicians.

Many technological breakthroughs that result from tackling one problem can then be taken on and developed by designers and technologists for use in other areas. For example, Teflon is a material first developed during research into space travel in the 1930s. Today, Teflon is used by textile designers and manufacturers as a protective coating for garments and soft furnishings. It enables fabric to be made waterproof, breathable and stain repellent.

Even when technological projects 'fail' (in the sense that they do not meet the needs of the problem they are designed to tackle), they may not be worthless. Lessons are learned and information passed on to others.

Role models

Every society has its ROLE MODELS - individuals whom others admire and try to imitate. Often, these role models influence style and fashion because their admirers copy the way they look and dress. An example is the singer Madonna. In the late 1980s, the clothes she wore made a big impact on the style of clothes many thousands of women chose to wear.

In the past, only the upper classes had enough money to buy fashionable clothes. It is no surprise, therefore, that the royal family was often regarded as leading the fashion in clothing. Although members of the royal family still influence some people, they are by no means the only role models. Film, television, music and sport celebrities, for example, all influence style and fashion. So do politicians - for example, during the Cultural Revolution in the 1960s almost everybody in China followed Chairman Mao's example and wore a simple peasant outfit.

Television and cinema

Television programmes and films are visual media and therefore often influence designs and styles and sometimes start trends. For example, in the 1955 film Rebel Without A Cause, James Dean (the star) wore a T-shirt, a garment originally designed for the American armed forces (see Figure 5). The film popularised the garment and many young people began to wear T-shirts. Since then, T-shirts have become a standard item in most British and American wardrobes.

Figure 5 James Dean

Costume dramas often lead to a revival of clothing from a particular era. For example, the film Evita which starred Madonna saw a surge of 1940s-style clothing on the catwalk and in retail outlets.

The purpose for which an item is required

A design will only be successful if it meets a particular need. It is important, therefore, to consider the purpose for which an item is required. For example, if an item is designed for hard, physical work, there is little point in designing it in a delicate material such as silk which is expensive and will soon disintegrate. Similarly, few people would want to be married in a wedding dress made of denim. The purpose for which an item is required, therefore, is an important influence on the sort of design which is generated.

activities

1. What is a role model? Name FIVE people who have been role models in the 1990s. Give TWO examples of role models who have influenced the style of clothes worn by you or your friends and relatives.

2. Look at the pictures above. Why do you think that these role models made such an impact on the clothing people choose to wear?

3. Explain the ways in which role models might influence the work of designers.

Ever since she married Prince Charles in 1981, Diana's 'look' has been the centre of media attention. Her hairstyle and clothes have been much imitated.

J.F. Kennedy became President of the USA in 1960. His wife, Jackie, was idolised as the ideal first lady (see left), especially after Kennedy was assassinated in 1963.

During the Cultural Revolution (1966-69), Chairman Mao was worshipped as if he was a god. To show their support, almost everybody living in China followed Mao's lead and wore simple peasant clothes.

FASHION SERVICES FOR PEOPLE WITH DISABILITIES

FASHION Services for People with Disabilities (FSPD) is a specialist clothing service which aims both to understand and to meet the clothing needs of disabled people. FSPD is a member of **'awear'** a national organisation of disabled people and clothing industry professionals which promotes greater awareness of the importance of clothes and related issues. The main aim of awear is to ensure that disabled people have direct and full access to fashionable, affordable clothes of their choice which fit well and are appropriate to their lives. Members of awear recognise that disabled people experience discrimination when trying to access clothes of their choice. They also recognise that appropriate clothing can promote independence, personal autonomy and social participation.

FSPD was set up to provide bespoke (individually tailored) garments for people who cannot buy ready-made garments in shops. Bespoke garments are expensive because the measuring, consultation, designing, pattern cutting and fitting stages are labour intensive and require a highly skilled staff. Able-bodied people do not pay these costs because they are covered by the savings made by mass production.

FSPD operates in two ways. First, the training centre offers disabled people, their relatives and helpers garment-making courses. These courses encourage self help and involve learning about fabrics, design, pattern making, fitting and garment construction. And second, the workshop offers a garment-making service for those people for whom a self help approach is inappropriate. Workshop staff also visit local homes, hospitals and centres to discuss clothing problems and to help in choosing fabrics, colour, style and designs. Each customer is assessed and fitted individually. Customers are charged only for materials and making up with the result that prices are kept in line with high street stores.

FASHION SERVICES
for people with disabilities

Original

Part of the cover of FSPD's brochure

Like other members of awear, FSPD is a user-led organisation. This allows disabled people to lead in the planning, delivery and management of all aspects of the organisation's activities. As a result, the designs that are produced are designs that aim to meet the particular needs that individual disabled people have. Each customer is consulted on design, colour and fabric choice. Measurements are taken and each garment fitted, if necessary, before completion.

Fitting a customer at the Style Centre, Disabled Living, Manchester

Activities

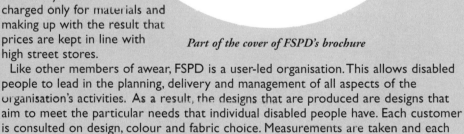

1. What is 'awear'. Why do you think it was set up?
2. What are bespoke garments and why are they most suitable for people with disabilities?
3. What influences the design of clothes made by FSPD?
4. To cover the cost of providing clothing for people with disabilities, FSPD relies on grants and donations. Why is this extra funding necessary? What would happen if it was not available?
5. Outline the differences in the work of a designer working for FSPD and a designer working for a company which manufactures mass produced fashion items.

Table 1 The main groups of fibres

Natural	Regenerated	Synthetic
Wool Silk Linen Cotton	Viscose Acetate Triacetate	Polyester Acrylic Polyurethane PVC Polypropylene Polyamide (nylon)

What are fibres?

Most textile items are made of TEXTILE FIBRES. Textile fibres are fine hair-like structures that are available in short lengths or as long continuous FILAMENTS. It is important to know about the different types of fibre and where these different types of fibre come from as this knowledge can then be used to choose the best fibre for a particular item.

Fibres can be grouped according to their origin. There are three groups. As the name suggests, NATURAL FIBRES come from natural, growing sources - both plant and animal. REGENERATED FIBRES come from natural non-animal, non-fibrous growing sources. The growing sources are treated with chemicals to produce fibres. SYNTHETIC FIBRES are made from chemicals only. These chemicals are usually taken from coal or oil. Table 1 shows examples of each group of fibres.

The processing and manufacture of fibres

Before fibres can be used, they have to be processed. All fibres are made up of groups of molecules called POLYMERS. These polymers are joined together to form the structure which affects the properties of the fibre. Different fibres have to undergo different processes before they can be made into fabrics.

Figure 1 Magnified image of a wool fibre

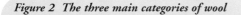

Figure 2 The three main categories of wool

1. Fine wool

The finest diameter wool comes from Merino sheep. It is used for high quality, smooth-handling fabrics and soft knitting yarns. It is highly valued by leading fashion designers.

2. Coarse wool

Several parts of Britain have given their names to popular coarse wool breeds - for example, Romney, Leicester and Dorset. Coarse wools are used mostly in carpets because of their strength and durability.

3. Crossbreed wool

The wide range of wools between fine and coarse is produced by crossing one breed of sheep with another. An example is the Corriedale. It is a cross between a Merino and a number of English longwool breeds. Crossbred wools are used in a variety of woven cloths and knitting yarns.

Natural fibres (1) - wool

The polymer that makes up a wool fibre is made up of protein molecules and produces a short (staple) fibre. A magnified image of a wool fibre is shown in Figure 1. This shows that scales are formed on each fibre. These scales help the fibre to 'mat' or stick together. Air is trapped and it acts as an insulator, making wool a warm fabric to wear.

Wool fibres come from sheep. Sheep farmers have learned to breed sheep that produce the best wool given a particular set of climatic and geographical conditions. As a result, there are many different breeds of sheep. Wool from different breeds of sheep varies in colour, length and diameter. Within a single fleece there is also some variation. Sheep's wool, can be divided into three broad categories (see Figure 2).

There are two basic methods of processing wool into yarn, though each method has many variations. The two methods are:
● the woollen process
● the worsted process.

For both processes the sheep is shorn and the fleece removed in one piece. The wool is classed or graded according to the length and fineness of the fibres. Longer wool normally goes into the worsted process. Combing the wool removes very short fibres and pieces of vegetable matter and it helps to ensure that the fibres lay parallel. The worsted process produces smooth yarn. Shorter fibres and wool 'skirts' (rough edges) are used in the woollen process. This produces bulky yarns with a fuzzy texture.

Sources of wool

Sheep are found in most countries in the world, but the main producers of wool for export are in the southern hemisphere. In 1995, for example, 28% of total world production of wool was produced in Australia and 11% was produced in New Zealand (see Figure 3). Australia is the major producer of Merino wool which is mainly used for clothing. New Zealand has a wetter climate more suited to Romney Sheep (which make up around 50% of the sheep population). Romney sheep produce a coarser wool suited to carpet manufacture. New Zealand is the biggest exporter of such wools.

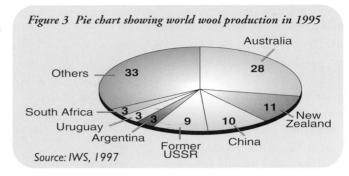

Figure 3 Pie chart showing world wool production in 1995

Others 33, Australia 28, New Zealand 11, China 10, Former USSR 9, Argentina 3, Uruguay 3, South Africa 3

Source: IWS, 1997

activities

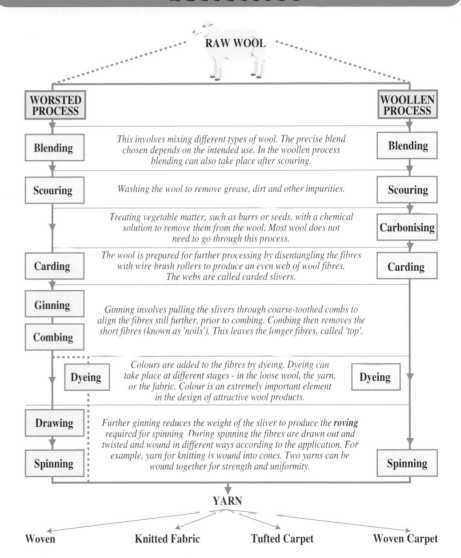

RAW WOOL

WORSTED PROCESS — WOOLLEN PROCESS

Blending — This involves mixing different types of wool. The precise blend chosen depends on the intended use. In the woollen process blending can also take place after scouring. — **Blending**

Scouring — Washing the wool to remove grease, dirt and other impurities. — **Scouring**

Treating vegetable matter, such as burrs or seeds, with a chemical solution to remove them from the wool. Most wool does not need to go through this process. — **Carbonising**

Carding — The wool is prepared for further processing by disentangling the fibres with wire brush rollers to produce an even web of wool fibres. The webs are called carded slivers. — **Carding**

Ginning / **Combing** — Ginning involves pulling the slivers through coarse-toothed combs to align the fibres still further, prior to combing. Combing then removes the short fibres (known as 'noils'). This leaves the longer fibres, called 'top'.

Dyeing — Colours are added to the fibres by dyeing. Dyeing can take place at different stages - in the loose wool, the yarn, or the fabric. Colour is an extremely important element in the design of attractive wool products. — **Dyeing**

Drawing / **Spinning** — Further ginning reduces the weight of the sliver to produce the **roving** required for spinning. During spinning the fibres are drawn out and twisted and wound in different ways according to the application. For example, yarn for knitting is wound into cones. Two yarns can be wound together for strength and uniformity. — **Spinning**

YARN

Woven   Knitted Fabric   Tufted Carpet   Woven Carpet

1. Describe the difference between a staple fibre and a continuous filament fibre. Give TWO examples of each.

2. a) What are the differences between the worsted process and the woollen process?

b) Describe the type of yarn produced by each process.

3. Name TWO animals apart from sheep which are used to produce textile fibres. Why do you think wool is produced in bigger quantities than fibres from other animals?

Wool technology

The International Wool Secretariat (IWS) is constantly trying to develop new technologies for the processing and finishing of wool. Working with the wool industry, its technical and marketing specialists create new wool products using the latest technical and scientific developments. New wool products and processes developed recently include:

● **cool wool** - lighter weight wool fabrics and garments
● **superwash** - a shrink resistant process which enables products labelled 'superwash' and 'machine washable' to be washed in washing machines without damage
● **zirpro** - a flame resistant finish for wool products used for protective clothing and aircraft upholstery.

The regulations governing product labelling allow the terms 'new wool' or 'virgin wool' to be used only for fibres shorn from a living sheep or lamb. Virgin wool products must be made from wool fibres which have not previously been:

● spun into yarn
● felted
● incorporated into a finished product.

The Woolmark is applied to pure new wool. As well as fibre content, the Woolmark guarantees a certain product quality level. The Woolblendmark is applied to blends where there is only one other fibre and a virgin wool content of at least 60% (see Case Study on p.124).

Other animals used to produce fibres

The alpaca and guanaco are two types of llama which are bred for their hair. They are shorn every two years and the hairs sorted by colour and fineness. The fibres are mainly fine, soft, lightly cropped and very warm. They are used in expensive knitted jackets, overcoats and blankets.

Cashmere comes from the coats of goats found in the Mongolian and Himalayan mountains. To withstand the extreme cold weather there, the goats have an unusually fine undercoat. At the annual coat change, the underhairs are separated

Figure 4 Camels

Camel hair is collected as it falls off the animal. It is never shorn. As a result, fabrics made with camel hair are very expensive.

from the coarser guard hairs and sorted by colour. Textile items made from cashmere are very soft, light and lustrous (shiny). Cashmere is the most expensive hair fibre.

Mohair is the hair of the angora goat which can be shorn twice a year. The best quality comes from animals in Texas, South Africa and Turkey. The hairs are long, lightly curled and have a silky lustre. They are white and

Figure 5 Silk production

A silk worm spins its cocoon. Most silk worms feed on mulberry bushes.

Silk cocoons before processing.

well suited for dyeing. Mohair is usually used to produce outerwear.

Angora fibre is the hair of the angora rabbit which is farmed in Europe and East Asia. The rabbits are shorn up to four times a year. The hairs are fine, very light and very absorbent. They are used in knitwear and for hats. The coarser guard hairs of the coat give angora fabrics their characteristic spiky appearance.

Natural fibres (2) - silk

The basic fibre substance of silk is fibroin. This is made from long-chain protein molecules which produce a continuous filament. Silk is made by the caterpillar of the silk moth (see Figure 5). The caterpillar spins a cocoon by producing a liquid which it secretes through a hole called a SPINNERET. This liquid sets into silk fibre which it winds around itself hundreds of times. Before the caterpillar grows into a moth (after around ten days), the cocoons are harvested and the pupae inside the cocoons killed with steam or dry heat. The cocoons are then placed into hot water to soften the gum. The filament ends are found and the filaments are wound onto a reel (an individual filament is too fine to be wound separately and so between seven and ten are collected and wound together). These filaments form the raw or 'greige' silk. The reeled silk is a bundle of continuous filaments around 1,000 metres long which comes from the middle part of the cocoon and is still cemented together by the gum. Later, several of these bundles are twisted together in the silk throwing process which increases their strength before spinning. Unwindable remnants from the cocoons are converted into spun yarns. They are made from the longer fibres and are separated by a combing machine. The silk fibre is long,

Figure 6 The silk seal

S Seide Silk Soie Seta

Table 2 Fabrics made from silk	
Chiffon	Duchesse
Crepe	Organza
Crepe de Chine	Satin
Damask	Taffeta.
Dupion	

smooth and it reflects light, giving it lustre. Since the fibres are continuous filaments, they are very strong.

Silk fibres can be made into a number of fabrics (see Table 2). The most important silk-producing countries are China, India, Japan and Thailand.

The internationally recognised silk seal (see Figure 6) is issued by the European Silk Secretariat. It shows that a product has been made from pure silk and guarantees a certain quality level.

Natural fibres (3) - cotton

Cotton is a natural fibre made from polymers of cellulose. Cotton grows on small

bushes. After the bushes flower, the seeds form pods called 'bolls' (see Figure 7) which burst open when they are ripe. In each boll there are about 30 seeds. The number of hairs on each seed ranges from 1,000 to 10,000 depending on the variety. Harvesting is done either by hand or using picking machines. If the newly harvested seed cotton is wet, it has to be dried using warm air. Ginning - the separation of the fibres from the seeds - then takes place. This is done using special machines (see Figure 9). The separated fibres called 'lints' have a staple length of between 15mm and 50mm, and 100kg of clean seeds yields around 35kg of fibre. The cotton fibres are compressed into large bales and sent to the cotton mill. At the mill, the fibre is carded (untangled) and combed (straightened). At this point, the fibres form a thin flat sheet which looks like a layer of cotton wool. The fibres are then drawn out to reduce their thickness ready for spinning.

Cotton is usually classified according to its variety and origin. Different varieties are grown in different countries. For example, the Giza

Figure 7

Cotton bolls

cottons of Egypt are a range of long-staple varieties. Sea Island cotton from the West Indies is a very high quality variety produced in small quantities. The most common variety is American Upland cotton.

Figure 8

The International Cotton Emblem

activities

Linen is a natural fabric made from the cellulosic fibres of the flax plant. Flax is pulled, not cut, during harvesting as the best fibres run right down into the root. Flax fibres are long, around 30-50 cm. To remove the fibres from the plant, it must first go through a process called 'retting'. The pectins (gummy substances) which bind the fibres and straw together are broken down through enzyme action by micro-organisms which occur naturally in the flax plant. For this process the plant is either laid out in the fields (dew retting) or steeped in warm water (water retting). 'Rippling' removes the seed capsules from the plant. 'Scutching' separates the fibre from the rest of the flax straw. This process is done mechanically in large turbines which roll, beat and break the straw, leaving the flexible flax fibres. The fibres are then 'hackled' (combed) so that the long fibres are parallel and the short fibres and impurities are removed. The fibre is then ready for spinning.
Source: The Irish Linen Guild, April 1997

Flax plants being harvested. The rows of flax are left in the field for retting

Flax fibre

IRISH LINEN

The Irish Linen trademark identifies 100% Irish linen and linen blends containing more than 50% flax fibres.

1. Draw a flow chart showing the various processes that take place in the production of linen fibres.

2. Name TWO vegetable sources for textile fibres. Describe the parts of the plant used for each fibre.

3. Compare the production of cotton and linen fibres. Describe the similarities and the differences.

4. Why do you think natural fibres are more expensive to produce than regenerated or synthetic fibres?

Table 3 Fabrics made from cotton		
Calico	Damask	Gabardine
Cambric	Denim	Oxford
Chintz	Drill	Poplin
Corduroy	Flannelette	Terry Towel
Velvet		

Figure 9 Cotton ginning

Cotton can be made into a large variety of fabrics (see Table 3). The International Cotton Emblem (see Figure 8) is an internationally registered symbol. It serves clearly to identify textiles made from pure cotton and implies good quality. It can only be applied to products which use 100% cotton fibres.

Other vegetable fibres

Other vegetable fibres include:
● linen (see activities on p.31)
● kapok
● hemp.

Kapok fibres come from hair cells which grow on the kapok fruit in Brazil, India, Indonesia and Mexico. The fibres are very weak and cannot be spun. They are soft and lustrous and are used as stuffing and wadding for items such as mattresses, cushions and life jackets.

Hemp fibres come from the hemp plant. Italy and Poland are the main producers of hemp. The fibres are strong, coarse and stiff.

Hemp is used for ropes and as backing for carpet (see activities on this page).

Regenerated fibres

Regenerated fibres are similar in composition to cotton. They are made from CELLULOSE which comes from natural sources such as wood pulp (wood chippings mixed with water). Before the fibre is made, the cellulose is extracted by a chemical so that the molecules can be reorganised into fibres. Regenerated fibres are classified according to the solvent system which is used to convert the cellulose raw material into a spinnable solution.

Viscose

The raw material for viscose is extracted from eucalyptus, pine or beech trees. After removing the bark, the wood is chipped into fragments from which resins and other impurities are extracted. The cellulose is purified and bleached and then pressed into solid sheets. For fibre production, the cellulose must be dissolved using the viscose process (see Figure 10). The cellulose sheets are first steeped in sodium hydroxide solution (an alkali). This penetrates into the molecular bundles and loosens their structure, forming soda cellulose. The excess liquid is pressed off and the soda cellulose is shredded and then allowed to age. Aging causes a reduction in the length of the cellulose molecules. Carbon disulphide is then added. This converts the cellulose to a form which is soluble. The cellulose is then dissolved in dilute sodium hydroxide to produce the spinning fluid. This fluid is degassed, filtered and extruded through fine spinnerets immersed in a coagulation bath. The cellulose is regenerated in the spinning bath and solidifies into

activities

The hemp plant and its cousins flax and linseed are fast emerging as the environmentally friendly crops of the late 20th century for making paper and clothes and for building timber and even car parts. Robert Lukies, a farmer and businessman in Essex, has developed a cost effective way of processing the hemp's fibre. Hemp from his farm will be made into jeans. Mr Lukies said: 'The beauty of hemp is that you can use the whole crop and it is so fast growing that it obliterates weeds and you don't need pesticides.' Unlike the hemp plants used for making illegal drugs, those on Mr Lukies' farm contain only 0.3% of mood-altering chemicals. Mr Lukies said: 'You could smoke a whole field of this stuff and only get a headache.'
Source: The Times, 11 April 1995

A field of hemp

1. What are the benefits of growing hemp?
2. Suggest reasons why few farmers in Britain grow hemp.
3. Give arguments for and against the view that the use of natural fibres will overtake that of synthetic fibres in the next 20 years or so.

Figure 10 Viscose production

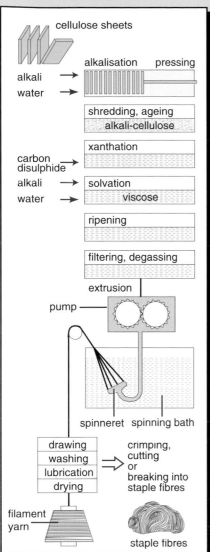

filaments which are drawn into filament yarn and wound onto a spool. The fibres are then washed and dried.

Filament viscose is used for effect yarns in woven and knitted fabrics, to make lustrous fabrics and for crepe fabrics. Many lining fabrics are made from viscose. Staple viscose fibres are usually used in blends with other fibres where their uniformity, lustre and absorbency are useful.

Acetate

Cellulose acetate is a combination of cellulose and acetic acid. It is a dry granular substance which can be dry spun (see Figure 11) when dissolved in acetone. Acetate fibres have a subdued lustre and produce fabric with an elegant drape.

Triacetate

Triacetate is made from glucose triacetate. It can be dry spun (see Figure 11) when dissolved in dichlormethane. Triacetate fibres are similar to acetate fibres.

Synthetic fibres

All synthetic fibres are made by similar processes involving different chemicals. Coal or oil are the raw materials from which all synthetic fibres are made. The production of synthetic fibres takes place in chemical plants. Simple chemicals (MONOMERS) are joined together to form complex chain molecules

('polymers'). This process is called POLYMERISATION. The polymers are used to make synthetic fibres. These fibres are produced by:

- WET SPINNING
- DRY SPINNING
- MELT SPINNING (see Figure 11).

Acrylic

Acrylic is made from simple chemicals derived from oil. Acrylonitrile is polymerised to form poly-acrylonitrile powder. The powder is then dissolved in dimethylformamide and either wet spun or dry spun into acrylic filaments. Acrylics are produced almost exclusively as staple fibres. They have a wool-like handle. Acrylic yarns are voluminous, very soft and warm.

Polyamide (nylon)

In the production of polyamide (nylon), two different monomers, an acid molecule and an amine molecule are joined together to form long chains. The most important polyamides are nylon 6 and nylon 6.6. The nylon polymer is then melt spun (see Figure 11). The polymer is melted and pumped through a spinneret (a hose with tiny holes like a shower head). The fibres are then dried in a stream of cold air.

Polyester

Polyester is synthesised from a simple substance obtained from oil. Like polyamide,

Figure 11 Wet spinning, dry spinning and melt spinning

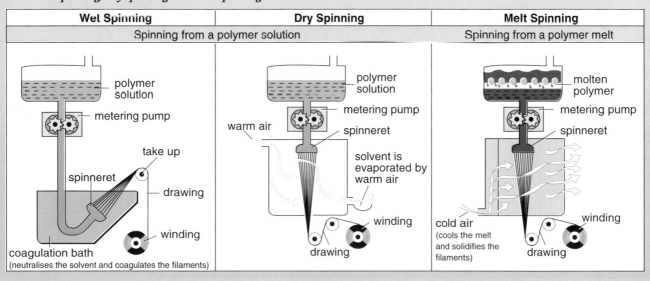

it is made from two monomers, an acid molecule and another molecule (ethylene glycol). These molecules are joined together to form the polyester polymer. The polyester is cast and cut into chips. These chips are melted at 280°C and melt spun (see Figure 11). After drawing them flat, the filaments are usually textured or cut into staple fibres. These staple fibres are mainly used in blends with other fibres.

Other synthetic fibres

Polyamide, polyester and acrylic are the most widely used synthetic fibres. There are many others, however, that are produced by a similar method using different chemicals. For example:

- polyvinyl chloride (PVC) - which is made from monomers of vinyl chloride.
- polypropylene (a hardwearing fibre used for carpets)
- elastane LYCRA® - a very stretchy fibre which is mixed with other fibres to improve elasticity.

In recent years, many new synthetic fibres have been developed, including TACTEL® (see Case Study, p.37). Some fibres are even made from recycled plastic bottles (see activities below).

Properties of fibres

The varying composition and structure of fibres give some indication of the different characteristics of each one (see Figure 12). People expect the textiles they use to have a wide variety of properties. For example, people expect clothing which is designed to be worn in cold weather to have good insulation qualities.

In general terms, the properties of fibres can be summarised as follows:

- fibres that are durable make fabrics that are hardwearing
- fibres that are strong make fabrics that do not break or tear when pressure is applied
- elastic fibres can stretch and then return to their original size
- absorbent fibres can soak up moisture
- fibres that are good insulators make fabrics that prevent heat passing through them.

Figure 12 Magnified fibres

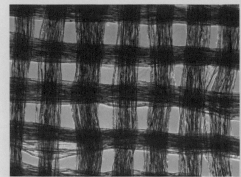

Electron micrograph of woven silk fibres (x80).

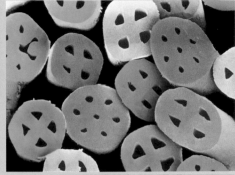

Electron micrograph of dacron polyester fibres used in sleeping bags (x300).

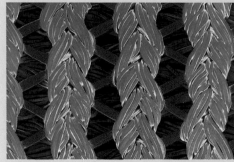

Electron micrograph of nylon stocking fibres (x150).

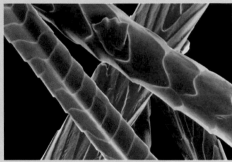

Electron micrograph of Angora wool fibres (x1,000).

activities

Berghaus has made a major commitment to the introduction of environmentally friendly fleece. All its standard fleece is produced in Malden's Polartec Recycled Fabric (89% recycled content). Recycled fabric is made from recycled plastic bottles which are broken down into chips, extruded into a fibre and spun into a polyester yarn which is then knitted to make a fleece fabric. Until recently, the only way to dispose of plastic bottles was to bury them or burn them. But this pollutes the atmosphere. Even when buried, they won't degrade. But now you can wear them.
Source: Berghaus August 1995

1. Is Malden's Polartec Recycled Fabric made of natural, regenerated or synthetic fibres?

2. Describe the process which is used to make the fibres used in Berghaus fleece.

3. a) 'The production of synthetic fibres on a large scale is dangerous to the environment'. Explain this statement.
   b) How might the development of recycled fibres improve matters?

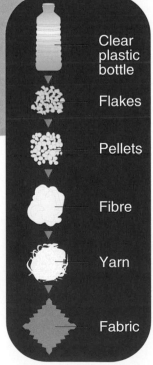

Clear plastic bottle

Flakes

Pellets

Fibre

Yarn

Fabric

The cost of raw materials, transport and the complexity of production all influence the final cost of producing fibres.

Mixing fibres

All fabrics have the same properties as the fibres from which they were made. Fabrics are often made from a mixture or blend of different fibres. For example, a polyester/cotton mix is often used to make shirts. The cotton makes the fabric absorbent and comfortable to wear. The polyester makes the fabric hardwearing and less likely to crease.

The development of new fibres

The earliest fibres to be used all came from natural sources. Regenerated and synthetic fibres have only been available this century. The development of new fibres is the result of:

● scientific advances in textile technology
● manufacturers' needs
● consumer demand.

Consumers want textile items made from fibres that have the properties of natural fibres but are stronger and easier to wash. Manufacturers want to produce fibres in the cheapest possible way. Scientific advance has led to the development of new synthetic fibres that have higher performance qualities than those produced before. For example, Microfibre is a new synthetic fibre that is light, strong and water repellent. It has good insulation properties and it feels, breathes and drapes just like silk. But it is much easier to care for than silk. Like other new fibres, Microfibre has been developed to meet consumer demand and manufacturers' needs. Its development, however, was only possible because of scientific advances.

activities

	Durability	Strength	Elasticity	Absorbency	Insulation	Cost	Ease of care	Crease resistance
Wool	**	*	****	****	****	***	*	****
Silk	**	****	**	****	***	****	*	**
Cashmere	**	*	****	****	****	****	*	***
Cotton	**	***	*	***	*	**	***	**
Linen	***	***	*	***	*	***	***	*
Viscose	*	**	*	****	**	*	**	*
Acetate	*	**	**	***	*	*	**	**
Triacetate	*	*	***	**	**	*	**	**
Polyamide	****	****	*	*	***	*	****	****
Polyester	****	****	****	*	***	*	****	****
Acrylic	***	**	***	*	***	*	***	****
PVC	*	*	**	*	***	*	****	****
Elastane	***	****	****	*	***	**	**	

Key to chart
The greater the number of ***, the greater the property in question. For example, a single * under cost means that the fibre is inexpensive while **** means that it is very expensive.

1. Using the table above, choose ONE natural fibre, ONE regenerated fibre and ONE synthetic fibre and write a description of each fibre's properties.
2. Suppose you have decided to make: (i) a nylon tent (ii) a cashmere jumper (iii) a pair of cotton socks and (iv) a top made of viscose. Explain why each fibre is suitable for the item you have decided to make.
3. You have been asked to make the following items: (i) a car seat cover (ii) a parachute (iii) a wedding dress (iv) a swimsuit (v) a sports shirt and (vi) a child's toy. What fibre or blend of fibres would you use for each item? Explain why.

Key Terms

Textile fibres - **fine hair-like structures.**
Filament - **a long fibre.**
Natural fibres - **fibres which come from plants or animals.**
Regenerated fibres - **natural fibres which have chemicals added to them.**
Synthetic fibres - **fibres made from chemicals only.**
Polymers - **groups or chains of molecules which make up fibres.**
Spinneret - **a tiny hole through which liquids are extruded to make fibres.**

Cellulose - **an organic substance found in all plant cells.**
Monomers - **single molecules.**
Polymerisation - **the process by which monomers are joined together to form polymers.**
Wet spinning - **the process by which polymers are extruded into a chemical bath which coagulates the filaments.**
Dry spinning - **the process by which polymers are extruded into a stream of warm air which solidifies the filaments.**
Melt spinning - **the process by which molten polymers are extruded into a cold air stream which solidifies the filaments.**

case study LYCRA®

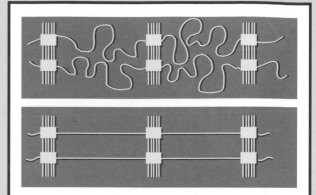

LYCRA® is an artificial elastic fibre invented and manufactured by DuPont. It belongs to the elastane group of artificial fibres and is described in chemical terms as a segmented polyurethane. Its properties of stretch and recovery enhance the characteristics of many fabrics.

LYCRA® can be stretched four to seven times its initial length without breaking and it instantly recovers its initial length when tension is relaxed. Compared to rubber, LYCRA® is stronger, more durable and has two to three times more restraining power with one third less weight. Unlike rubber, LYCRA® is resistant to both sun and salt water.

LYCRA® is always combined with other fabrics. Whatever the blend, a fabric enhanced with LYCRA® always retains the natural appearance and feel of its primary fibre. Whether knitted or woven, a fabric with LYCRA® becomes more lively, supple and drapeable and the garment therefore feels more comfortable to the wearer. LYCRA® yarns are produced in dull white, semi-transparent bright and clear versions. They come in a range of different thicknesses or yarn counts - from 11 to 1880 decitex. The decitex measurement indicates weight in grams of 10,000 metres of yarn (the lower the decitex number, the finer the yarn). Textile yarns can also be measured in deniers - the weight in grams of 9,000 metres of yarn.

LYCRA® is made up of soft segments bonded together with hard segments. This molecular structure provides the fibre with its capacity to stretch and recover.

Covering LYCRA®

Covering LYCRA® with another fibre ('sheathing') ensures that the visual and tactile characteristics of a fabric are not affected by the LYCRA®. It also temporarily stabilises the LYCRA®, making certain weaving and knitting techniques possible. LYCRA® can be combined with other fibres in three ways.

1. Single and double covered LYCRA®
The stretched LYCRA® is wrapped in either a single strand or two strands of non-elastic filament yarn. If two strands are used they are wrapped in opposite directions to balance the yarns' tendency to spiral.

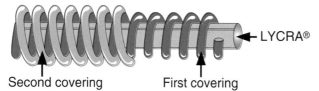

Second covering   First covering   —LYCRA®

2. Core-spinning
A non-elastic fibre - natural or artificial - is spun around stretched LYCRA®. The resulting yarn has the

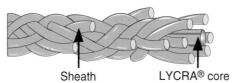

Sheath   LYCRA® core

appearance and feel of the yarn used to cover the LYCRA® (eg wool, cotton, nylon, silk).

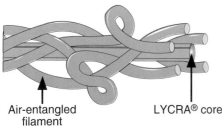

Air-entangled filament   LYCRA® core

3. Interlacing
A non-elastic multi-filament yarn is fed through an air jet together with stretched LYCRA®. The jet causes the yarns to intermingle, partially covering the LYCRA®. Because of the random loops on its surface, LYCRA® hooks onto the other yarn - a useful feature in some knitting constructions where a smoother elastic might slip.

LYCRA® makes all fabrics elastic. The direction and amount of stretch depends on the percentage of LYCRA® and the construction of the fabric. As little as 2% of LYCRA® is enough to improve fabric quality - contributing liveliness, drape and better shape retention. Where body-hugging fit and high performance stretch are required (eg in swimwear), fabrics contain between 14% and 40% of LYCRA®.

1880 decitex LYCRA® (top), a human hair (cente) and 11 decitex LYCRA®

Activities

1. Suggest FOUR textile items whose fabric might contain LYCRA®. Explain the advantage of using LYCRA® in each case.
2. Why might the use of LYCRA® be preferred to the use of rubber in garments?
3. Give TWO reasons why LYCRA® is always combined with another fibre.
4. Why is LYCRA® produced in so many different thicknesses?
5. How can LYCRA® be combined with non-elastic fibres? What is the result?

LYCRA® is a registered trademark of DuPont.

case study TACTEL®

In 1938, DuPont invented nylon. At first, the new fibre was used for mundane products such as fishing lines, bristles and tow-ropes. The development of nylon stockings, however, revolutionised its use. Its strength and easy-care properties, as well as its low price, encouraged other parts of the clothing and furnishing markets to use it. All sorts of nylon products were made - including nylon shirts and nylon sheets which many people found uncomfortable to wear or sleep in. During the 1960s, other synthetic fibres such as polyester and acrylic were developed and nylon began to lose its appeal. ICI realised the limitations of nylon and understood that, if it was to become successful again, a new fabric needed to be developed - a fabric which met customers' changing needs. Research revealed that comfort was the most important factor as far as customers were concerned and a new fibre, TACTEL®, was designed to meet this need. TACTEL® (from the Latin word 'tacto' meaning 'I touch') was first launched in 1983. It is made from a high quality polyamide yarn. Building on the useful properties of nylon, TACTEL® makes fabrics which have outstanding softness and are exceptionally lightweight. TACTEL® yarns are 30% lighter than cotton or polyester and have the highest strength to weight ratio of any fibre - natural or artificial. Clothes made of TACTEL® can also be breathable and waterproof.

Initially TACTEL® was launched in the skiwear market. Its excellent performance properties and exciting aesthetics provided highly functional yet fashionable garments. Within two years, TACTEL® had captured 50% of the skiwear market. This success led to the development of a whole range of TACTEL® yarns - from robust, hardwearing outdoor clothing at one end of the range to soft, luxurious hosiery and lingerie at

Fleece fabrics using 100% TACTEL® yarns, in addition to having thermal insulation and outstanding softness, have inherent moisture management properties.

The versatility of TACTEL®

TACTEL® Micro was launched in 1988. TACTEL® Micro fibres are 60 times finer than human hair but six times stronger than silk, one of nature's toughest fibres. This ensures garments are softer and more comfortable and have better performance. Again skiwear was the target area, but it was in the hosiery sector that TACTEL® Micro made the biggest impact.

TACTEL® Diabolo is a fibre with a cross-section shaped like a diabolo toy. It produces a wonderful lustre and is notable for its sensual drape, fluidity and outstanding softness. It has been used extensively for lingerie and sportswear.

Fabric profile

LIGHTWEIGHT

ABRASION RESISTANCE

STRENGTH TO WEIGHT RATIO

AESTHETIC/COMFORT

— New high performance fabric in TACTEL®
— Standard nylon
— Polyester

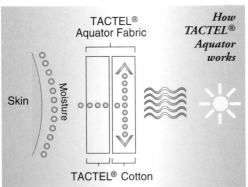

How TACTEL® Aquator works

TACTEL® Aquator Fabric

Skin

Moisture

TACTEL® Cotton

TACTEL® Aquator uses TACTEL® yarns as an inner layer which moves moisture away from the body to the outer layer (see diagram, left). This promotes efficient evaporation and increased comfort. TACTEL® Aquator is used for sportswear and functional underwear.

the other. Many designers are now experimenting with TACTEL®. Paul Smith, Helen Storey, Jean-Paul Gaultier and Issey Miyake, for example, all agree that it is a welcome alternative to the traditional and often more limiting natural fibres and they use it in their collections.

In July 1993, DuPont acquired ICI fibres' worldwide nylon businesses and, with it, the TACTEL® brand. DuPont are delighted with the success of TACTEL® but recognise that trends are constantly changing. At DuPont Nylon Textile Centre in Gloucester, textile scientists and designers are therefore researching and developing new ideas for TACTEL®.

Activities

1. a) Is TACTEL® a natural or synthetic fibre?
    b) What are the properties of TACTEL®?
2. Why was TACTEL® developed?
3. Why do you think TACTEL® was successful?
4. What is the difference between TACTEL® Micro, TACTEL® Aquator and TACTEL® Diabolo? Give TWO examples of new clothes each might be used for.

TACTEL® is a registered trademark of DuPont.

Fabric construction

From fibre to yarn

Most fabrics are made from yarns. A yarn is made by spinning fibres together. This involves twisting straightened fibres together so that they cling to each other to form a continuous thickness.

To spin staple fibres (natural fibres such as cotton, wool and linen - see Unit 6), the yarn must be:

- cleaned to remove dirt and waste;
- carded to untangle the fibres and align them parallel to each other
- drawn into a 'sliver' or a 'strand' ready for spinning.

Yarns that are produced by spinning staple fibres have to be twisted together quite tightly

Figure 1

Staple   Continuous filament

to stop them being pulled apart. The ends of the fibres can be seen sticking out at the side of the yarn, giving it a 'fuzzy' appearance (see Figure 1).

Spinning continuous filament fibres (synthetic fibres and silk) is less complicated and results in very fine, sheer yarns and fabrics (see also Figure 1). Before spinning, continuous filaments are drawn or stretched to make the fibres stronger.

Figure 2 A traditional spinning wheel. Today, industrial spinning machines spin large quantities of yarn rapidly.

Texturising fibres

Fine, straight filament fibres produce yarns and fabrics that lack bulk. Bulk can be added in two ways:

- by chopping up the long filaments into staple size fibres and then spinning them

in the way described above - a lengthy and expensive process
- by texturising the fibres (a common technique with synthetic fibres).

TEXTURISING fibres means crimping them by twisting and folding them and then setting them by heat (a process similar to curling and crimping hair). Texturising fibres

activities

1. Scouring

The fleece is passed through a washing plant to extract grease and dirt. 'Lanolin', a by-product used in soap and cosmetics, is produced.

2. Carding

Twigs and burrs are removed and the long fibres are separated and straight-ened. A ribbon of loose, untwisted fibres is produced - the 'carded sliver'. The fibres used for wool are spun at this point.

3. Combing

As the worsted process uses only the long fibres, the carded sliver is combed to separate out the long fibres, producing the 'combed top'.

4. Spinning

The combed top is twisted slightly before being placed on a spinning frame . It is then drawn out and twisted into a fine single ply yarn.

The pictures, above, show the four stages in the production of worsted yarn after the sheep has been sheared (see also p.29, Unit 6).

1. Why does the wool pass through each of these four stages?
2. How would you expect worsted yarn to differ from woollen yarn?
3. Compare and contrast the production of worsted yarn, polyester yarn and cotton yarn (use the information on cotton and polyester in Unit 6).

makes yarns and fabrics more elastic and gives them a more interesting and varied appearance. This method of adding bulk is much cheaper.

How fibres are spun into yarns

Traditionally, spinning was done by hand, using a weight. Spinners twisted the yarn manually with their fingers or used a spinning wheel where the twist is put into the yarn by the rotation of the wheel (see Figure 2). Both methods produce yarns which are not uniform in thickness. Today, yarns are spun for the mass market by machine. Yarn is spun very quickly. The yarn produced is of a predetermined, uniform thickness.

Twisting yarns

Yarn is twisted to hold the fibres together. The more a yarn is twisted, the stronger it will be. Yarns of different texture can be produced by spinning them either very loosely or very tightly. Worsted yarn is wool that has been spun very tightly to produce yarn that makes very fine, hardwearing fabric. Wool fibres that are spun together less tightly produce yarns and fibres that are not so hardwearing and have a less regular texture.

When a yarn is spun, it is twisted anticlockwise, the S twist or clockwise, the Z twist (see Figure 3). The direction a yarn is twisted is important when making more complex yarns. Yarns made with an uneven balance of Z and S twists relax unevenly and distortion of the yarn and fabric occurs.

Figure 3 The 'S' and 'Z' twist

Forming complex yarns

A single yarn or 'thread' is made by twisting a group of fibres together. When a number of single yarns are then twisted together, a two, three or MULTIPLE PLY YARN is produced. This is also known as 'plied yarn'. Two ply yarn is made by twisting two single yarns together. Yarns that are used for knitting go up to four ply. The label on a ball of hand knitting wool states what the ply is.

When two plied yarns are twisted together, a CORDED YARN is produced. This is a very strong yarn, used in the production of embroidery threads and rope (see Figure 4).

Mixed fibre yarns

Plied and corded yarns are usually made from yarns of the same fibre. By twisting two or more yarns made from different fibres together, a wider variety of yarns can be produced. Bouclé yarn, for example, is formed by combining three yarns, each made from fibres with different characteristics. One of the yarns is used to form loops (see Figure 5), giving bouclé yarn its characteristic texture.

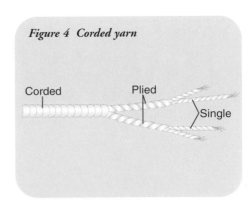

Figure 4 Corded yarn

Novelty yarns

Novelty yarns are made from three different plied yarns (often made of different fibres). Novelty yarns can be single or multi-coloured. They are

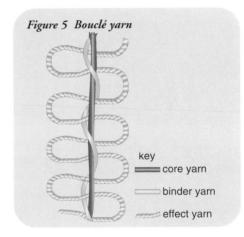

Figure 5 Bouclé yarn

key
— core yarn
— binder yarn
— effect yarn

activities

1. What is the difference between bouclé yarn and three ply yarn?

2. When would you use the three types of yarn pictured right?

3. What type of yarn would you use:
(i) to mend a button, (ii) to make a tow rope, and (iii) to make a baby's jumper? Explain your answers.

The four ply yarn (left) is made by spinning together four fibres made of nylon, acrylic and wool. The three ply yarn (middle) is made by spinning together three courtelle fibres. The bouclé yarn (right) is made by spinning together two acrylic fibres and one nylon fibre.

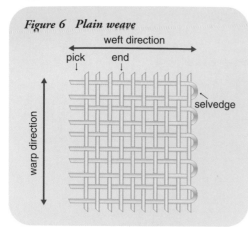

Figure 6 Plain weave

weft direction

pick   end

selvedge

warp direction

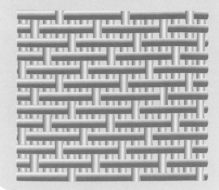

Figure 7 Twill weave

Figure 8 Sateen weave

interesting because of their varied appearance, texture and colour mixes. Metallic yarns are sometimes incorporated into novelty yarns.

Fabric construction

There are three main ways of making fabric:
- weaving yarn
- knitting yarn
- bonding fibres.

A fabric's properties (how it behaves and what it is capable of - see Unit 8) depend on what fibre or fibres it is made from and how it is constructed.

Woven fabric

Weaving is the most popular method of producing fabric. Fabric is formed by interlacing a series of yarns at right angles to each other. Woven fabrics are held together by the friction created where the yarns cross each other. If the weave is loose and there is not enough friction between the yarns, the fabric will easily be distorted.

Woven fabric is produced on looms. These range from small-scale hand-operated looms to sophisticated computerised looms that produce fabric on a mass scale at high speeds. All looms work on the same principle.

Woven cloth is made from two sets of yarns - WARP YARNS (running the full length of the cloth) and WEFT YARNS (running the width of the cloth). When the woven cloth is made on a loom which uses a shuttle to weave the weft yarn over or under the warp yarn, an edge or SELVEDGE (also called a 'selvage') is formed where the weft yarns wrap around the end warp yarn. Modern shuttleless looms, however, do not weave fabrics with selvedges. Fabric made on these machines has edges that have yarn ends sticking out.

All woven cloth has a GRAIN or direction in which the yarns travel. The grain runs parallel or at right angles to the selvedge. Woven fabric does not stretch significantly when pulled along the grain. It stretches most across the BIAS (diagonally across the grain).

By changing the order in which the weft yarns travel over or under the warp yarns, fabrics of different texture can be created. The four main weaves are as follows.

Plain weave

Plain weave is the simplest weave. The weft yarn passes over and under alternate warp yarns, two rows forming the pattern. Plain weave is used to make fine fabrics such as calico which is used to make shirts. The weave in Figure 6 is a plain weave.

Twill weave

Twill weave (see Figure 7) is recognised by diagonal lines across the fabric. The weft yarn passes over two and under two warp threads,

activities

Fabric is woven on a traditional loom by threading the warp yarns from the warp beam, through the heddles, through the reed to the cloth beam, where it is fastened. The weft yarn is wound onto a pirn which fits into the shuttle. The heddles move in alternate directions, separating the weft yarns and making a gap (a 'shed') through which the shuttle passes. The reeds beat the weft yarns into place on the cloth beam. When the shuttle turns round the last warp thread, the heddles move, creating a new shed, forming the selvedge.

1. What function do heddles serve when weaving?
2. How is tightly woven fabric made?
3. Suggest THREE types of fabric that might be woven on a traditional loom?
4. What are the limitations of the traditional loom?

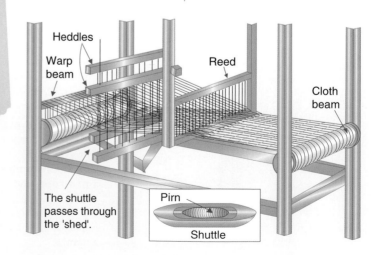

Heddles

Warp beam

Reed

Cloth beam

The shuttle passes through the 'shed'.

Pirn

Shuttle

Figure 9 Weft knitting

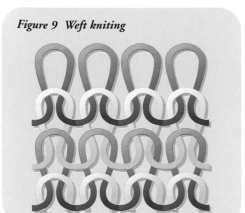

Figure 9 Weft knitting

the order moving one thread to the next row. Four rows of weft yarn form the pattern. Twill weave makes dense, hardwearing fabric - for example, denim used to make jeans and workwear.

Sateen weave

Sateen weave is recognised by its shiny right side. The weft threads go over between four and eight warp threads and then under one. Sateen fabrics are sheer and delicate as the long length of the weft threads on the surface of the fabric are exposed and can easily be snagged. Sateen woven fabric is used to make luxury items - for example, underwear. Satin is made using this weave.

Jacquard weave

The most complicated weaves are made on jacquard looms which can be set to weave in different sequences to produce patterns. The fabrics produced on jacquard looms are high quality and expensive.

Knitted fabric

Knitting is the second most popular method of producing fabric. There are two ways to knit fabric - WEFT KNITTING and WARP KNITTING.

Weft knitting

Knitted fabric made from one long length of yarn is called 'weft knitting'. The basic principle of weft knitting is that loops are formed along a length of yarn and the interlocking of these loops above and below each row holds the fabric together. This is called weft knitting since the yarn runs across

the rows from left to right like weft yarns in woven fabric (see Figure 9). All knitting done by hand is weft knitting.

Warp knitting

'Warp knitting' is so called because the yarns run and interlock with each other vertically up and down the length of fabric, each piece of fabric coming from a separate source (see Figure 10). All warp knitted fabric is produced by industrial knitting machines. The lace used for bras, for example, is knitted using this method. The fabric produced has slightly different properties from weft knitted fabric. Warp knitting cannot be done by hand.

Non-woven fabrics

Non-woven fabrics are made from fibres without first being made into yarns. The fibres are bonded together in different ways depending on the fibre used and what the fabric is to be used for. Fibres are bonded

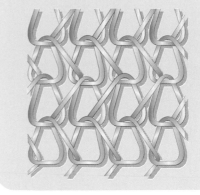

Figure 10 Warp knitting

together by:

- **sticking** with adhesive
- **heating** (heat is used to fuse together thermoplastic fibres)
- **stitching** together a web of fibres
- **punching** a web of fibres with hot needles.

As non-woven fibres are not made from yarns, they do not have an ordered structure or grain like woven and knitted fabric. They therefore have quite different properties.

activities

This photo shows fabric made by weft knitting (left) and warp knitting (right).

A lace bodice and a handknitted jumper

1. Which of the two items pictured above is likely to be made of weft knitted fabric and which is likely to be made of warp knitted fabric?
2. How would you expect the properties of the two items to differ?
3. What are the advantages and disadvantages of handknitting a jumper?

The properties of weft and warp knitted fabric

Weft knitting
- easy to unravel
- ladders and runs if cut or pulled
- curls at the edges when cut
- very stretchy
- looses shape easily
- has a right side and a wrong side

Warp knitting
- difficult to unravel
- does not ladder or run
- lies flat when cut
- elastic but stable
- keeps shape well
- both sides are the same

Non-woven fabrics are stiff and do not DRAPE well. This is because the arrangement of fibres is random and the fabric has no grain. Non-woven fabrics are not very strong since the fibres are not twisted together (fibres can easily rub or pull out). They do not stretch and, if pulled, the shape does not recover.

The uses of non-woven fabrics are therefore limited by their properties. One of the main advantages of non-woven fabrics is that they can be produced easily and cheaply. As a result, they are used for disposable items such as wash cloths and operating theatre gowns. Alternatively, they are used in conjunction with other fabrics. For example, they are used as interlining to stiffen woven and knitted fabric or as underfelt for carpets (see Figure 11). Advantage is taken of their dense structure and insulating properties by using them, for example, as thermal lining in coats and jackets.

Many fibres are used to make non-woven fabrics, but the commonest are synthetic fibres such as polyester, nylon and viscose.

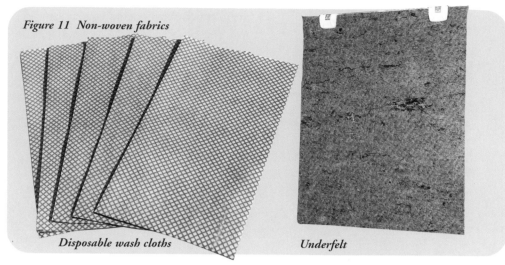

Figure 11 Non-woven fabrics

Disposable wash cloths   *Underfelt*

Felting

Most non-woven fabrics are made from synthetic fibres, but wool has been made into non-woven fabric for centuries. Non-woven wool fabric is known as 'felt'. Felting is one of the oldest methods of making fabric. The fibres of wool felt together when treated with

moisture, heat and pressure. Felt cloth has a thick, matted appearance with no straight grain. It does not fray when cut. The wool fibres felt together because of the structure of the fibres. The scales on the surface of wool fibres lock and tangle together (see Figure 12). This is also why knitted or woven woollen items can shrink if they are not washed properly. Felted wool is used to make hats and

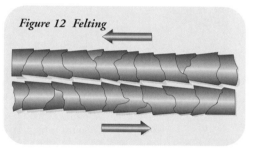

Figure 12 Felting

soft toys and it is used as as protective layer on the underside of rigid items such as trophies and lamps.

Laminated fabric

Laminated fabric is made by joining two or more fabrics together in layers. Foam is often used to provide an insulating layer and PVC is sometimes joined to woven fabric to produce a fabric that is waterproof. Laminated fabrics are used to make outdoor coats, protective coverings and mattress covers.

Net and lace

Net and lace fabrics are made from fine yarns which are twisted together with a very

activities

Non-woven fabrics are often used to make disposable textile items. They are used extensively in hospitals, especially in operating theatres and X-ray departments. The surgeons in the picture (right) are wearing face masks made of non-woven fabric. The patient's gown is made of non-woven material.

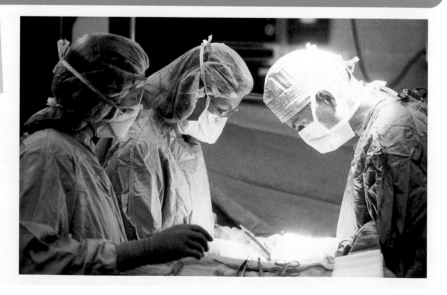

1. How do the properties of woven and non-woven fabrics differ? Why?

2. Describe THREE situations when it would be appropriate to use non-woven fabric.

3. Why do you think hospitals make extensive use of items made of non-woven fabric?

Figure 13

A lace dress

open structure. A decorative pattern is created by the shape and position of the holes in the fabric. Net and lace are used to make net curtains, decorative tablecloths and clothing for special occasions, such as wedding dresses. Lace fabric was traditionally made by hand, using very complicated designs and patterns. Today, however, it is more commonly made by machine.

Fabric with pile

Some fabrics, such as velvet and corduroy, are made with a furry texture. They have a 'pile'. These fabrics are made by weaving or knitting. Velvet can be produced in two ways. First, it can be produced by weaving two thicknesses of fabric together, with extra warp threads travelling between the two. As the double layer fabric is woven, the pile is carefully cut, separating the two layers and creating a fabric similar to a very smooth carpet. After being cut, piles are sheared, brushed and steamed to make them stand up. The second way of making velvet involves passing the weft yarns over wires forming loops. When the wires are pulled away, the loop is then cut, forming the pile.

The pile in all pile fabrics goes one way. The fabric therefore looks slightly darker if the light catches it upside down or if the pile is smoothed by hand. Because of this, pile fabrics are said to have a NAP - a one directional brushed surface.

Ecological considerations and large-scale fabric production

Before the industrial revolution, all textile items were produced on a small scale. People produced fabric on a loom in their home or in small workshops. This is often described as 'cottage industry'.

Developing technology resulted in the mechanisation of fabric production Early machines were steam driven. The steam was made by burning coal and the smoke from the coal caused pollution. Although modern machines are driven by electricity, fabric construction still has an ecological impact.

First, although natural fibres come from renewable sources, many synthetic fibres are derived from fossil fuels, a resource which cannot be renewed. Second, most synthetic fabrics are not biodegradable and it is difficult to dispose of them in an ecologically friendly way once their useful life has ended. And third, fabrics are often treated with chemicals which can have a harmful effect on the environment if released as either gas or liquid.

activities

1. Describe how the fabric for each of the items pictured here is made.

2. Suggest reasons why this method of construction is used.

Fuzzy felt

Nylon tights

Velvet curtains

Denim jeans

Key Terms

Texturising - crimping and then setting fibres to add bulk.

Multiple ply yarn - a number of single yarns twisted together to form a new yarn.

Corded yarn - a number of plied yarns twisted together.

Warp yarn - vertical yarn running the length of a woven fabric.

Weft yarn - yarns which run horizontally across a woven fabric.

Selvedge - the very edge of woven fabric (the end warp yarn).

Grain - the direction of the construction of a piece of fabric.

Bias - an imaginary line drawn diagonally across the grain of woven fabric.

Weft knitting - creating fabric by forming loops along a single length of yarn.

Warp knitting - creating fabric by interlocking a number of yarns along the length of the fabric.

Drape - a fabric's ability to form folds or pleats.

Nap - a one directional brushed surface.

Properties of fabrics

Selecting fabrics

When selecting fabric for designing and making textile items, it is essential to choose the fabric that has the right PROPERTIES. For example, when making outdoor winter clothing, it is necessary for the fabric to have good insulating properties. Similarly fabric used for children's clothing needs to be able to withstand frequent washing.

The properties of fabrics

The properties of a fabric depend on three factors:
- the fibres from which the fabric is made (see Unit 6)
- the construction of the fabric
- the processes which are applied to the fabric during or after construction (fabric finishes - see Unit 11).

In theory, any fibre can be used for any method of fabric construction. In practice, however, there are exceptions. For example, towelling is not usually made from nylon yarn because the fabric is designed for maximum absorbency and nylon has very low absorbency. Cotton and cotton blends are normally used for towelling.

Generalisations can be made about the properties of fabrics by taking into consideration the way in which they were constructed. However, variations and exceptions must be acknowledged.

Woven fabric

Woven fabric has four main properties:
- it does not stretch significantly along the grain of the fabric, but it will stretch when pulled diagonally across the bias

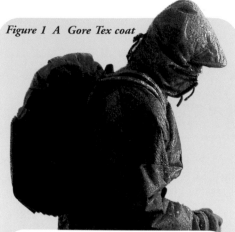

Figure 1 A Gore Tex coat

This coat is made from three layer Gore Tex. The Gore Tex membrane is sandwiched between two layers of nylon. Gore Tex is waterproof, windproof and breathable. It is also thin, lightweight, strong and durable.

- depending on the closeness of the weave, it is quite resilient
- because of the grain, it usually has some degree of drape, but the closeness and variety of weave affects this
- it usually does not insulate as well as

activities

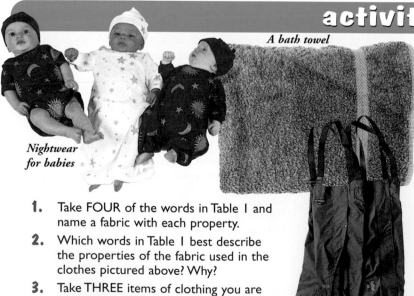

Nightwear for babies

A bath towel

Salopettes

1. Take FOUR of the words in Table 1 and name a fabric with each property.
2. Which words in Table 1 best describe the properties of the fabric used in the clothes pictured above? Why?
3. Take THREE items of clothing you are wearing and describe the properties of the fabric used in each item.

Table 1 The properties of fabrics
Absorbent - can soak up moisture.
Abrasion resistant - does not wear out easily.
Colourfast - retains its colours after washing or exposure to sunlight.
Conductor - allows the passage of heat through it.
Crease resistant - does not easily crease.
Elastic - will stretch and return to its original shape and size.
Insulator - prevents the passage of heat through it.
Mothproof - is resistant to clothes moth.
Non-flammable - does not catch fire or burn easily.
Non-irritant - is comfortable against the skin.
Non-shrink - does not reduce in size when washed.
Resilient - returns to original shape after pulling or crushing.
Showerproof - keeps a small amount of water out.
Strong - can resist a great deal of strain without tearing.
Washable - can be washed without damaging the fabric.
Waterproof - keeps water out completely.

knitted fabric. In woven fabric, there is less space in which to trap air.

However, closely woven fabrics can be used to prevent cold air currents passing through a garment.

Knitted fabric

All knitted fabric:
- stretches to some degree because of its loop construction
- is absorbent
- easily sheds creases.

Non-woven fabric

Due to the random arrangement of fibres in non-woven fabric (the fibres are not twisted together), non-woven fabrics are not very hardwearing and have very little drape or flexibility.

Testing a fabric's suitability

Before making a decision about which fabric to use, its suitability can be assessed by testing the fabric. One of the most useful ways to evaluate a fabric is to test its CHARACTERISTICS (the way it looks, feels and behaves - see Table 2).

Look at the fabric to see:
- how the fabric is made - what weave or knit method is used?
- whether the fabric has an obvious grain
- whether the construction is dense (close) or open
- whether the yarns are staple or filament
- whether the fabric will easily snag or ladder.

Feel the fabric to find out about:
- crease resistance - squeeze a

piece of fabric in your hand for 30 seconds. If the fabric creases, do the creases remain? Can they be smoothed away?
- elasticity - pull the fabric in all directions and check if the fabric returns to its original size and shape
- comfort or irritation - hold the fabric against a sensitive area of the skin such as the inside of the wrist or neck
- weight - does the fabric feel heavy or light?
- stiffness or drape - hold the fabric up by a corner. The fabric will either form folds or it will stick out stiffly.

Another important way to evaluate a fabric is to read the information on the label (see Figure 2, left). The label describes the fibre content of the fabric and provides important information about the fabric's properties.

Table 2 The characteristics of fabrics

Colour/pattern - is the fabric the same on both sides?

Construction - how much space is there between threads? How firmly are the threads held in place?

Dimensional stability - how stable is the fabric? Fabrics which slither about and lose shape are difficult to cut out.

Drape - is the fabric stiff or floppy?

Hole recovery - does the fabric recover from needle or pin marks? Some fabrics do not.

Fraying - how easily do the yarns come apart? If they come apart easily, this can make seams weaker.

Snagging - are there loose threads which are liable to catch and pull out yarns from the fabric?

Texture - what is the feel and physical appearance of the fabric?

Thickness - is the fabric bulky or thin?

Non-irritant - is the fabric comfortable against the skin?

Transparency - is it possible to see through the fabric? Fabrics can be transparent (see-through), opaque (not see-through) or translucent (in between).

Weight - is the fabric heavy or light?

Figure 2 A label showing a fabric's characteristics

SOFT & SHEER TIGHTS
WITH A HIGH LYCRA® CONTENT
FOR A BETTER FIT AND DURABILITY
REINFORCED BODY & TOE

	HIPS		HEIGHT	
	cms	inches	cms	ft/inches
SMALL	87-92	34-36	152-163	5'0"-5'4"
MEDIUM	92-99	36-39	157-170	5'2"-5'7"
LARGE	99-107	39-42	157-175	5'2"-5'9"
EX LARGE	107-132	42-52	157-175	5'2"-5'9"

HAND WASH AND DRY SEPARATELY

94% NYLON 6% LYCRA® ELASTANE
EXCLUDING WAISTBAND

* DUPONT'S REGISTERED TRADEMARK
FOR ITS ELASTANE FIBRE

activities

Suppose you had chosen to go on the holiday advertised to the right. You decide to buy some clothes to take with you, but you have limited space as you will have to carry your luggage.

Two weeks in Florida
14-28 August.
Fly to Orlando & drive from there.
Flight, room and car hire - £1,489.
Source: Lunn Poly, Ormskirk, April 1997

1. Name TWO fabrics which you might well avoid because they crease too easily.

2. How would you test the suitability of the clothing before buying it?

3. Suggest FIVE items of clothing that you would take with you. Explain why the properties of the fabric used for each item are particularly suitable for this holiday.

Testing abrasion resistance

The following test involves damaging the fabric. It is therefore not appropriate to do it on pieces of fabric that are to be used. Rather, scraps should be used.

Samples of fabric are secured to a table using sticky tape. The fabric samples are then 'worn' by stroking them with a sanding block wrapped in fine emery paper, using strokes of equal pressure and length. The number of strokes needed to produce noticeable wear is recorded as is the number of strokes required to make a hole. The fabric with the highest score is the most hardwearing.

Testing water repellency

Fabric samples are fixed in embroidery frames so that the fabric is taut and not touching any surfaces. The surface of the fabric is then made wet with water, using a dropping pipette (see Figure 3). The same number of drips are dropped onto each sample. The amount of time taken for each sample to absorb the water is recorded. If the water remains in bubbles on the surface, the sample is waterproof. The longer a sample

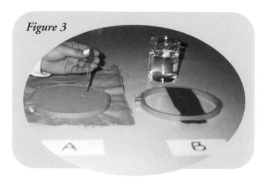
Figure 3

takes to absorb the water, the more water repellent it is. Those which take longest to absorb the water are probably showerproof.

This test can also serve as a rough guide to how absorbent a piece of fabric is. Absorbent fabrics are more comfortable to wear than non-absorbent fabrics.

Testing flammability

This test is done to establish whether or not a fabric is flammable. Non-flammability is an

especially important quality in items such as children's nightwear.

Strips of fabric (5cm x 20cm) are securely attached to a metal rod with a clip which is, in turn, securely fixed to a stand (see Figure 4). A flame is applied to the bottom of each sample for two seconds. The fabric is then observed as it burns to find out:

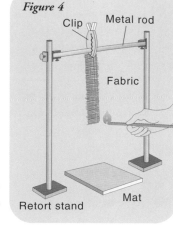
Figure 4
Clip
Metal rod
Fabric
Retort stand
Mat

● how fast the flame travels
● whether ash is formed or the sample melts into a hard ball
● how long each sample takes to burn
● how much smoke is produced.

activities

1. Name a fabric which is:
   i) hardwearing
   ii) delicate
   iii) waterproof
   iv) showerproof
   v) highly flammable
   vi) non-flammable
2. Using Tables 3-5 describe the properties of the following fabrics:
   i) denim
   ii) gaberdine
   iii) flannelette.
3. Which fabric might be suitable for the following items:
   i) a shirt to wear to work
   ii) a child's anorak
   iii) a chef's overalls?
   Explain why.

Table 3 Abrasion test results

Table 3 Fabric	Nº of strokes to wear fabric	Nº of strokes to make a hole
Denim	4	13
Polyester satin	1	4
Gaberdine	5	13
Flannelette	3	7
Cambric	3	9
Close weave nylon	5	14

Table 4 Water repellency test results

Table 4 Fabric	Absorbs water	Nº of seconds taken to absorb water
Denim	Yes	12
Polyester satin	Yes	10
Gaberdine	Yes	24
Flannelette	Yes	6
Cambric	Yes	16
Close weave nylon	No	

Table 5 Fabric	Speed of flame (fast 5, slow 1)	Ash or hard bead	Smoke or fumes?
Denim	3	grey ash	burning paper
Polyester satin	4	hard brown bead	chemical smell
Gaberdine	1	ash	smell of burnt hair
Flannelette	5	grey ash	burning paper
Cambric	4	grey ash and hard brown bead	burning paper and sharp chemical smell
Close weave nylon	3	stringy bead	chemical smell

Table 5 Flammability test results

Figure 5
WARNING
HIGH FIRE DANGER
KEEP AWAY FROM FIRE

Fabrics with open, loose textures are easily flammable. Wool and silk are the most flame resistant fibres. Some fabrics are labelled if a fabric is flammable (see Figure 5) so that the item is kept away from heat sources.

Enhancing the properties of fabrics

Fibres are often mixed or BLENDED to produce fabric that

has the combined benefits of two or more fibres and also to minimise the negative qualities that any single fibre might have. Fibres are blended or mixed:

● when yarns are spun
● when fabrics are woven or knitted.

Fabrics are also combined or LAMINATED for the same reasons.

Blending fibres

Two or more fibres can be mixed together at the spinning stage. For example, polyester and cotton are often spun together, producing a yarn and then a fabric which has the desirable qualities of polyester (it is crease resistant and hardwearing) and the desirable qualities of cotton (it is cool, absorbent and easy to care for).

Other examples of blended fibres are:

● wool and nylon
● wool and cotton (viyella)
● linen and polyester
● cotton and elastane
● bouclé yarn.

Cotton and elastane (LYCRA®) is combined by wrapping cotton fibres around filaments of elastane to provide a yarn and then fabric which has the desirable qualities of cotton and the ability to stretch and

Figure 6 Blended fibres

Bouclé yarn

recover its shape. This fabric is also less likely to crease as it is usually knitted.

Bouclé yarn can be made from three different fibres (see p.39 and Figure 6 above). The core yarn is made from a strong fibre. The binder yarn is made from a fine fibre. And the effect yarn provides the texture.

Mixing yarns

After fibres have been made into yarns, they can be combined together to make fabric with two or more fibres. Woven fabrics can be made by using a yarn made from one fibre in the warp and a yarn made from a different fibre in the weft. Mixing different yarns like this is sometimes called a UNION. An example of this is linen union which is made by weaving linen and cotton together. Linen union is used for tea towels. The union makes the tea towel absorbent and hardwearing and

the fabric can be laundered at high temperatures. Linen union is also less expensive than 100% linen fabric.

Laminating or layering fabrics

Fabrics can be combined in layers after they have been made (see also Unit 11). Layered fabric can be recognised by its different front and back or it may be possible to peel the layers apart. Quilted fabric is an example of a layered fabric. Wadding (polyester or cotton) is sandwiched between two layers of woven or knitted fabric (see Figure 7). The wadding provides a layer of insulation. The outer layer prevents the wadding from disintegrating and provides a decorative surface. Layering and laminating fabrics can be a way of combining the desirable properties or characteristics of two or more fabrics. Sometimes, however, layering and laminating cancels out a property of one or more of the fabrics. For example, when knitted fabric is quilted, the resulting fabric will not stretch.

Figure 7 Quilted material

Key Terms

Properties of fabric - **the way in which a fabric behaves in different circumstances.**
Characteristics of fabric - **the way a fabric looks, feels and behaves.**
Blending fibres - **mixing different fibres before making yarn.**
Laminating fabrics - **combining different fabrics in layers.**
Union - **weaving fabric using a different yarn on the weft and the warp.**

activities

Look at the results of the survey (right).

1. Describe the different properties of each fabric mentioned in the survey.
2. Give THREE reasons why polyester-cotton was the most popular fabric. Why do you think that nylon was the least popular?.
3. Conduct a survey of your colleagues to find out which fabrics are most commonly used in coats. Draw bar charts showing your results and write a passage analysing your findings.

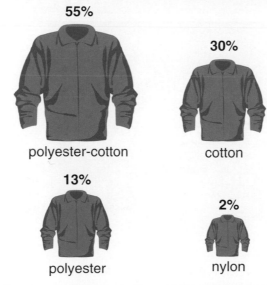

55%
polyester-cotton

30%
cotton

13%
polyester

2%
nylon

Results of a survey of office workers' shirt labels carried out in Harrow by the authors in October 1996.

unit
9 Care of fabrics

Soiling

If fabrics are to last, it is necessary to take steps to care for them. Over time and as a result of being put to use, all textile items soil (become dirty). Soiling happens when the fabric comes into contact with dirt. Some sources of dirt do not cause obvious stains. Others do. A common way for textile items to become soiled is for moisture and oil from the body to be absorbed into clothing. This attracts dirt and dust. Many textile items also absorb smells. A jumper worn in a smoky atmosphere, for example, will smell of smoke the next day. A shirt will pick up the smell of the wearer's sweat or perfume.

Few textile items are disposable. The vast majority are made to be used again and again. To return a textile item to the state it was in before being used, it is usually necessary to wash it, to dry it and to iron it.

All manufactured textile items contain a label showing the fibre content. This information has to be there by law (the Indication of Fibre Content Regulations, 1973). It is necessary to have this information before making decisions about the care of a fabric. For example, if a label shows that a jumper is 100% wool, then it is important not to wash it at a high temperature since the heat would make it shrink.

Washing

Water and a detergent are used to dissolve dirt and stains. Agitation is required to loosen dirt and to wash it away from the item. The item is then rinsed in clean water to remove the detergent and the dirty water. Information about the correct washing temperature can usually be found on the item's label (see Figure 1) and on fabric detergent containers.

It is the chemical structure of the detergent

molecule which enables it to tackle dirt. Detergent molecules have a 'head' and a 'tail'. The tail is attracted to grease whilst the head is attracted to water. Water needs some help to penetrate and soak fabric and the detergent acts as a wetting agent. It lowers the surface tension of water droplets, letting the water make close contact with the fibres and the dirt. At the same time, the detergent molecules attach themselves to particles of dirt. With agitation, the particles of dirt are detached. They are then prevented from getting back onto the fabric by a coating of detergent molecules.

Detergents used at low temperatures often contain ENZYMES - organic substances which break down protein, fat and starch stains into particles small enough to allow the detergent to be effective. Detergents that contain enzymes are called BIOLOGICAL DETERGENTS.

Although most washing is done using a

Figure 1
Washing symbols

Symbol	Wash Action	Fabric
95°	Normal (maximum)	White cotton or linen without special finishes.
60°	Normal (maximum)	Cotton, linen or viscose without special finishes. Colourfast at 60°C.
50°	Reduced (medium)	Nylon, polyester/cotton, viscose with special finishes. Cotton/acrylic mix.
40°	Normal (maximum)	Cotton, linen or viscose. Colourfast at 40°C but not 60°C.
40°	Reduced (medium)	Acrylics, acetate, triacetate, wool mixes, polyester/wool blends.
40°	Much reduced (minimum)	Wool, wool mixes, silks.
(handwash)	Handwash (do not machine wash)	Delicate fabrics.
(crossed)	Do not wash	
No bar	Normal (maximum) machine action	Normal spinning
▬	Reduced (medium) machine action	Short spin
▬ ▬	Much reduced (minimum) machine action	Normal spinning

activities

Bio-tex powder is a washing product formulated to remove dirt, fats and biological stains. It is designed for use in the pre-wash programme and for soaking. Bio-tex contains enzymes but not bleach or optical brighteners, so the ingredients reinforce the cleaning power of the enzymes. To save time, Bio-tex provides a number of quick, easy and concentrated biological stain removers to apply directly to spots or stains before the main wash.
Source: The Bio-tex Information Bureau, 1996

1. What task do enzymes peform in fabric detergents?

2. What kinds of stains might Bio-tex stain remover be used on?

3. What are the advantages of using enzymic stain removers rather than other solvents?

washing machine, delicate fabrics need to be washed by hand because they require very low temperatures and very little agitation.

After washing, the water is removed by WRINGING (squeezing the fabric) or SPINNING (the use of centrifugal force to remove the water). Most natural fibres need to be spun fast because they absorb a great deal of water. Many synthetic fibres, on the other hand, can be spun slowly because they do not absorb so much water. Spinning often causes the fabric to crease.

Drying

Drying can be achieved by hanging the item on a clothes line outside, hanging the item on a frame next to a heat source or placing the item in a tumble drier. In a tumble drier, fabrics are dried as they are rotated (tumbled) in a drum which has hot air blowing through it. At the same time, damp air is removed by a filter. Some clothes should not be tumble dried. This is made clear on the label.

Ironing

Some synthetic fibres do not crease and therefore do not need to be ironed. Most fabrics, however, become creased during the washing and drying process and do need to be ironed. Passing a hot iron over a fabric removes creases, especially if steam is used (steam relaxes the creases).

The temperature of an iron is controlled by a sensitive THERMOSTAT and can be altered to suit different fibres. Labels on clothing or fabric provide advice about the

correct temperature to use when ironing. Iron temperatures are represented by dots inside a symbol (see Unit 16).

Dry cleaning

In dry cleaning, soiling and stains are removed from textile items by the use of an organic solvent, not water. Water does not easily remove grease or oil, but dry cleaning solvents are able to dissolve them and remove them from the fabric.

The advantages of dry cleaning are:
- there is no risk of wool fibres shrinking
- colours and dyes are unlikely to run.

The disadvantages of dry cleaning are:
- it is a complicated process compared to ordinary washing and cannot be done at home.
- the solvents are expensive (and so dry cleaning is much more expensive than ordinary washing)
- not all solvents work on all stains or fibres.

Symbols on fabric labels indicate whether a fabric can be dry cleaned and what solvent is recommended (see Figure 2).

Bleaching

Bleach removes stains and soiling from most fabrics. But it also removes colour. As a result, it is usual only to use bleach on white fabrics - unless there is a need to remove colour. Wool and silk can be damaged by strong bleach. Symbols on fabric labels indicate whether a fabric can be bleached (see Figure 3).

Figure 2 Dry cleaning symbols and explanation.

Dry cleaning

◯ The circle symbol shows that the article can be dry cleaned.

⊖ A bar placed underneath the circle means that extra care is needed during the process.

Ⓐ Normal goods dry cleanable in all solvents.

Ⓟ Normal goods dry cleanable in perchloroethylene, solvents 113 and solvent 11.

Ⓕ Normal goods dry cleanable in solvent 113 and white spirit.

⊗ Do not dry clean.

Stain removal

There are three categories of stains:
- surface dirt - dust, mud, smoke
- absorbed dirt - coffee, tea, food
- compound stains - paint, oil, grease.

Some stains cannot be removed from fabric by washing or dry cleaning, particularly absorbed dirt and compound stains. These stains can only be removed by the use of special stain removers which contain specific solvents to remove specific stains. Acetone, for example, is used to remove adhesive and nail varnish. Methylated spirit is used to remove ink marks and grass stains. The stain remover is applied to the stain before the item is washed. Stain removers are toxic. The following steps should be taken to ensure safety:
- use in a well ventilated room
- keep away from flames
- wash hands after use
- keep away from children.

Figure 3 Bleaching symbols

△cl The letters cl indicate that the article may be bleached with chlorine bleach.

△✕ Do not bleach, eg wool, silk.

Key Terms

Enzymes - proteins which break down dirt into particles.
Biological detergents - detergents that contain enzymes.
Wringing - squeezing fabric to remove water.
Spinning - the use of centrifugal force to remove water.
Thermostat - device for controlling temperature.

activities

1. What are the advantages of using symbols on care labels?

2. Explain the care symbols on the label (right). What additional care instructions are given?

3. Draw a care label for a 100% lambs' wool, hand knitted sweater.

TO FIT WAIST TOUR DE TAILLE	
76cm	30in

TO FIT HIPS TOUR DE HANCHES	
102cm	40in

80% COTTON/COTON
18% NYLON/POLYAMIDE
2% ELASTANE LYCRA®
ELASTHANNE

40 WOOL CYCLE   ✕   WARM   Ⓟ

DO NOT TUMBLE DRY
PULL TO LENGTH WHILE DAMP

WEAVING - HARRIS TWEED

ONE of the best known wool textiles in the world is Harris Tweed. Harris Tweed is produced in the Outer Hebrides, north of mainland Scotland, mainly on the islands of Harris and Lewis. To qualify as Harris Tweed, cloth must be: 'a tweed made from pure virgin wool produced in Scotland, spun, dyed and finished in the Outer Hebrides and handwoven by the islanders at their own homes in the islands of Lewis, Harris, Uist, Barra...all known as the Outer Hebrides'. Harris Tweed is used to make suits, jackets and coats for both men and women. It is also used for hats, luggage and furnishings. Harris Tweed is available in a number of weights - standard, light and bantam/feather. This gives it a great deal of versatility.

Harris Tweed is hand-woven by around 400 weavers in their own homes. To qualify as 'hand-woven', cloth must be produced on a loom powered by an individual rather than by an external source (such as electricity). The weavers are supplied with materials through the Harris Tweed Distribution Centre which allocates work. The warp yarns and weft yarns are delivered to the homes of the weavers who also receive the design instructions and a pattern sample. Each loom is the weaver's own property and responsibility. Until the 1920s weavers

Figure 1 Harris Tweed

Figure 2 Single width loom

used wooden hand looms (just one weaver continues to use this sort of loom today). Between the 1920s and early 1990s, weavers used single width looms like that in Figure 2. More recently, however, double width looms like that in Figure 3 have been introduced. Double width looms have two main advantages. First, the weaver produces cloth which is 150cm wide (rather than 75cm wide). This allows clothing manufacturers to cut out a whole suit from a single piece of cloth (with the 75cm wide cloth it was necessary to cut out two pieces and try to match them). And second, the double width looms are quicker and more efficient than the single width looms and they are better for producing lightweight cloth. Single width looms work by a tidal motion (the weaver pushes their feet up and down on the pedals) whereas the double width looms work by a cycle motion (the weaver works the pedals in a circular motion as if riding a bike). In addition, the single width looms are shuttle looms whilst the double width looms are rapier looms. With shuttle looms, the patterns made using the shuttle are limited to two threads and it is necessary to stop and refill the shuttle. With rapier looms, the rapier picks up single threads, allowing greater scope for pattern design and losing less time with stopping and refilling. By May 1997, over 100 weavers were using double width looms and the Harris Tweed Authority (HTA) estimated that all Harris Tweed weavers would be using double width looms within five years.

Figure 3 Double width loom

Activities

1. What is distinctive about Harris Tweed?
2. Draw a diagram to show how the production of Harris Tweed is organised.
3. What are the differences between a single width loom and a double width loom?
4. Why do you think all weavers are likely to be using double width looms within five years?
5. In recent years, Harris Tweed has become an important fashion fabric. Suggest TWO garments that might be made from Harris Tweed and draw a thumbnail sketch of each.

In November 1996, Jo Edwards, a fourth year student at Brighton University, entered a knitwear competition organised by Marks and Spencer PLC. Marks and Spencer representatives showed entrants mood boards illustrating three or four trends. Entrants had to pick one trend and come up with knitwear designs for children's hosiery. They had two weeks to complete the project. Jo noticed that one of the Marks and Spencer mood boards included a picture of an old-fashioned sampler and decided to use this as the basis for her designs. After researching old-fashioned stitching, Jo created her own mood boards (Figure 1) and began experimenting with some designs. She soon decided that the lettering used on old embroideries might work well on a knitting machine and she began to work out how the stitching might work, thinking through her ideas on paper (Figure 2). The next stage was try out the ideas on a knitting machine. Jo used a Brother 910 electronic knitting machine (Figure 3). Eventually, she came up with nine different designs, three of which are shown in Figure 4. For the samples in Figure 4, Jo used lace knitting and three colour jacquard knitting techniques. Jo won second prize in the competition and three of her designs were taken up to be used in Marks and Spencer's 1997 collection.

Figure 1

A mood board

Figure 2

Ideas for design. By working out the design on graph paper, it is possible to see how the stitches will work when knitted.

Figure 3

Jo Edwards working on her designs

Figure 4

This photo shows a drawing of the finished product on the left and three samples. For the two samples in the middle of the photo, the three colour jacquard design (the main body of knitting) was programmed into the computer and knitted automatically. However, Jo had to transfer stitches manually to make the holes which produce the lace effect (the blue stripes, top, and the 'V' shapes below). The design on the right was programmed in and knitted automatically.

Activities

1. a) What is a mood board? Why is it useful?
    b) What was the advantage of using an electronic knitting machine?
2. Draw a flow chart to show the processes carried out by Jo Edwards from initial idea to final product.
3. Why were Jo's design ideas particularly appropriate for knitting?
4. You have entered a knitwear competition which requires you to design a woollen jumper. Produce a mood board and design drawings and explain how you would knit your design.

Components

What are components

In addition to fabric, most textile items need additional materials or COMPONENTS (see Figure 1) if they are to be made into usable products. Components used in the construction of textile items fall into the following categories:

- **thread** - components used to join two fabrics or a piece of fabric and a component together permanently
- **fastenings** - components used to securely fasten and unfasten textile items repeatedly
- **linings and interlinings** - materials used to help an item made from textiles keep its shape and improve its appearance and performance
- **structural components** - components used to alter the shape, fit or definition of an item made out of textiles
- **decorative components** - components used to enhance the appearance of textile items (they may also be a fastening or used to join the fabric).

Thread

The performance of a textile item is strongly influenced by the the thread used to join the fabric together. A good sewing thread will have the following properties:

- strength
- colour
- elasticity
- resistance to rot.

Sewing thread can be made from a variety

Figure 1 Examples of components

of different fibres or blends of fibres. Most modern threads (see Figure 2) are made from polyester, though cotton is still widely used (cotton is more expensive than polyester). Linen and silk threads are used only for specialist items. Viscose is used mainly for embroidery.

Polyester thread has all the desirable properties - it is strong, dyes easily, has a high degree of elasticity, does not shrink and is resistant to rot. Polyester thread made from filament yarns, however, is not normally used since the heat of a sewing machine needle

activities

This table shows the results of a test to find out how strong different threads were when placed under tension. 'Tenacity' measures how much pressure a thread can withstand before breaking. The thread is hung from a stand and weights are added until it breaks. 'Extension' measures how far the thread will stretch under tension. A 10cm piece of thread was put under a set amount of pressure and then measured. The amount it stretched is given as a percentage over its original length.

Source: Textiles, Vol.2, 1991

Comparison of the tensile properties of sewing threads		
Thread type	**Tenacity**	**Extension (%)**
Cotton	23 - 28	5 - 8
Spun polyester	25 - 38	12 - 20
Core spun polyester	30 - 43	14 - 24
Filament polyester	41 - 53	15 - 30
Filament polyamide	45 - 56	15 - 30

1. What is the difference between tenacity and extension at break?

2. Which thread is the strongest and most elastic?

3. How do the properties of spun polyester differ from those of filament polyester?

4. What are the advantages of using polyester thread instead of cotton?

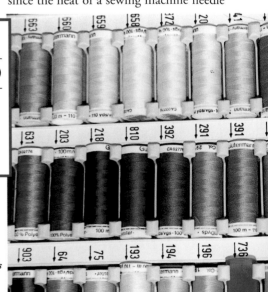

Figure 2 Threads

(generated by friction) would cause the thread to melt and break. To overcome this problem, polyester filaments are covered with cotton (core spun) or 'staple' polyester is used. Staple polyester (or 'spun polyester') is polyester whose filaments have been cut into short pieces so that they are a similar length to staple fibres. By spinning these shorter pieces, greater strength and resistance to heat is achieved.

Fastenings

A wide range of fasteners is available for use on textile items. The particular fastener chosen depends on the function and design of the particular item. Some fasteners need to be functional rather than decorative. Some need to be discreet (not obvious).

Buttons

Buttons are one of the oldest fasteners to be used. They are very often decorative. Size is measured in millimetres and shapes vary, though most buttons are round. Some buttons have SHANKS (stems) and some do not. Buttons without shanks are attached to the fabric by thread through two or four holes. Buttons with shanks have a stem with a hole which is used to attach the button to the fabric with thread.

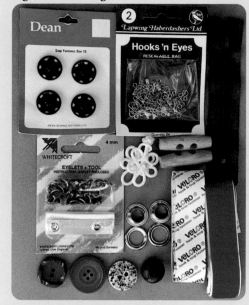

Figure 3 Fastenings

Frog and toggle

Frog and toggle fasteners are similar to buttons, but there is no hole in the fabric. The toggle is secured by a length of cord or a leather thong (the frog). This method of fastening is used on heavyweight items such as coats and waistcoats.

Hook and eye

Hook and eye fasteners are a simple form of fastening. They are not commonly used in industry as they are fiddly and have to be attached by hand. As a result, they are too expensive for many mass produced items. When attached properly, they are a secure discreet fastener. They are often used for skirts and trousers and are situated at the top of a zip fastener to prevent the garment from slipping down if the zip becomes undone.

Zips

Zips have replaced buttons in many items. 'Teeth' are fixed to tapes and the teeth lock and unlock by the action of a 'slider'. The first zips had metal teeth which were very strong and hardwearing but bulky. Most modern zips are made from lightweight nylon which can be dyed to match the colour of the tape. Zips where the teeth are not visible when closed are used for tailored trousers and skirts. For decorative effects, zips with large plastic coloured teeth are used - particularly for outdoor clothing and children's wear. Zips come in any length and can be open ended or closed.

Velcro

Velcro is a hook and loop fastening tape (see Case Study, p.57).

Press fasteners and gingersnaps

Press fasteners and gingersnaps both work on the same principle. A smaller

activities

An anorak

Shoes for a child

A tent

1. What fastenings are used on each of the above items?

2. What are the advantages of using each of the fastenings shown above?

3. Which of the fastenings shown above are functional? Which could also be decorative?

4. For each of the items, suggest an alternative fastening that could be used. Why do you think the alternative was not used in the items above?

circular piece on one side snaps into a larger circular piece on the other side. They come in various sizes and can be made of metal or plastic. Gingersnaps need a special tool to attach them to the fabric. Press fasteners are attached using thread. They are used to fasten items which need to be opened and closed quickly.

Laces and eyelets

Laces and eyelets are used to fasten items in the same way that shoe laces are used to fasten shoes. Holes or 'eyelets' are made in the fabric and finished off with stitches (like a small button hole) or with a metal eyelet which is fixed like a rivet. Laces are then threaded through these eyelets and tied up. Laces can be decorative or functional depending on the use of the item being fastened. This fastening is not commonly used to fasten modern clothing, but it is used to fasten bags and footwear.

Decorative ties and ribbons

Decorative ties and ribbons (see Figure 4)

Figure 4 Ribbons

are used as a decorative fastening for items such as children's clothing and duvet covers. They have the advantage of being easy and cheap to use, but they are not very secure. Items such as bath robes and dressing gowns are often fastened using ties. These garments are easy to put on and take off and do not need to be fastened securely.

Choosing the right fastening

It is necessary to take into account several factors when choosing which fastening to use:

- the appearance of the item - does the fastening need to be discreet or invisible?
- will the fastening form a design feature of the item?
- how secure does the fastening need to be? Some fastenings are more secure than others. Some are more durable and more difficult to replace than others. For example, zips are more difficult to replace than buttons.
- who will be using the item? Children or people with physical disabilities may find some fastenings difficult to manipulate.
- the cost of the fastening. Expensive fastenings such as zips and Velcro can add to the overall cost of producing an item. A cheaper alternative may be acceptable.

Some textile items require more than one method of fastening. Take for example high performance outdoor clothing. A coat which is to withstand very cold conditions is likely to have a heavy duty zip to keep it securely fastened, a flap or guard over the zip that is secured by press fasteners or Velcro to prevent wind and rain coming through the zip, Velcro fasteners around the wrists to keep them tight and a tie around the waist to draw in the coat and prevent the wind penetrating from below.

Linings and interlinings

LININGS are used on many textile items for a variety of reasons:

- to give greater insulation and opacity so that textile items are warmer and not see through
- to make clothing easier to put on and take off (linings make the insides of jackets, trousers and skirts smoother and they reduce friction, making the clothing more

activities

Fumbling attempts by youngsters in winter and the general annoyance of not being able to grasp and pull up the zipper on your jacket could well be a thing of the past thanks to an innovative new zip product from Coats. Exactly 102 years after the first zip fastener was invented, Coats have launched a brand new version which is set to take the manufacturing industry by storm. The company's new Grip Zip does away with tiny, fiddly connections in open zip applications like jackets. It has lightweight, flat ends which slot so easily into place that jackets can be zipped up by the coldest of hands in the bulkiest of mittens. 'We haven't reinvented the wheel, but we have taken the whole concept of the zip fastener one stage further with Grip Zip. It makes the whole process of zipping up much easier and quicker and works in one positive action', commented marketing manager Brian Schubert. 'Another huge advantage is that the shape will allow manufacturers to add branding, thus making it a fashion accessory rather than a simple component.'
Source: Coats Newslink, Issue 4, Summer 1996

1. Would it be correct to describe the Grip Zip as 'a new type of fastening'? Explain your answer.
2. What are the advantages of the Grip Zip?
3. Does the Grip Zip have a functional use, decorative use or both? Explain your answer.
4. Suggest THREE items that are fastened with a zip but could not use a Grip Zip. Explain why they could not use a Grip Zip.

comfortable to wear)

- to protect the textile item from perspiration, rubbing and staining, making it more hygienic
- to improve the hang or drape of the textile item, preventing static cling and creasing
- to extend the life of a garment by preventing wear and tear
- to enhance the appearance of the inside of a textile item by hiding the construction details.

The type of lining required depends on the item that is being lined. For example, clothing linings have requirements which are different from linings for furnishings such as curtains.

Linings for clothing

It is important that the lining for clothing (see Figure 5) is a similar colour to the outer fabric. It should not be a colour that will show through or alter the shade of the outer fabric (unless that is a deliberate design idea). It is also important that the lining for clothing can withstand the same wear and tear as the outer fabric and that it requires the same care - dry cleaning or washing. The lining should not deteriorate before the outer fabric.

Some linings are put into garments principally to make the clothing warmer - for example, quilted or brushed fabric is used to line outdoor jackets and coats to increase thermal insulation. In more expensive items, linings can be removable.

Linings for furnishings

It is usual to line curtains. Also, some fabrics used for upholstery have a backing fabric to improve wear and tear when delicate fabrics are used.

Curtains are lined:

- to reduce the amount of light being let into a room (some linings have a 'black-out' quality and do not allow any light to pass through the curtains)
- to insulate the room against heat loss through the windows (some linings have a special finish that reduces the heat loss through curtains, but this does make the lining very bulky and cumbersome).

Curtain lining can either be joined to the curtain fabric or it can be separate and removable in lighter, warmer weather. Lining that is attached to the curtains must not shrink when the curtains are washed or dry cleaned.

Interlinings

An INTERLINING is an extra layer of material placed between the ordinary lining and the outer material. Interlinings are used mainly in clothing, although there are some applications for home furnishings.

The main function of an interlining in a garment is to give body, depth and shape to the outer fabric. Interlinings keep certain parts of a garment stiff - for example, collars on shirts stand up because they have an extra layer of stiff material between the outer fabric and the lining.

A large range of interlining materials is available to satisfy a large range of performance requirements such as:

- elasticity
- padding
- stiffening
- formability
- after care
- tolerance to manufacturing processes.

The fabric used for interlining can be either woven, knitted or bonded. Interlinings can be sewn into the garment or they can be glued to the outer fabric. Interlinings which can be glued are known as FUSIBLE INTERLININGS. The majority of interlinings are fusible. They have a layer of adhesive on one side. The interlining is then ironed onto the back of the garment's outer fabric. The adhesive used must provide an adequate bond to the outer fabric and it must be able to withstand washing and dry cleaning. Fusible interlinings are quick and easy to apply, but they are slightly more expensive than non-fusible interlinings.

The factors which affect which interlinings are used include:

- cost
- design of the garment
- compatibility with the outer fabric.

Over 70% of interlinings used are made from non-woven fabric because they are cheaper and give a soft handle to the finished garment.

Figure 5 Lining

Interlinings are available in a variety of weights. The weight used depends on the weight of the outer fabric. Interlinings are used to stiffen collars, cuffs, belts, pocket flaps, epaulettes, button stands, facings and yokes.

Structural components

Structural components are components used to alter the shape, fit or definition of an item made out of textiles.

Shoulder pads

Shoulder pads are used to alter the shape and change the definition of the shoulder line in clothes such as suits and coats. They are usually fixed between the lining and the outer fabric. Some shoulder pads are made to be removable, particularly in women's clothing. Like linings and interlinings, shoulder pads must be durable, comfortable and able to withstand cleaning processes.

Bondaweb

Bondaweb is used to fuse two fabrics together. It is a layer of adhesive mesh that, when placed between two layers of fabric and ironed, joins the two layers together. Bondaweb can be used to attach non-fusible interlinings to outer fabric or to attach appliqué motifs before sewing.

Elastic tape

Elastic tape is used to reduce fullness. Sections of fabric are gathered up to hold the item secure. Elastic tape can be set in a casing or channel of fabric or it can be sewn directly onto the fabric (whilst it is stretched) using a zig-zag stitch. SHIRRING ELASTIC (elastic thread - core-spun elastic covered in cotton yarn) is used to gather lightweight fabric.

Using elastic means that other fastenings are not usually needed. Garments with an elasticated waistband, for example, do not need a zip or buttons. This makes the garment cheaper to make, easier to put on and take off, and more comfortable.

Boning

Boning is a fine strip of rigid but flexible polyester tape. It is used to give structure and shape to textile items - for example, it is used in ball gowns and corsetry to mould the body to the required shape. It is also used to give shape to pelmets and curtain tie-backs. Boning can either be inserted in a casing or sewn directly on to the fabric.

Bias binding

Bias binding is fabric cut into strips diagonally across the bias. Bias binding has the ability to stretch and follow curves

Figure 6 Decorative components

without creasing. It is used to edge textile items or inside seams.

Decorative components

There are many components that are available to enhance the appearance of textile items. Decorative components are chosen to complement the outer fabric both aesthetically and practically. Some decorative components have an additional functional role - for example, buttons might act as a fastening as

well as serving as a decoration.

Decorative components are divided into the following categories:

- EMBROIDERY (decorative stitching) can be added to any textile item (the threads used are chosen only for their appearance and whether they can be used by hand or by machine)
- beads and sequins are sometimes included in designs to provide an item with colour and sparkle
- braid, fringing and piping can be sewn on the edges of clothing or furnishings (they add an interesting finish to the design and sometimes cover raw edges).

Decorative components add to the overall cost of an item. They are often expensive in themselves and it is time consuming to attach them, particularly if they have to be attached by hand.

activities

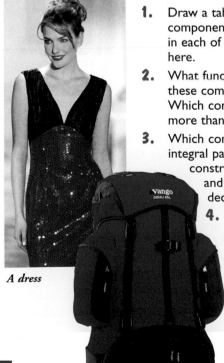

A dress

A rucksack

1. Draw a table listing the components likely to be used in each of the items shown here.

2. What functions do each of these components serve? Which components serve more than one purpose?

3. Which components form an integral part of the construction of an item and which are only decorative?

4. Which other components could have been used to suit the same purpose? Why do you think the alternative components were not used?

A dinner jacket and dress shirt

Key Terms

Components - materials added to fabric to make a textiles item.
Shanks - stems on some buttons.
Lining - an extra piece of material attached to the inside of a piece of fabric.
Interlining - an extra layer of material placed between the ordinary lining and the outer material.
Fusible interlining - an interlining which can be glued.
Shirring elastic - elastic thread comprising core-spun elastic covered in cotton yarn.
Embroidery - decorative stitching.

 VELCRO

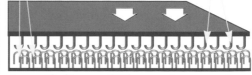

Figure 1 How Velcro works

Loops   Hooks

A magnified image of Velcro can be seen on the cover of this book.

Pieces of Velcro

VELCRO was invented by a Swiss engineer, Georges de Mestral, who began by investigating why burdock burrs clung to his clothing. Under a microscope, Mestral saw how tiny hooks on the burrs caught in loops in the fabric. This gave him the idea for Velcro. Velcro is a hook and loop fastener consisting of two tapes. One tape is covered in thousands of tiny hooks. The other is covered in thousands of tiny loops. When pressed together, the hooks grip the loops to form a tight, secure closure (see Figure 1). The strips can be separated by peeling them open from either end. Velcro tape is durable and can be opened and closed thousands of times. It can be cut, without fraying, to any length or shape and it can be attached to most other substances by sewing, moulding-in, adhesives or staples. Velcro fasteners are made of nylon. This makes them washable, dry cleanable and virtually unbreakable. Under normal conditions, Velcro will outlast the life of the garment or other item to which it is attached. The tables below examine Velcro's characteristics and the different ways in which it is used.

Table 1 Some of the uses of Velcro fasteners

Home furnishings

Velcro can be used to secure carpets and rugs, to close cushion covers or to attach pelmets.

Sport and leisure

Velcro can be used to fasten items such as golf gloves or cricket pads. It can be used in camping and caravanning and for skiwear.

Clothing and footwear

Display

Velcro can be used to fix promotional and display material in exhibitions that can be moved or replaced with the minimum of effort.

Medical and orthopaedic

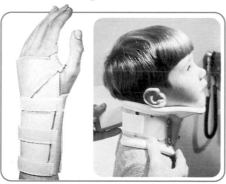

Velcro is used for apparatus such as blood pressure cuffs, tourniquets, surgical collars and splints.

Because of its durability, Velcro can be used as an alternative to zips, buttons and press studs. It is commonly used as a fastener for workwear and uniforms and is used as a quick and reliable fastener for outdoor clothing.

Table 2 Characteristics of Velcro fasteners

- Can be washed and dry cleaned
- Can be sterilised or autoclaved (sterilised using high pressure steam)
- Melting temperature = 204°C
- Hand ironing up to 163°C
- Most oils do not affect closure strength
- Retains 50% closure strength in water, 100% when dried
- Acids will cause the deterioration of tape
- Vibration increases closure strength
- Closure strength increases when pressure is applied

Activities

1. Explain how Velcro works as a fastener.
2. Table 1 discusses the uses of Velcro. Suggest FOUR other items which might use Velcro.
3. What advantages does Velcro have over other fasteners?
4. Velcro can be used to make the lives of people with physical disabilities easier. Explain how this might be so. Consider the following: clothing, mobility, leisure, transport and living at home.

Fabric finishes

What are fabric finishes?

The properties and characteristics of fabrics are dependent on the method of construction used and on the fibres used to make the fabric (see Units 6 and 8). The properties of fabric can be changed or enhanced further by applying a FABRIC FINISH. A fabric finish is applied by physical (mechanical) or chemical means. The finish applied can be **permanent** (it will last as long as the fabric), **temporary** (it will only last until the fabric is cleaned), **durable** (it will wear off eventually) or **renewable** (the finish can be reapplied).

There are three basic reasons for finishing fabric:

● changing the surface of fabric (raising, smoothing or embossing)
● altering wearing properties (staining, creasing, draping)
● modifying aftercare characteristics (ironing, shrinking).

Physical finishes

With physical finishes, the finish is applied by a mechanical process that modifies the surface of the fabric.

Raising

RAISING is a technique designed to give fabrics a soft and fluffy texture. Fabrics with a raised surface are warm because of the increased volume of enclosed air. Fibre ends are teased from the fabric to form a pile which obscures or hides the fabric weave. This is achieved by the action of wire-clad rollers which hook into the fabric as they rotate (see Figure

3). The raising action must not be too strong, however, or it will weaken the fabric. Raising is a permanent fabric finish.

Calendering

CALENDERING is a technique designed to smooth the surface of the fabric, compact it and improve its lustre. Fabric is passed between pressure rollers (see Figure 1). The effect created varies depending on the roller surfaces, the temperature of the rollers and the relative speed of the rollers. Chintz fabric, for example, is made by calendering plain weave cotton fabric to make it lustrous. Moiré and embossed fabrics are produced when fabric is calendered with special engraved rollers. The effects of calendering are not usually permanent. It is a durable finish.

Tentering

TENTERING (or 'stentering') is a technique designed to pull fabric back into shape after construction. It is one of the final finishing processes. The fabric is dipped into a chemical bath and then the selvedges (edges

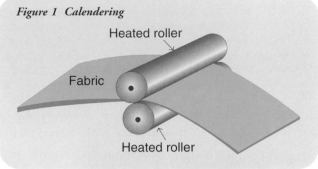

Figure 1 Calendering

Heated roller

Fabric

Heated roller

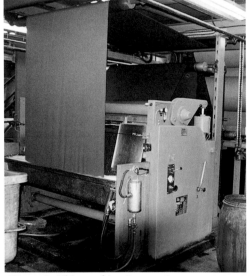

Figure 2 This machine is tentering cotton fabric which has just been dyed.

of the fabric) are gripped by tiny pins or clips (see Figure 2). This stretches the fabric into shape whilst it is dried (hot air is blown on it). This is a durable finish. Unless it is preshrunk (a separate process), fabric may shrink back during pressing or laundering.

Filling

FILLING is a technique designed to fill up the gaps in loose-weave poor quality fabrics. The gaps in construction are filled up by soaking the fabric in starch solution before calendering. This makes the fabric look very smooth and lustrous and

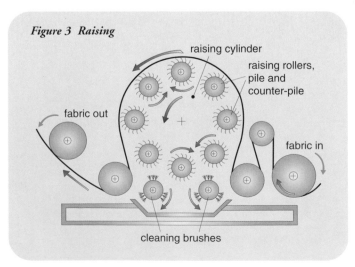

Figure 3 Raising

raising cylinder

raising rollers, pile and counter-pile

fabric out

fabric in

cleaning brushes

also adds stiffness. This finish is applied mainly to cotton fabrics. It is a temporary finish - the starch washes out after the first wash, leaving the fabric slack and lifeless.

Chemical finishes

Chemicals can be applied at any stage in the production of fibre, yarn or fabric.

Mercerising fibre and fabric

Cotton fibres are MERCERISED to make the fabric more lustrous. The process can be applied to fibres, yarns or to fabric, before dyeing. The fibres, yarns or fabric are stretched tight and soaked in a concentrated sodium hydroxide solution. This makes the flat cotton fibres swell up and straighten out. The fibre, yarn or fabric becomes softer, stronger and more absorbent and so it is able to absorb dyes more easily. This is a permanent finish and it is commonly applied to sewing threads, dress and shirt fabrics and furnishing fabrics. The process was invented by J. Mercer in 1866.

Flame-proofing

A FLAME-PROOF finish can be applied to some yarns or fabrics to make them less flammable (see Figure 5). This finish is applied to the yarn or fabric after other finishing processes have been completed. Different fibres and fabrics react differently to fire (see Unit 8). Asbestos and glass fibres are completely resistant to burning, but are not used for everyday textile items. All other fibres burn. The behaviour of fibres when they are removed from a flame varies a great deal (see Table 1) and is an important factor.

The yarn or fabric is saturated with chemicals which prevent the fabric catching fire if it is placed near a spark or a flame. Flame retardant fabric finishes tend to make the fabric stiff and they can be damaged if they are not washed under the right conditions.

There are regulations regarding the

Table 1 Flammability of selected fibres		
Fibre	**Burn easily?**	**After flame removed?**
Modacrylic	No	Stops burning immediately
Wool	No	Stops burning immediately
Silk	No	Stops burning immediately
Polyester	Yes, slowly	Continues to burn slowly
Nylon	Yes, slowly	Continues to burn slowly
Acrylic	Yes	Burns quickly
Cotton	Yes	Burns quickly
Viscose	Yes	Burns quickly

flammability and treatment of fabrics used for soft furnishings.

Figure 4 This machine is used to mercerise cotton fabric. The fabric travels along the machine and is immersed in a chemical bath.

Waterproofing

For use in wet conditions, some fabrics are treated to make them WATERPROOF. Chemicals, usually silicones, are applied to stop water soaking into the fabric. Instead, the water remains in droplets on the surface of the fabric. This treatment allows air to pass through the fabric and water will pass through when the surface becomes saturated. The process is carried out on densely woven fabrics which are used for raincoats, anoraks and umbrellas (see Figure 5). It is an invisible finish which is durable and renewable. The process can be applied either when all other finishes have been applied or when the item has been made.

activities

The relative flame retardant characteristics of fibres are sometimes compared using the Limiting Oxygen Index (LOI) which gives the minimum percentage of oxygen needed to support combustion of the fibre in question. Fibre with a LOI of less than 21% will burn freely in air. The higher the LOI, the more flame retardant a fibre will be.
Source: Textiles, Vol. 1, 1992

1. Judging from the information (above and right) which fibre is (i) most flame retardant and (ii) least flame retardant?
2. What are the advantages and disadvantages of flame retardant finishes?
3. What fibres are furnishing fabrics commonly made from? Explain why it is usual for furnishing fabrics to have a flame retardant finish.

The Limiting Oxygen Index (LOI)	
Fibre	**LOI (in %)**
Modacrylic	26-31
Wool	25
Nylon	22
Polyester	22
Cotton	19
Viscose	19
Acrylic	18

Figure 5 A range of finishes (1)

Flame retardant

Waterproof

Crease resistant

Resisting stains and dirt

A finish similar to that used to waterproof fabrics can be applied to fabrics to make them stain repellent. The aim is to prevent grease and dirt clinging to the fibres. This finish is used on, for example, furnishing fabrics, curtains and shoes (see Figure 7). Scotchgard is an example of a commercial finish that can be applied as the fabric is being manufactured or it can be sprayed on after manufacture.

Crease resistance

Some fibres make fabrics which crease easily. A finish can be applied that makes the fabric crease resistant and therefore reduces the need to iron. This finish is applied to cellulosics - cotton, linen and viscose. The fabric is treated with a resin and then dried on a tenter machine. After the item has been made, it is baked in an oven to 'cure' the resin. This finish is applied to fabrics that are used to make trousers and shirts (see Figure 5). It is a very durable finish, but care is needed with washing and ironing.

Mothproofing

Protein fibres (wool and silk) can be treated with chemicals to make them mothproof. These fibres are susceptible to attack from the larvae of the clothes moth and carpet beetle.

To mothproof fabric, chemicals are added to the dyebath. These chemicals change the flavour of the fibres so that the larvae no longer like the taste. This is a permanent, invisible finish that is applied to fabrics used for clothing, furnishing, carpets and rugs (see Figure 7).

Shrink resistance

Wool fabrics are prone to shrink when washed, due to the felting of the fibres. To inhibit or prevent this, wool fibres can be treated to make them shrink resistant. Fibres are either treated with chlorine or with other chemicals. These chemicals either eat away the tips of the scales on the fibre which interlock with each other or a thin coating of synthetic resin fills up the space between the scales and the fibre. These finishes can be applied at any stage from fibre carding (see Unit 7) to the finished article. Shrink resistant finishes are permanent invisible finishes. Wool items with the label 'machine washable' or 'superwash' have been treated in this way (see Figure 6).

Anti-static finishes

Fabrics can be treated with an ANTI-STATIC FINISH to prevent a build-up of static charge that makes the fabric cling to itself, attracts dust and dirt particles and causes sparks and mild electric shocks. This finish is applied to acetate and all synthetic fabrics. The chemicals make the fibres a little more absorbent and so they take in water from the atmosphere. Water is a good conductor of electricity and helps to rid the fabric of its electric charge. This is a permanent, invisible finish that is applied to

Figure 6 Labels

Items with a particular finish are often labelled, as above.

Figure 7 A range of finishes (2)

Moth proof   *Anti-static*   *Stain resistant*

Figure 8 Coated fabrics

fabrics used to make carpets and clothing (see Figure 7).

Coated fabrics

The properties of fabrics and therefore the items they make can be radically altered by coating them with a different material. COATING a fabric means adding another layer on top of the fabric. Coating fabrics may serve a functional purpose - for example, to improve a fabric's resistance to soiling or penetration by water. Alternatively, fabric may be coated for aesthetic reasons - for example, to simulate leather.

The overall characteristics of the coated fabric depend on the thickness of the coating, the nature of the base fabric and the technique used to apply the coating to the fabric. Commonly used coatings are:

● polyvinyl chloride
● neoprene
● silicone rubber
● polyurethane.

These coatings are polymers (long chain

activities

The photo below shows cotton fibres after they have been mercerised.

Mercerisation means soaking cotton fibres in concentrated sodium hydroxide solution to make them swell up. The fibres change from being flat, ribbon-like twisted fibres to plump, rounded and straight fibres.

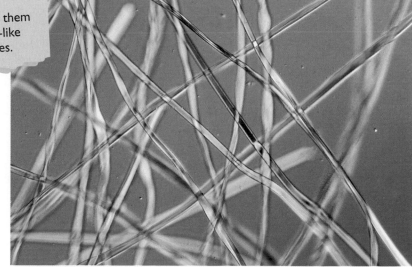

1. a) Why do you think that cotton is mercerised?
   b) What effect does the process have on the fibres and fabric?

2. Draw a diagram showing how the cotton fibres would have looked under the microscope before they were mercerised.

3. Note down THREE other finishes that might be applied to cotton and describe one in detail.

molecules) and give off toxic chemicals when fixed by heat.

Coated fabrics are used to make clothing for sport, protective and working clothing, highly visible (fluorescent) fabrics, shoe uppers, luggage, car seats, book bindings and floor and wall coverings (see Figure 8). The coating is permanent.

Breathable waterproof fabrics

It used to be the case that whilst waterproof fabrics prevented water penetrating the fabric they also did not allow perspiration to escape. As a result, the wearer still ended up wet, despite being protected from the rain. Today, however, BREATHABLE FABRICS have been developed (see Figure 9) which have a waterproof layer that does not allow water in but, at the same time, does allow perspiration to escape. Breathable waterproof fabrics work because the barrier layer is designed to distinguish between extremely tiny water molecules present in vapour emitted from the body and the much larger water droplets present in mist, rain and other forms of precipitation.

The waterproof layer is either laminated to the outer fabric or its lining, or it is sandwiched between the two.

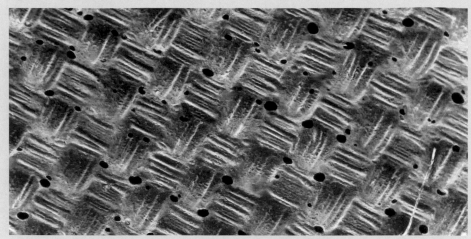

Figure 9 Breathable waterproof fabric

An electron micrograph of the surface of a waterproof fabric used in outdoor clothing. The coating is polyurethane and has many tiny pores. These allow humid air and water vapour to come out of the garmet, but the small size prevents liquid water from entering due to surface tension.

Key Terms

Fabric finish - a means of changing or enhancing a fabric's properties.
Raising - a technique designed to give fabrics a soft, fluffy surface.
Calendering - a technique designed to smooth a fabric's surface.
Tentering - a technique designed to pull fabric back into shape after construction or dyeing.
Filling - a technique designed to fill up the gaps in loose-weave poor quality fabrics.
Mercerising - a technique designed to make cotton fibres more lustrous.
Flame-proofing - a technique designed to make yarn or fabric less flammable.
Waterproofing - a technique designed to make fabrics repel water.
Anti-static finish - a finish which prevents the build-up of static electricity.
Coating - adding another layer on top of a fabric.
Breathable fabrics - fabrics which protect against preciptitation whilst, at the same time, allowing perspiration to escape.

activities

Direct coating or 'spreading' is the most straightforward technique. A polymer compound is applied directly onto the surface of the fabric. This method is suitable for strong, stable fabrics which do not distort under the high tension required to pull the fabric through the coating machine. Fabrics selected for direct coating are usually manufactured from tough synthetic yarns and are tightly woven to prevent the coating compound from sinking into the textile material.
Source: Textiles, Vol.2, 1992

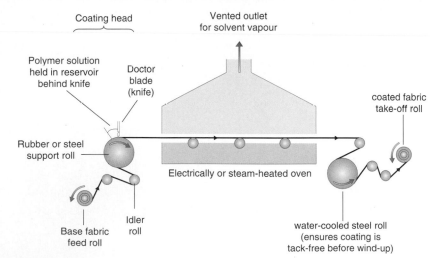

1. Describe how the direct coating process works.
2. Why might environmentalists be concerned about this process?
3. Suggest THREE items that might be made from a fabric which has a coating produced in this way.

The Rossendale Search and Rescue team was sponsored by J.B. Broadley in 1996. Jackets and salopettes with a Permatex lining were donated to the team.

PERMATEX is a weatherproof, breathable membrane system developed and produced by J.B. Broadley. It is used as linings and outer fabrics in high performance clothing and footwear, industrial wear and sports and fashion wear. The idea of breathability is really a simple one. It rests on the fact that rainwater drops are several hundred thousand times bigger than individual water molecules in perspiration. With a suitable barrier layer in the fabric, it is possible to ensure that in all but the most extreme conditions, perspiration can escape but rain cannot enter. Permatex is a lightweight, hydrophilic polyurethane material. A hydrophilic system is non-porous (solid). The molecules of water vapour diffuse chemically through the membrane allowing moisture vapour to escape whilst blocking water droplets from entering (see Figure I). The solid membrane is tough, durable and resistant to abrasion. A non-porous system is used because porous systems sometimes become clogged up with dirt or detergents. The Permatex membrane can be transfer coated or laminated and has been developed to meet customers' specifications. It can be used on a wide range of synthetic or natural products including wool, cotton, nylon, polyester and foam. Permatex can be used in four different ways (see Table 1 below).

Figure 1 A hydrophilic membrane system

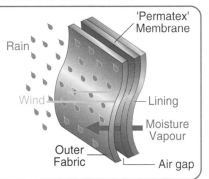

Hydrophilic Membrane

air

50μ*

direction of vapour

H₂O molecules in vapour phase

skin

* 1 micron = 0.001mm

Table 1 Four ways in which Permatex is used

1. Lining system

Permatex is laminated onto the lining fabric. It is used as a lining for sweaters, sports/leisure suits and in technical outdoor garments.

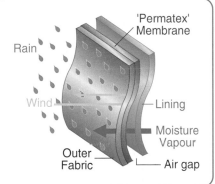

Rain / Wind / 'Permatex' Membrane / Lining / Moisture Vapour / Outer Fabric / Air gap

2. Dropliners

The separate membrane is placed between the outer fabric and the lining. It offers designers complete freedom of choice in fabric and colour and can therefore be used in almost any existing garment design. The system is used where a soft handle and natural drape are required - eg in leisure suits, high fashion and country clothing.

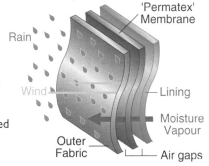

Rain / Wind / 'Permatex' Membrane / Lining / Moisture Vapour / Outer Fabric / Air gaps

3. Two ply

The membrane is transfer coated or laminated to the inner surface of an outer fabric, offering a lightweight, waterproof shell. The result is high performance, durable garments used in the outdoor and workwear markets.

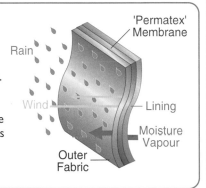

Rain / Wind / 'Permatex' Membrane / Lining / Moisture Vapour / Outer Fabric / Air gap

4. Three ply

When constructed as a three ply system, very tough and durable garments with high performance properties result. Owing to various fabric combinations, this three ply system can be used in extreme climates and diverse conditions for both the outdoor and the technical and industrial wear markets.

Rain / Wind / 'Permatex' Membrane / Lining / Moisture Vapour / Outer Fabric

Activities

1. What makes Permatex particularly suitable for outdoor clothing?

2. Give TWO specific examples of garments that might be made using Permatex in each of the ways described in Table 1.

3. How does the hydrophilic system work? What are the advantages of using a hydrophilic system?

4. Why do you think J.B. Broadley sponsored the Rossendale Search and Rescue team with jackets and salopettes?

Disassembly of textile items

The starting point for designing and making textile items is often the evaluation of an existing product. This can be done by DISASSEMBLY - taking the product apart to see how it has been made and what materials and components have been used in its construction.

Usually, the first section that can be removed is the last piece to be added during construction. For example, cuffs are sewn onto sleeves after the sleeve has been joined together and the cuff opening finished off. Cuffs have to be removed from the sleeve before the sleeve seam can be undone.

The whole point of diassembling textile items is to learn about different construction techniques and to gain knowledge and understanding of design features.

Who uses disassembly?

When designing a new product, a textiles manufacturer might disassemble similar products made by other companies to find out more about the competition. The company would analyse and evaluate the results before launching its own product.

Trading standards officers disassemble products to check that manufacturers are meeting legal requirements and packaging claims.

Disassembly may also be a useful activity for students since it enables them to see exactly how an item was constructed.

Disassembly is expensive, however, as it

Figure 1 This banner was designed and sewn by the Hammersmith branch of the Women's Social and Political Union in 1911.

usually means the destruction of the item. On occasions, it is simply impossible to disassemble a textile item. The banner in Figure 1, for example, is unique and therefore very valuable. Disassembly would destroy it and therefore is not an option.

Recording results

Before disassembling a product, it is necessary to design a PRO FORMA or template to record the results. This could be as simple as that in Figure 2 or more complicated.

Using a pro forma ensures that the same method of analysis is used for each sample and it allows like to be compared with like. The pro forma will vary depending on the investigation, but it is likely to include questions on the following subjects:

● fabric construction

activities

After inspecting the seams, the stitching and the overlocking with a hand lens, Steve unpicks the seam which attaches the lining on the inside of the jacket to the arm and shoulder.

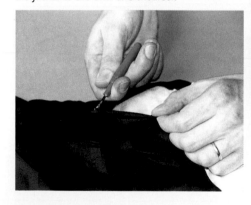

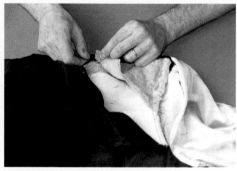

After removing the lining in the shoulder area, Steve unpicks the shoulder pad and then examines the interlining and material to which it is attached. He examines samples with a hand lens and cuts off a small piece of material to be subjected to a flammability test.

The photos above shows steps in the disassembly of a jacket.

1. Design a pro forma that will help Steve to assess the jacket.
2. a) What do you think Steve hoped to find by disassembling this jacket?

b) How might the information be useful?
3. Describe THREE circumstances in which disassembly might be useful and TWO when it would be impossible.

- sewing techniques
- patterns and colours
- choice of materials
- choice of components
- production processes
- the quality of the product
- whether the product meets its intended purpose
- value for money.

How to disassemble a textile item

First, look carefully at the item. Before unpicking anything, work out the order of construction by looking at seams and edge finishes. Then, using a small pair of scissors, a pin or a stitch cutter, carefully unpick the last seam to be sewn - it should not be locked into another seam. Continue to remove each section in order, remembering to number them as you do so. Once the sections have been separated, unpick all darts, pleats and seams formed within the construction and iron the pieces flat. Once this has been done, it should be possible to calculate the exact sequence or order in which an item has been put together.

In addition to establishing how a textile item has been constructed, it is sometimes important to find out what sort of fabric the item is made of. If the fibre content of the fabric is unknown, various tests can be done to identify the fibre content.

1. **Microscope test** - fibres can be identified under a normal laboratory microscope if they have a distinctive appearance (eg wool and cotton). A cross-section of synthetic fibres, however, is dependent on the shape of the spinneret used in manufacture. As a result, it is not possible to identify exactly what synthetic fibres are present using a normal microscope.

2. **Burning test** - the fibre content of fabric can be identified by observing how the fabric or yarn reacts when it is burned.

3. **Tearing test** - when fabric is snipped and torn, the length of the broken fibre ends can be observed. Some fibres behave differently when wet than they do when they are dry - for example:

- cotton has short fibre ends when torn dry and has high strength when torn wet
- linen has long fibre ends when torn dry

Figure 2 A simple pro forma

Product	Method of construction	Components used	Colour/Pattern

- viscose has low strength when torn wet.

The tearing test will provide different results depending on the method of construction of the fabric (see Unit 7). Woven material will tear across the warp or the weft, but not easily along the bias. Knitted fabric is usually more difficult to tear as it will first stretch and pull out of shape. Non-woven fabric tears easily and in any direction, depending on where the pressure is applied.

Maintaining quality

When developing new textile items manufacturers must consider the profit they hope to make. It is also vital that quality standards are maintained to protect the company's reputation.

In recent years, the problem of the production of counterfeit (fake) products has become a major headache for large clothing manufacturers. According to Mike Roylance of Adidas' anti-counterfeiting group, £1 million worth of Adidas counterfeit gear was seized in the UK in 1995 alone. This, he estimates, was just 5% of that in circulation.

When clothing suspected of being counterfeit is seized, disassembly can help to prove whether or not the clothing is counterfeit.

activities

Although companies like Nike and Adidas are commercial competitors, they cooperate in the fight against counterfeit products. Both companies are members of the Anti-Counterfeiting Group. This group shares information and resources and helps trading standards officers and customs officials. Mike Roylance used to be a quality controller with Adidas. Now, his main job is to identify counterfeit Adidas products. If, after he has examined it, there is any doubt about whether a product is genuine or not, it is sent to a laboratory and the following tests carried out:
- the garment is weighed to check it is the correct weight
- a sample of fabric is tested to make sure that it contains the correct blend (eg 70% cotton and 30% polyester)
- the number of stitches per cm and the number of threads per cm are counted
- the seams are compared to those on a genuine Adidas product
- the labels are examined to check that they have been sewn on correctly
- the chemicals used in the dyes are analysed to see if they are those used by Adidas.

Mike Roylance says that clothing made up 99% of counterfeit Adidas goods seized in 1996 - mainly T-shirts, sweatshirts, woollen hats and sports socks.
Source: interview with Mike Roylance, 18 February 1997

1. a) Why do you think the Anti-Counterfeiting Group was set up?

   b) Write a job description for somebody working for the Anti-Counter-feiting Group.

2. a) Judging from the passage, how would you expect a counterfeit garment to differ from a genuine garment?

   b) How might disassembly help to prove that a garment was counterfeit?

Key Terms

Disassembly - **taking apart products to find out how they are made.**
Pro forma - **a standard sheet designed to record answers to the same questions for a number of different samples.**

Application of colour

The importance of colour

Colour is particularly important when choosing fabrics or textile items. Colour catches the eye. Indeed, when it comes to first impressions, colour is often more important than other factors (such as design, size, properties and uses). Most people have strong preferences for certain colours and not for others.

Colour

All colours come from three **primary colours** - red, blue and yellow. **Secondary colours** are made when two primary colours are mixed together in equal proportions - for example:

- red + yellow = orange
- red + blue = purple
- blue + yellow = green.

Tertiary colours are made when a primary colour and a secondary colour are mixed together. For example, if red and purple are mixed, violet is produced. A violet pigment, therefore, contains three parts - one part blue and two parts red (since purple is a mixture of red and blue).

The colour wheel (Figure 1) shows how different colours can be formed and their relationship with one another. Colours opposite one another on the wheel are known as 'complementary' or 'contrasting' colours. They do not contain any of the same primary colours. Colours that are found next to each other on the wheel are known as 'toning' colours. They have a primary colour in common and when they are used together - for example, in the decoration of a room - the effect is harmonious.

Colour is used to create feelings, change environments and moods, and to give out signals or messages. For example:

- red is a warm colour or indicates danger
- yellow symbolises cowardice
- green suggests envy
- blue is a cool colour.

Colours are associated with important events - eg black for death and white for weddings. Colour therapy can help healing - eg blue for the throat, green for the heart and lungs. Colour is used to package goods attractively. The colour of the decor in rooms may evoke a warm cosy atmosphere or a cold, impersonal atmosphere. Dark colours make rooms appear smaller and ceilings lower. Lighter colours create the illusion of space.

Figure 1 A colour wheel

WARM COLOURS

Tertiary Secondary Tertiary Secondary Tertiary Secondary Tertiary Secondary Tertiary Secondary Tertiary Secondary

COOL COLOURS

activities

1. What mood is created by the use of colour in each room?
2. Find an example of a toning colour and a contrasting colour. What is the effect of each?
3. Are the colours appropriate to the use or function of the room? Explain your answer.
4. What colour scheme would you choose if you were decorating (i) a ward in a hospital (ii) a school staff room and (iii) a restaurant? Explain why.

Adding colour to textiles

All fibres in their raw, untreated state make fabrics which are dull and uninteresting colours. Fabrics made from fibres which have not been treated are known as LOOMSTATE. Very few fabrics are used that have not undergone some treatment to change their colour. Techniques used to colour and decorate fabric can be classified under three main headings:

- DYEING
- PRINTING
- embroidery.

Both dyeing and printing involve changing the colour of fabric by using a concentrated pigment. In most cases, this pigment is absorbed into the fibres.

Dyes

Dyes have been used for centuries to colour fabrics. Originally, dyes were made from natural sources ('natural dyes'). These pigments come mainly from plants (see Table 1). It was only in the 19th century that synthetic dyes were discovered. Today, the vast majority of dyes used are synthetic dyes, though natural dyes are still sometimes used for textiles produced on a small scale.

A common problem that occurs when using natural dyes is that they are not COLOURFAST. This means that the colour easily fades or washes out. A MORDANT is used to make the dye fast. Mordants are chemicals that are used in small quantities in the dyebath. The most common mordants are:

- alum
- chrome
- iron
- tin.

Mordants are toxic and so care must be taken when they are used.

Synthetic dyes

The first synthetic dyes were discovered in 1856 by a chemist called William H. Perkin. These dyes were different because they produced bright and intense colours, unlike the colours from natural dyes. Synthetic dyes are cheaper to produce and easier to make than natural dyes and, because they are made to a scientific formula, colours can be matched exactly every time. In addition, many different colours can be produced - far more than those obtained from natural substances. Different fibres react differently to synthetic dyes and colours are not always fast. As a result, a mordant may need to be used.

Since the first synthetic dyes were discovered, a range of dyes has been developed to suit the properties of different fibres and fabrics. The chemicals used to make the dyes and the way in which the pigment is fixed in the fibres depends on the physical and chemical properties of the fibre or fabric being dyed.

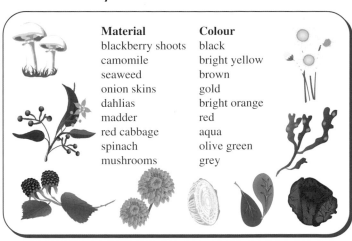

Table 1 Natural dye sources and their colours

Material	Colour
blackberry shoots	black
camomile	bright yellow
seaweed	brown
onion skins	gold
dahlias	bright orange
madder	red
red cabbage	aqua
spinach	olive green
mushrooms	grey

Dyeing

Dyeing means changing the colour of fibres or fabrics by immersing them in liquid pigments, allowing them to soak up the colour.

Depending on the fibre, dyeing can be done at almost any stage in the production of a piece of fabric:

spin dyeing - colour is added to artificial fibres while they are still liquid, before they have been spun (see Unit 6, p.33)

stock dyeing - fibres are dyed before being spun into yarns (cotton and linen are never stock dyed)

yarn dyeing - yarn is dyed before being made into fabric

activities

British scientists are hoping to recultivate woad, the weed used by the ancient Britons to dye themselves blue, as well as other plants which produce dyes - such as madder, weld, golden rod, yellow camomile and ox-eyed daisies. The success of synthetic dyes means that these plants have never been improved. 'The scope for development is huge. In the past 40 years, wheat production has been increased fivefold. That sort of improvement would make woad economic', says Dr David Cooke of Long Ashton Research station near Bristol. The market for natural dyes is about 5% of the total at present, but is forecast to rise to 15% in the next ten years.
Source: The Times 17 June 1995

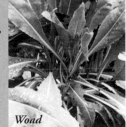

Woad

1. Give TWO reasons why natural dyes are not used on a large scale in Britain.
2. Explain why it may be advantageous in the long term to produce dyes from natural sources.
3. What changes do you think the dyeing industry would have to make if they made the move back to using natural dyes?

piece dyeing - pieces of fabric are dyed before cutting and assembly

garment dyeing - the whole garment is dyed.

Creative use of dyes

When a piece of fabric is immersed in a dyebath in the right conditions the colour is changed completely. It is possible, however, to treat a piece of fabric so that dye is prevented from being absorbed into parts of it. This means that dyes can be used creatively to make patterns and designs on the fabric. There are two main ways of doing this:

● tie and dye
● BATIK.

Tie and dye

Tie and dye is one of the oldest methods of applying a colourful design to fabric. Parts of the fabric are isolated so that they do not take up the dye. Fabric is tied or bound with string, knotted or stitched to prevent the dye penetrating.

A wide variety of designs can be produced by tie dyeing (see Figure 2), but it is not a very precise method of applying a design to fabric - no two designs are ever alike.

Any fabric can be used for tie and dye as long as the correct type of dye and mordant are used. Most new, woven fabrics have a finish or dressing which has to be washed off first as it may prevent the fabric which has not been tied from taking up the dye.

Many different effects can be created by tie and dye. For example, more than one colour can be used. It is important to remember, however, that colours are accumulative. Red dye applied over yellow would make orange, for example. If the fabric was tied differently each time the red and yellow dyes were applied, a design of three colours would result.

The following equipment is needed for tie and dyeing:

● a watertight container
● rubber or surgical gloves
● a protective cover for the work surface
● stirrers for the dyebath

Figure 2 An example of tie and dye

Source: Dylon International

● a spoon for measuring the dye
● a cooker or hot plate for hot dyeing
● a kettle
● thread or bands for tying

Equipment that is used in direct contact with dyes should not be used again in the preparation of food. Dyes and mordants are toxic.

The best method to tie and dye is as follows:

1. Bind the fabric with thread or elastic bands very tightly.
2. Soak the fabric in water - this ensures the dye is absorbed evenly.
3. Dye the fabric following instructions on the dye's packaging.
4. Rinse out excess dye with cold water until the water runs clear.
5. Spin dry.

Batik

The word 'batik' comes from Indonesia and means 'wax writing'. Indonesia is famous for its batik fabric which is traditionally produced on the island of Java. The principles behind making a batik are simple. Hot wax is applied to fabric. The areas of the fabric that have been waxed do not then accept the dye (see Figure 3).

Batiks are most successful when the technique is applied to natural absorbent fabrics. Silk, cotton and linen give the best results. Synthetic fabrics find it difficult to absorb hot wax and cold dyes.

Different waxes (for example, beeswax and paraffin wax) have different melting points. Some are more pliable and less likely to crack

activities

Before you dye, ask yourself three questions: What fabric? What does it weigh? What colour? It is important to choose the correct dye for the correct fabric (see table, right). The amount of dye to be used depends on the dry weight of the fabric. Dyeing smaller or larger amounts of fabric will give stronger and lighter shades. In addition, the final colour will depend on the original colour of the fabric - eg blue dye on yellow fabric makes green. Patterned fabric can be dyed but the pattern will not be covered, it will only change colour.
Source: Dylon 1997

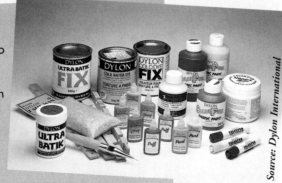

Source: Dylon International

Fabric	Dye
Cotton, linen, viscose	All dyes
Wool, silk	Hand, cold water or multi-purpose dye
Nylon, elastane	Multi-purpose dye
Polyester	None

1. Why is it necessary to weigh fabric before it is dyed? What would happen if the item being dyed was heavier than is recommended on the instructions?

2. Give THREE reasons why an item being dyed needs to be washed first.

3. What dye would you recommend to dye the following items: (i) white cotton bedding (ii) wool socks, and (iii) a batik design on white cotton calico? Give reasons for your choice.

when set than others. For batiks, it is best to use batik wax (50% beeswax and 50% paraffin wax). Batik wax is sold as fine granules that can easily be measured out and melt quickly on contact with heat.

The temperature of the wax should be carefully controlled. It should not exceed 137°C. It is important to take appropriate precautions when heating wax. Keep a fire blanket close at hand.

Before the wax is applied to the fabric, the fabric must be attached to a batik frame - a wooden frame that keeps the fabric taut and above the work surface.

There are two ways of transferring wax onto fabric - by using TJANTINGS and brushes. A tjanting is a tool for drawing with wax. It consists of a small metal cup with a handle attached. The cup has a spout (or sometimes more than one spout) and is filled with molten wax. The wax is then poured through the spout onto the fabric. Detailed and intricate designs can be created using tjantings. Alternatively, hot wax can be brushed onto the fabric using paint brushes. Very detailed work is not possible using brushes as the wax quickly sets.

Fine design can be created by 'reverse batik'. Fabric is stretched over a frame and the surface completely coated with hot wax using a large paint brush. When the wax has set, it can be scraped away using a sharp object. The fabric is then immersed in a dyebath or the exposed areas of fabric are painted with fabric paint.

In batik, cold water dyes are always used as hot water dyes would melt the wax.

When the fabric has dried after dyeing, excess wax is scraped off. To remove wax that has been absorbed by the fibres, the fabric should be ironed between sheets of absorbent paper. Even after ironing the fabric will remain stiff. The remaining wax can be removed by placing the fabric in boiling water for several minutes. Dyes and paints need to be completely fast at this point, otherwise the colours will bleed. Dry cleaning solvents can also be used to remove wax.

Printing

Designs can also be applied to fabric by printing. Colour is applied to particular areas in the form of a paste which sticks to one side of the fabric. There are three main types of printing:

- Block and roller printing
- Screen printing
- Transfer printing.

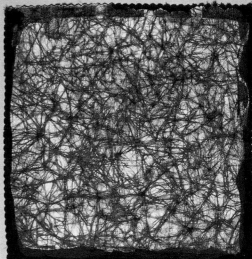

Figure 3 An example of batik

Source: Dylon International

These began as handcrafts, but since the 19th century have become mechanised. Today, the printed fabrics used to make clothing and furnishings are printed in factories which print thousands of metres at a time.

Block and roller printing

One way of printing is to cut a design out of a block of resistant material (traditionally wood) so that it stands out in relief. Colour is then applied to the surface and the pattern printed on the fabric. Each colour needs a different block. This is a very time consuming technique and therefore very expensive.

For large-scale production of printed fabric, rollers are used. The principle, however, is the same as using blocks. Engraved rollers are made with a copper surface. A separate roller is needed for each colour. The maximum design repeat is the circumference of the engraved roller (see Figure 4).

Screen printing

Screen printing is the most widely used method. It accounts for around 78% of all fabric printing. There are two main elements in screen printing:

- a stencil which blocks off part of the screen where no printing is to occur
- a fine mesh screen which ensures that when the dye does reach the fabric, it is applied evenly.

activities

A modern, easy alternative to traditional batik is Dylon Acrobatik. As a ready-to-use substitute for hot wax (no heating required), Acrobatik creates a crackle-free resist to the dye. It is a quick and simple way of creating batik-style effects on fabric. Ideal for children and beginners, Acrobatik can be applied by freehand, by using a brush, by sponging or by stencilling.
Source: Dylon 1997

Source: Dylon International

1. Why is Acrobatik 'ideal for children and beginners'?
2. In what ways is Acrobatik similar to and different from traditional batik?
3. What arguments might somebody who does a great deal of batik use in support of the traditional methods?

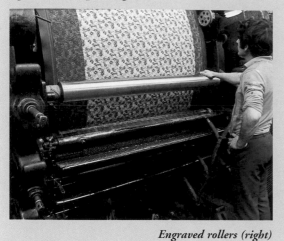

Figure 4 Roller printing

Engraved rollers (right)

Stencils are used to produce positive or negative images - positive when the dye is pushed through and negative when a resist paste is used. For a negative image, after the resist paste has been applied, the fabric is then dyed. When the resist is removed, a pattern is revealed.

In industry, the screen is coated with a light-sensitive material and then selectively exposed to ultraviolet light using a photographic stencil. Exposed areas are made insoluble. Unexposed areas are washed away. Alternatively, the screen is coated in an insoluble polymer which is then etched away in selected places by a computer-driven laser beam.

A separate screen has to be made for each colour - which adds to the cost of the process. The maximum design repeat is the size of the screen. Consequently, large screens may be used in industry.

For industrial flat screen printing, the fabric is held firm and flat on a surface using a tacky

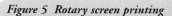

Figure 5 Rotary screen printing

For a picture of flat bed screen printing see p.137.

adhesive. The conveyor moves the screen along the fabric one screen width at a time, lowering the screen onto the printing table. Printing paste is supplied to the screen and forced through the gaps in the screen using a squeegee or roller. The screen is then lifted and the next cycle begins.

The rotary screen printing system allows continuous production. The printing paste is pumped from reservoirs to the inside of a cylindrical screen. From there it is continuously squeezed through the screen onto the moving fabric by a blade or a roller squeegee. Rotary screen printing is more common in industry as it is faster and cheaper and yet equally intricate designs can be produced (see Figure 5).

The main advantages of screen printing are:

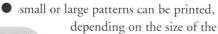

- screens are relatively cheap to make and so it is economical to print small amounts of fabric
- small or large patterns can be printed, depending on the size of the screen
- screen printing is easy to do on a small scale using a fine mesh screen, a squeegee and a stencil.

Transfer printing

In transfer printing, the design is first printed on a special type of paper, using a special kind of dye. The design is then transferred to the fabric by means of a heated calender. The high temperature makes the dye change into gas and since the fabric is close to the paper and is under pressure, the gaseous pigments attach themselves to the fibres of the fabric. Transfer printing is most successful on fabric made from synthetic fibres.

The advantages of transfer printing are:

- multi-coloured designs can be transferred onto fabric in one step
- colours can be pale and delicate or bright
- colours are permanent - there is no need for a separate fixing process
- the equipment used is relatively simple and therefore comparatively low cost.

The disadvantages are:

- the high temperatures needed can damage some fabrics
- it is difficult to judge what the colour will look like until it has been transferred.

Other printing methods

There are three other, less common, methods of applying a printed design:

- **flock printing** - fabric is printed with an adhesive and cut fibre snippets are applied - a method used for wallpaper and other furnishings.
- **discharge printing** - a plain dyed fabric is overprinted with a paste which destroys, decolourises or changes the colour of the dye
- **resist printing** - fabric is painted with a resist paste. When the fabric is dyed, the printed area is not coloured.

Embroidery

Fabric can be decorated using threads of different colours and textures. This is known as 'embroidery'. Decorating using embroidery is an ancient tradition. The earliest examples date back to 5000 BC. Today, embroidery in industry is a highly mechanised process using computer technology. Traditionally, it was done by hand.

Embroidery can be incorporated into designs that involve other methods of applying colour. It is often the finishing touch.

For hand embroidery, the fabric should be secured in a TAMBOUR (embroidery frame), to prevent the fabric becoming distorted when stitched. Special scissors, needles (see Unit 16) and threads are used. Any fabric can be used, however, so long as the thread is the correct weight and will not strain it.

Many domestic sewing machines can perform a range of decorative embroidery stitches (see Figure 6). Some have in-built software that can be programmed to sew complicated embroidery designs. Some can be connected to computers. Designs can then be scanned in or created on screen and transferred to the sewing machine.

Industrial embroidery machines, usually controlled by computer software, are used to embroider fabric on a large scale. The development of this technology means that fabric with detailed embroidery is affordable to most people.

Appliqué

When pieces of fabric are sewn by hand or by machine onto a background fabric to

Figure 6   Embroidery stitches

LAZY DAISY STITCH

SEED STITCH

DOUBLE SATIN STITCH

DOUBLE CROSS STITCH

FRENCH KNOT

LONG AND SHORT STITCH

CHAIN STITCH

SATIN STITCH

STEM STITCH

BULLION STITCH

BUTTONHOLE STITCH

BACK STITCH

CROSS STITICH

BULLION OR "GRUB" ROSE

HERRINGBONE STITCH

create a collage effect, this is known as APPLIQUÉ. Appliqué is not just used for decoration. It can be used to strengthen items or to repair them. Hand appliquéd items are often attached using embroidery stitches, the edges of the fabric being turned under to give a neat, non-fraying edge. Machine appliqué is stronger and quicker to do. The edges are sewn down using satin stitch (see Figure 6). The edges do not need turning under as they cannot be seen under the stitches.

activities

The Husqvarna Orchidea comes with a Sewing Adviser with which you select materials and sewing techniques. When you have made your selections, the machine itself makes the proper settings so your result will be perfect. You no longer need to consult complicated operating instructions. You can sew beautiful patterns just by pressing a button. Different embroidery cards containing various decorative embroidery stitch types are available. Using a personal computer, you can install the embroidery system and create your own designs. These can be stored and sewn by the machine.
Source: Husqvarna, 1995

1. Describe the advantages and disadvantages of (i) hand embroidery and (ii) using a machine like the Husqvarna Orchidea.
2. What skills and knowledge would be necessary to achieve the best results from using a machine like the Husqvarna Orchidea.
3. List THREE textile items that might be embroidered. Draw a design for one of the items and say which stitches you would use.

Key Terms

Loomstate - untreated fabric.
Dyeing - soaking fabric in a pigment to colour it.
Printing - marking fabric with a decorative design in colour.
Colourfast - the colour will not easily fade or wash out.
Mordant - a chemical used to fix a dye.
Batik - applying wax to fabric before dyeing to make a pattern.
Tjantings - tools for drawing with wax.
Tambour - embroidery frame.
Appliqué - sewing fabric onto a background fabric to make a collage effect.

Measuring and marking

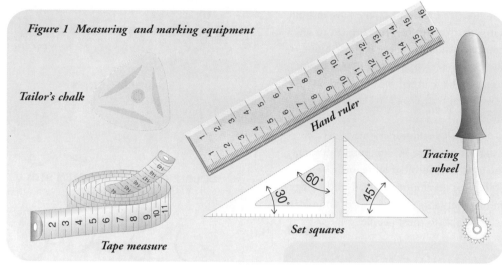

Figure 1 Measuring and marking equipment

Tailor's chalk

Hand ruler

Tracing wheel

30° 60°

45°

Set squares

Tape measure

Measuring

It is very important to measure accurately when marking out a piece of material to be cut. Plans should show measurements in centimetres or metres.

When making textile items, measurement plays an important part in the quality of the finished product. An item of clothing must fit the body for which it has been designed. The upholstery on a chair must cover and fit the frame of the furniture for which it is designed. A tennis racquet bag must be able to hold a tennis racquet.

Most textile items are made from flat two-dimensional sections which are joined together to form a three-dimensional textile object. It is, therefore, essential that all the measurements are accurate. Otherwise, the various sections will not fit together properly.

Instruments for measuring

The instruments used for measuring textile items vary according to the item which needs to be measured. A TAPE MEASURE is a flexible ruler used to measure the body. Most tape measures are made from a flexible plastic and have millimetres, centimetres and metres

marked on them. The end of the tape measure is usually reinforced with metal to ensure a straight starting point. A 30cm hand ruler is useful when marking the 1.5cm seam allowance on patterns or fabric. A metre ruler is used when measuring out large amounts of fabric and drawing long lines on fabric or on patterns. Set squares are useful when measuring angles. Figure 1 shows the main measuring instruments.

Measuring for clothing

Most items of clothing are made from a series of two-dimensional shapes which are joined together to make a three-dimensional structure. The size and shape of these two-

dimensional pieces are all part of the design of the final product. Exceptions to this basic format are items of clothing such as the sari - which is a single length of fabric wound around the body using intricate folds and pleats to form a garment.

When making clothing, a designer uses body BLOCKS. These are the the basic shapes used to make garments. The shapes are joined together to make simple garments which fit the body but have no style or decoration. Blocks are usually made from stiff card or, in industry, from thin sheets of metal. Each block shape is drawn onto paper and then these shapes are adapted to include specific design features. The altered shapes become the pattern pieces of a garment. A PATTERN is a set of working instructions and accurately shaped pieces from which textile items can be made. Patterns are used to transfer the shape of the design from drawings onto the sheet material. They show how much material is needed and they allow the material to be used in the most economical way.

Before blocks can be made, a series of measurements must be collected from the person for whom the item of clothing is to be made (see also Unit 20). Measurements must be taken closely but not tightly and they should be taken over as few layers of clothing

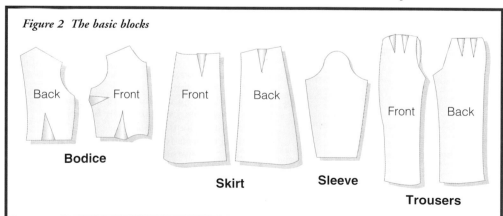

Figure 2 The basic blocks

Back   Front

Bodice

Front   Back

Skirt

Sleeve

Front   Back

Trousers

Figure 3 Bodice measurements

1. Chest - measure around the body, above the bust and under the arms.
2. Bust - measure around the fullest part of the chest (make sure the tape does not slip down the back).
3. Waist - measure around the natural waist line (to find the natural waist line, loosely tie a length of string around the body).
4. Hips - measure around the fullest part of the hips (around 20cm below the waist).
5. Upper hips - measure around the hip bones (around 10cm below the waist).
6. Back length - measure from the nape (base of the neck) to the waist line.
7. Front length - measure from the base of the throat to the waist line.
8. Back width - measure from the edge of one arm hole to the edge of the other arm hole.
9. Shoulder - measure from the neck to the point at which the arm begins.

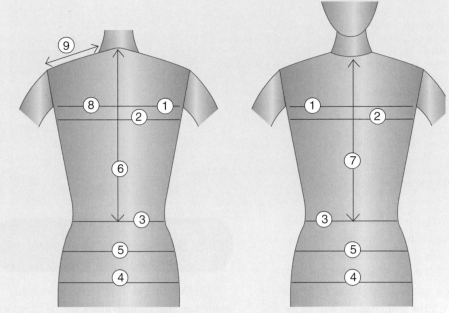

Figure 4 Measurements for trousers

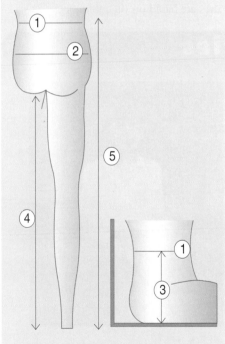

1 & 2. waist and hip measurements - as with bodice.
3. Body rise - measure from the waistline down to the seat of the chair over the contour of the hips.
4. Inside leg length - measure down from the crotch to the level of the outside ankle bone.
5. Outside leg length - measure down from the waist, over the hips to the ankle bone.

as possible. A person should never attempt to measure themselves as this could lead to inaccurate measurements.

The particular item of clothing for which the pattern is being designed will determine what measurements are required. Figures 3-6 (on pages 73 and 74) show how to take the necessary body measurements to make the blocks and to adapt patterns to fit to a particular person.

Standard sizes

If you are making a piece of clothing for a friend or relative, it is easy to take their measurements and to devise a pattern accordingly. When producing clothing on a large scale, however, it is simply not practical (or economical) to measure out each piece of clothing so that it is an exact fit for each customer. People come in all shapes and sizes and it would be impossible to mass produce clothes if all the variations of sizes were catered for. Since large-scale production is necessary because it ensures that clothes are affordable, mass producers produce clothes in standard sizes. These standard sizes are laid down by the British

activities

Many companies require their staff to wear a uniform. Designers therefore need to create a standard design of clothing that can be worn by both sexes and by many different sizes of people. A unisex coverall is an ideal solution.

1. Why is it important that someone else takes your measurements?
2. a) Draw up a table of the measurements you would require to make a unisex coverall.
   b) With a partner, take two sets of measurements (yourself and your partner) and fill in the table.
   c) Which measurements are most difficult to take?
3. Why do you think a unisex coverall is an ideal solution for a uniform?

Figure 5 Sleeve measurements

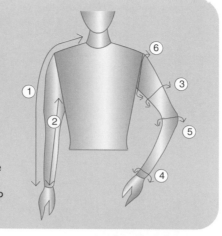

1. Neck to wrist length - measure from the side of the neck, along the shoulder, down the arm to the wrist.
2. Under arm length - measure from under the arm to the wrist.
3. Biceps - measure around the widest part of the upper arm.
4. Wrist - measure around the widest part of the wrist.
5. Elbow width - measure around the elbow with the arm bent.
6. Shoulder width - measure around shoulder, high up into the armpit.

Table 1	Standard sizes (women)				
Size	**8**	**10**	**12**	**14**	**16**
Bust	80	83	87	92	97
Waist	61	64	67	71	76
Hips	85	88	92	97	102
Back (all figures in cm)	40	40.5	41.5	42	42.5

Standards Institute (BSI). All companies producing clothes for the British market have to make sure that their clothes are made to the sizes laid down by the BSI. This makes sure that a size 12 dress produced by one company is the same size as a size 12 dress produced by another company. Table 1 shows the measurements of the different standard sizes for women. From time to time, these measurements change. This reflects the changing shape of the population as a whole. For example, people are, on average, taller today than they were 50 years ago. If trousers were still made to the standard sizes of 50 years ago, they would be too short for most people. It is the job of the BSI to monitor changes in the size of the population and to adapt standard sizes accordingly.

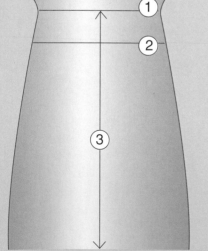

Figure 6 Skirt measurement

1 & 2. Waist and hip measurements - as with bodice.
3. Skirt length - measure from the waist down the centre front to the length required.

Commercial patterns

COMMERCIAL PATTERNS are ready-made templates which allow textile items to be made easily and quickly. The patterns have been designed and tested to ensure that they work. Commercial patterns allow items to be made without the use of blocks and without the need for intricate measurements. They are available from shops and by mail order.

Commercial patterns usually come in envelopes. The front of the envelope normally shows the items which can be made using the pattern. Often a number of garments can be made from the same pattern. The envelope in Figure 8 shows how each garment might look if it was made in different fabrics.

Clothing patterns are sold in a variety of sizes. As with industrial clothing manufacture, the sizes are based on the tables of

activities

Sushima is size 12

Sara is size 10

1. a) Why do clothing producers make clothes in standard sizes?
   b) What are the advantages and drawbacks of this system?
2. Suppose the two women above each bought a jacket and a skirt. What would the waist/hips/bust measurements be?

3. Why might women with the following measurements - (i) chest 94cm, waist 71cm, hips 94cm, back length 40cm and (ii) chest 81cm, waist 69cm, hips 107cm, back length 48cm, outside leg 125 cm - find it difficult to find clothes which fitted well? How might they overcome this difficulty?

Figure 7 A pattern envelope (1)

1. The yardage chart
This chart tells the maker how much material is needed to make the garment. These measurements are often given in yards and inches as well as metres and centimetres. The varying amounts depend on the widths of the fabric chosen and whether the fabric has a NAP or not. The amount of any lining, interfacing, elastic or trim are also included.

2. Suggested fabric list
This guides the maker in selecting fabric which will produce the best results. Patterns have to take into account features and style of the garment. For example, if the garment has numerous making up details (pockets, seams or pleats) a fabric with a bold design would be unsuitable. Also, some garments need stiff fabric to give them the best appearance whilst others need soft draping fabric for the best effect.

SIX SIZES IN ONE

Size	8	10	12	14	16	18	
European Size	34	36	38	40	42	44	
Bust	80	83	87	92	97	102	cm
Waist	61	64	67	71	76	81	"
Hips	85	88	92	97	102	107	"
Back-neck to waist	40	40.5	41.5	42	42.5	43	"

Long Sleeve Jacket

	8	10	12	14	16	18	
115cm**	2.20	2.20	2.20	2.20	2.20	2.30	m
150cm**	1.50	1.50	1.50	1.50	1.50	1.60	"

Short Sleeve Jacket

	8	10	12	14	16	18	
115cm**	1.60	1.80	1.90	1.90	1.90	1.90	m
150cm*	1.40	1.40	1.40	1.50	1.50	1.60	"

Interfacing - Long or Short Sleeve Jacket - 0.80m of 90cm woven or non-woven

Dress

	8	10	12	14	16	18	
115cm**	1.80	2.00	2.00	2.00	2.00	2.10	m
150cm***	1.20	1.20	1.20	1.20	1.20	1.20	"

Top

	8	10	12	14	16	18	
115cm**	1.00	1.00	1.20	1.20	1.40	1.40	m
150cm***	1.30	1.30	1.30	1.30	1.50	1.70	"

Interfacing - Dress or Top - 0.40m of 90cm woven or non-woven

Trousers

	8	10	12	14	16	18	
115cm**	2.20	2.30	2.40	2.50	2.50	2.50	m
150cm*	1.30	1.30	1.30	1.30	1.50	1.70	"

Interfacing - Trousers - 1.00m of 90cm woven or non-woven

GARMENT MEASUREMENTS
Finished back length from base of neck:

Jacket	65.5	66	66.5	67.5	68	68.5	cm
Dress	88.5	89	89.5	90	91	91.5	"
Dress width	113	116	120	125	130	135	"
Top length	58.5	59	59.5	60.5	61	61.5	"
Pants side length	98.5	99	100	100.5	101	102	"
Pants leg width	32	33	34.5	35.5	37	38	"

SUGGESTED FABRICS: Cotton and Cotton Blends, Crepe, Linen and Linen Blends, Wool and Wool Blends, Dress and Top also in Silks and Silk Types. Not suitable for obvious diagonals. Allow extra fabric for matching plaids or stripes. For pile, shaded or one-way design fabrics, use with nap yardages/layouts.

*without nap **with nap ***with or without nap

REQUIREMENTS: Jackets Five 2.2cm buttons, 1.3cm deep set-in shoulder pads. Dress: 55cm Zipper, hook and eye. Pants: 18cm Zipper, one 1.3cm button.

3. Standard body measurements
These are the standard sizes laid down by the BSI. They are useful when choosing the correct size of pattern and when making pattern adjustments.

4. Finished garment measurements
These, like the standard body measurements, are useful when making any pattern adjustments.

5. Requirements
This is a list of all the extras needed to make the textile item. These may include buttons, zippers, seam bindings and shoulder pads.

measurements produced by the BSI. After taking the appropriate measurements of the person for whom the clothing is being made, the clothes maker should choose the pattern whose sizes come nearest to these measurements.

The back of the pattern envelope contains a great deal of information. This is examined in Figure 7.

The pattern instruction sheet

Commercial patterns have two main elements - the pattern instruction sheet and all the pattern pieces. The pattern instruction sheet guides the maker through each step - from the laying out of the pattern pieces to cutting out sections and assembling to constructing the item. It contains:

● **Line drawings** - simplified sketches of all the views of items included in the pattern. They show all the design details (eg darts and buttons).

● **Select pattern pieces** - simplified diagrams of each of the pattern pieces. Each piece is identified by a letter or a number.

Figure 8 A pattern envelope (2)

activities

1. What blocks would be used to make the pattern for each of the items of clothing pictured above?

2. What design features would have to be included on the patterns of each of the garments shown?

Figure 9 Symbols and directions found on patterns

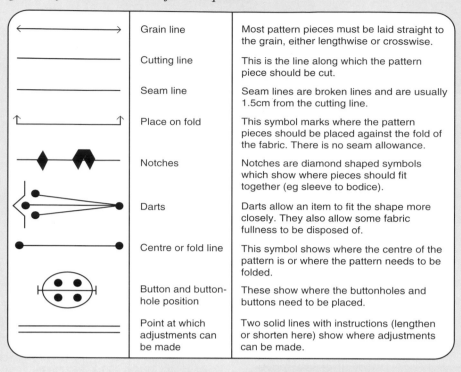

← →	Grain line	Most pattern pieces must be laid straight to the grain, either lengthwise or crosswise.
——————	Cutting line	This is the line along which the pattern piece should be cut.
- - - - - -	Seam line	Seam lines are broken lines and are usually 1.5cm from the cutting line.
↑ ↑	Place on fold	This symbol marks where the pattern pieces should be placed against the fold of the fabric. There is no seam allowance.
◆ ⬠	Notches	Notches are diamond shaped symbols which show where pieces should fit together (eg sleeve to bodice).
◁•	Darts	Darts allow an item to fit the shape more closely. They also allow some fabric fullness to be disposed of.
•—————•	Centre or fold line	This symbol shows where the centre of the pattern is or where the pattern needs to be folded.
⊙	Button and button-hole position	These show where the buttonholes and buttons need to be placed.
—————	Point at which adjustments can be made	Two solid lines with instructions (lengthen or shorten here) show where adjustments can be made.

- **How to use your pattern** - an explanation of the most common pattern symbols and how to make simple adjustments. Tips on marking and cutting are included (see Figure 9).
- **Cutting layouts** - diagrams showing the maker how to place the pattern pieces on to the fabric in the most economical way. Different layouts are shown for different widths of fabric.
- **Sewing information and directions** - an explanation of common sewing procedures and set by step instructions on how to construct each item.

The pattern pieces

Every pattern piece has written symbols and directions which show the maker how to place the pattern piece and help with the construction of the item (see Figures 9 and 10).

Adjusting pattern pieces

Commercial patterns are based on the standard sizes laid down by the BSI. Since different people have different shapes, commercial patterns may have to be altered to cater for the particular size of an individual. Most commercial patterns show where adjustments can be made. By using personal measurements, the maker can adjust the pattern to ensure a perfect fit (see Figure 10).

Marking out patterns

Once a particular pattern has been chosen, it is necessary to transfer the information on the pattern to the fabric. This can be done in a number of ways.

TAILOR TACKING (temporary stitching) can be used for transferring pattern markings onto double fabric. This enables both layers to be marked together. Double thread is used to sew two stitches, leaving long loops. The two layers of fabric are then gently pulled apart and the stitches can be cut, leaving half the thread in each layer of fabric (see Figure 11). Different coloured thread can be used to mark different features such as buttonholes and darts.

TAILOR'S CHALK can be used if the garment is to be tacked together and made up straight after cutting out (the chalk wears off with handling). Only one layer of fabric can be marked up at a time.

Carbon paper may be used on washable fabric. The paper is placed between the fabric and the pattern with the carbon side against the fabric. The markings can be transferred from the pattern to the fabric using a pencil or a tracing wheel. Only one layer of fabric can be marked up at a time.

activities

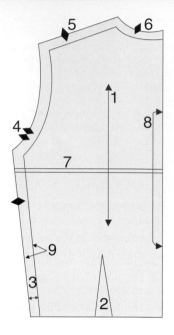

Look at the pattern piece above. The numbers on the diagram correspond to the questions below.

1. What is the function of this marking?
2. What is the pattern telling you to do? Why?
3. What is the distance? What is it called?
4. What is the name of the marking? What does it tell you to do to the fabric? Why?
5. Why is this marking here?
6. Why is this marking here?
7. What do these fine parallel lines mean? What do they give you the opportunity to do?
8. What does the bent double-headed arrow mean?
9. What is the bold outer line called? What is the broken line which lies parallel to it called?

Figure 10 Instructions commonly found on patterns

How To Use Your Multi Size Pattern

FIRST PREPARE YOUR PATTERN

Select the pattern pieces according to the view you are making.

This pattern is made to body measurements with ease allowed for comfort and style. If your body measurements differ from those on the pattern envelope adjust the pieces before placing them on the fabric.

Check your nape to waist and dress length, if necessary, alter the pattern. Lengthening and shortening lines are indicated.

TO LENGTHEN: Cut pattern between printed lines and place paper underneath. Spread pattern the required amount and pin to paper.

TO SHORTEN: Fold at the printed lines to form a pleat half the amount to be shortened, ie 1/2" (1.3cm) deep to shorten 1" (2.5cm).

STUDY YOUR PATTERN MARKINGS

STRAIGHT GRAIN: Place an even distance from selvage or a straight thread.

FOLD: Place on fold of fabric.

LENGTHENING AND SHORTENING LINES.

5/8" SEAM ALLOWANCE: 5/8" (1.5cm) unless otherwise stated.

NOTCHES: Match notches.

CUTTING LINES: Multi patterns have different cutting lines for different sizes.

CUTTING DIRECTIONS

FOR FOLDED AND DOUBLE LAYER FABRIC - Place fabric with right side inside and pin pattern on wrong side of fabric. FOR SINGLE LAYER - Pin pattern on right side of fabric.

NOTE: Pattern pieces may interlock more closely for smaller sizes.

Cut notches out from cutting line.

BEFORE removing pattern from fabric, transfer all pattern markings using tailor tacks or dressmaking tracing paper.

TAILOR TACKS With double thread make two loose stitches forming loop through fabric layers and pattern leaving long ends. Cut loop to remove pattern. Snip thread between fabric layers. Leave tufts.

Laying out using patterns

Patterns must be laid on the fabric in the right direction and in the most economical way. If the fabric has a nap or a pile (velvet, for example), it is important to make sure that all pieces are facing in the same direction. If the fabric has a bold design, the pattern pieces must be arranged to ensure that the designs match on pieces which will be sewn together.

Commercial patterns provide ideal layouts for pattern pieces. When, however, you have designed and made your own pattern, it is necessary to plan your own layout. Care should be taken to ensure that the fabric is laid in the right direction and that there is as little waste as possible.

activities

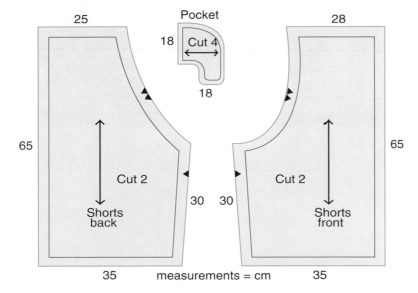

1. Copy the pattern pieces onto pattern paper. Do not forget to include all the pattern markings. You can scale down the measurements.
2. Work out how much fabric you would need to make one pair of shorts if the width of your chosen fabric was 115cm.
3. A manufacturer has been commissioned to supply 100 pairs of these shorts for a local sports club. The fabric it will use is 153cm wide. How much material will be needed to make the shorts. What method of cutting is the manufacturer likely to use?

Figure 11 Tailor tacking

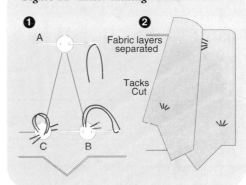

Key Terms

Tape measure - a flexible ruler.
Blocks - basic shapes used to make pattern pieces.
Pattern - a flat set of working instructions from which a 3-D textile item can be made.
Commercial patterns - ready-made templates which allow textile items to be made quickly and easily.
Nap - a raised surface which needs to be used in one direction.
Tailor tacking - temporary stitching used to mark fabric.
Tailor's chalk - fine chalk used to mark fabric temporarily.

EMMA BROSTER - PAINTING FABRIC

During her studies at Brighton University, Emma Broster (right) spent a year gaining work experience. Between April and July 1996, she worked in a design studio in Como, Italy owned by Nicoletta Linate. The studio employed eight full-time designers. Emma was one of three students to work there at that time. Emma's job was to invent designs and to paint them onto pieces of fabric. Although Nicoletta suggested themes to Emma, Emma was left to work at her own pace and in her own style. During her time at the studio, she produced between two and 20 designs per day depending on the intricacy of the design. The designs were produced on pieces of fabric roughly A2 size and were sold either directly to fabric manufacturers or to companies who build up a collection of designs which they then sell on. The market was mainly Italian, but American, Japanese and German companies all bought designs. Many of the designs were then used in the mass production of garments. Some of Emma's designs were used for swimsuits produced by a German manufacturer, for example. The studio received a straight fee for each design sold and the individual designer then received a commission.

For most of her designs, Emma painted directly onto fabric using soft brushes. The fabrics she used were crepe de Chine, georgette, organza and cotton. Each of these fabrics has a different surface

Emma in Italy

and therefore different properties that need to be taken into account when painting. Emma used Deka silk paint, a special fabric paint and luma inks - ink that bleaches out well in various colours. She also used Gutta, an outlining liquid. When Gutta is painted onto fabric through a fine nib it creates a seal which paint is unable to penetrate. The photographs on these pages explore the various painting techniques which Emma used.

This design was adopted by a German swimwear manufacturer. A piece of crepe de Chine was divided randomly into sections and different patterns were drawn in black Gutta to make the outlines. Each area was then painted with Deka silk paints. On the tulips, the colour was faded out by adding more water to the brush.

For this design, a piece of crepe de Chine was painted and then left to dry crumpled up. This ensured that, once it was dry, it left creases of a darker colour. Layers of thin colours were then applied on top of each other. White Deka Silk was used to highlight certain areas (the white Deka Silk is more opaque than the other colours). The overall effect is translucent, though the white highlights provide greater substance.

When Emma was asked to come up with a nautical design, she produced this design on crepe de Chine. She used Gutta to draw the outline and then wet the fabric before painting so that the colour bled easily from light to dark. The Gutta provided the barrier for the shapes.

When Emma was asked to come up with a tropical design, she produced this design on georgette. First, the background was painted onto the fabric. Then, using a thick brush, leaves were painted, leaving spaces to paint in simple floral shapes. Tones were kept simple because this was a busy design.

In this design, white cotton was painted with black ink and water. The rose design was then painted on using a fine brush dipped in bleach. The thicker areas were those painted first. As the bleach thinned on the brush, the finer stem lines were drawn. The bleach burned away the ink, leaving the rose design (black ink was used so that the marks left by the bleach would stand out).

This design was influenced by designs made by William Morris. The flower shapes were drawn by hand on paper, photocopied and placed under the fabric (crepe de Chine). The outline was drawn in transparent Gutta and the shapes filled in using Deka Silk paint. Some areas were faded out by adding water to the paint. The background was then painted in quickly.

Activities

1. What is Gutta? Why is it particularly useful for a fabric designer?
2. Emma used a number of different techniques when painting her designs.
   a) Make a list of the different techniques.
   b) Take any TWO designs and explain what effect Emma was trying to create. How did the techniques she chose help her to achieve this effect?
3. How might a company which prints fabric make use of Emma's designs?
4. You are asked to produce a design for crepe de Chine using the theme of 'the four seasons'. Draw your design on paper and explain the techniques you would use to produce it on fabric.

case study APPLYING COLOUR – DAVID EVANS

David Evans has been producing silk fabrics since 1843. It is the only company still using Ancient Madder to colour silk. Most of the silk used at David Evans comes from China. It is imported in its grey state, still containing the natural gum 'sercin'. At David Evans, the silk goes through six processes (see below). Around 60% of the printed silk is then exported.

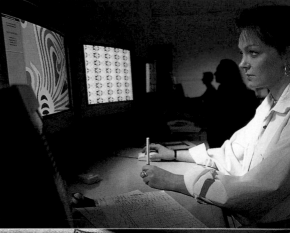
Designing at David Evans

Washing
The first stage is to remove the sericin from the cloth. This is achieved by boiling it in baths containing varying strengths of natural soap. The cloth is then immersed in a solution of soda to remove all soap residue. It is vital that the silk is completely clean before being dyed.

Dyeing
For designs that have a large area of background colour, the fabric is dyed in the dyehouse. The silk fabric is dyed using perforated beam dyes (it is wound around a beam and then lowered into vats of dye). The dyes are synthetic dyes mixed with gum and water. About 350 print colours can be obtained from 20 dye shades. The mixing is computerised.

Printing
Two methods of printing are used - one semi-automated and the other computerised. Both methods make use of a screen made of polyester mesh stretched over a steel frame. Each screen provides a different colour in the finished design. The silk is stretched out on printing tables treated with gum (to hold it in place). To ensure it lies flat a large industrial rolling pin or a warm iron is used. A vernier gauge (movable measuring device) enables the printer to ensure that the repeat size of the design is accurate to within 1mm. The screen fits into a metal frame which goes up and down the table by means of a metal carriage. Dye is poured on the screen and pushed through by a squeegee. On computerised machines, a printer has to programme the machine. Computerised machines are no faster than semi-automatic, but they are more accurate.

Steaming
When the printing is complete, the silk is left on the table to dry. Hot air is blown on it. Once dry, the silk is steamed to 'fasten' (fix) the dye.

Washing
The printed silk is then thoroughly washed again. Chemical waste is taken away in tanks.

Finishing
There are around 260 different finishing processes.

Activities

1. What sort of printing takes place at David Evans? Describe TWO advantages and TWO disadvantages of this method.
2. List the points in the colouring process where computers are used. What are the benefits of using computers?
3. Why does dye need to be fixed? What would happen if it was not fixed?
4. Pick one of the designs in the picture above and describe how a headscarf in that design would have been coloured.

Silk printed by David Evans

SIMPLICITY PATTERNS

Patterns for making clothes have been used for many centuries. In ancient Egypt, for example, the Pharaoh's tailors used guides or blocks cut from slate to shape the pieces of royal garments. Patterns for home sewing, however, are a comparatively modern innovation. Commercial patterns were first made in the 1870s. The pattern industry emerged as sewing clothes changed from necessity to enjoyment. The Simplicity Pattern Company was founded in New York in 1927 by James J. Shapiro. His aim was to produce and sell patterns which were easy to follow and affordable.

The manufacture of commercial patterns is a complex procedure requiring 10 steps. These are outlined in the flow chart below.

1. The idea
Ideas for patterns emerge after many months of research. The sources used by designers include:
• the ready-to-wear market
• haute couture (high-class dressmaking)
• films and television
• music
• street style.

2. The draping department
The design is first produced in muslin using basic pattern shapes called 'staples'. Half the garment is draped on a standard size mannequin. Alterations are made where necessary. When the drape is approved, a full muslin model is made and tried on a live model of the same size. Alterations are made as necessary.

3. The master pattern
The muslin garment is taken apart and used by the pattern maker to cut a master pattern. Heavy paper is used to cut out each shape. View numbers, guidelines and dressmaking instructions are written on each pattern piece.

5. Grading
The master pattern is made only in one size. Now it is graded into a variety of sizes. This involves fine mathematical calculations based on measurements for standard figure types.

6. Primer
Using the designers' sketches and the test garment, writers and illustrators prepare the instructions for making the garment. Construction symbols (such as notches) are now added.

4. Testing
The outlines and construction details of the master pattern are first traced onto fabric and then the garment is made up and tested on a live model. Any necessary alterations are made.

7. Measuring
The graded pattern pieces are placed on a flat table and manipulated to find the most economical amount of fabric needed to make the garment.

8. Illustrating
While the master pattern is being produced, illustrations are being made for the envelope and catalogues. The illustrators use the test garment and samples of fabrics and colours.

9. Printing the pattern
The master pattern is covered with transparent glassine and the outlines, markings and instructions on each piece are traced. The glassine is placed in a vacuum frame over a sensitised zinc sheet. Bright arc lights transfer the markings to the zinc plate which is then developed in a chemical bath. The pattern lines are etched onto the zinc surface. The pattern pieces are then printed from the plate onto tissue paper and cut.

10. Folding
The pattern pieces are assembled, folded and placed into an envelope.

Activities

1. What is a 'staple'? Why are staples made?
2. Make a list of all the different jobs done during the production of a commercial pattern. Write a job description for any THREE jobs outlining the skills needed.
3. Today, computers play an important part in the production of commercial patterns. At which stages in the production do you think computers could be used? Explain your answer.
4. Suppose Simplicity decided to produce a pattern for a shirt. What measurements would need to be taken?

Cutting techniques

When a design has been decided on, fabric and components have been selected and a TEMPLATE produced, the fabric must be cut out in the correct shape.

If a one-off prototype is to be made, the equipment needed to cut out the fabric is relatively simple:

● sharp scissors
● pins
● a large flat surface
● a tape measure
● marking chalk.

Placing the template pieces on the fabric, however, is something that requires some knowledge of fabric and fabric construction.

Preparation

First, the fabric should be laid out and the creases smoothed. It may be necessary to iron the fabric. Second, if using a commercial pattern, the cutting layout on the instruction sheet inside the envelope should be consulted. The fabric may need to be folded so that duplicate shapes can be easily cut out. The templates should be positioned for the most economic use of fabric. If a template for a newly designed prototype is being used, then a layout plan will have to be made. It is best, therefore, to experiment, moving the pattern pieces around the fabric to see which is the most economical positioning. For more complex designs, a scale drawing will help.

It is important to take note of grain lines on templates. These run the length of the template piece and mean that the piece should be placed parallel to the selvedge. When cutting fabrics which have a one-directional pattern or fabrics such as corduroy or velvet that have nap (a one-directional

pile), template pieces must be placed in a single direction. For fabrics with a pile, the direction can be found by stroking the fabric - the smoothest direction means that the fabric is being stroked from top to bottom and should be used in this way. It may be necessary to use greater quantities of fabric with nap than fabric without nap.

Figure 1 Cutting by hand

Positioning the template pieces

The next stage is to place the template pieces on the fabric and to smooth them out so that there are no creases in either the fabric or the templates. The template pieces should be pinned to the fabric. The pins should be positioned as follows:

● at the corners
● matching notches
● every 10 cm on straight sections.

More pins should be used round curves so that there is no risk of the template moving. All the template pieces should be pinned onto the fabric before any of the pieces are cut out.

activities

Cutting layout for a woman's blouse (without nap)
- For with and without nap layouts ensure that the fabric is placed with nap or design running in the same direction.
- Cut out all pieces except pieces which extend beyond the folded fabric. Then open out the fabric and cut in positions shown.
- A = front; B = button loop; C = front facing; D = front insert; E = back; F = sleeve; G = continuous lap; H = cuff

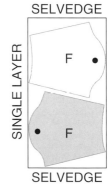

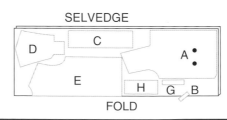

1. What would happen if the fabric was cut out when it was very creased and would not lie flat?

2. Why is the fabric folded selvedge to selvedge for the body and facing, but not for the sleeves?

3. Where would you put tailor's tacks? Explain why.

4. Suppose you used a fabric with nap. Draw out a cutting layout for the same blouse. Explain the differences.

assembly...assembly...assembly...assembly...assembly

Cutting

When cutting carefully around the template pieces, care should be taken to ensure that the fabric does not move too much. Smooth, long strokes should be made with the blade of the scissors. Where there are matching notches, cut a notch outwards.

For fabrics that fray easily, pinking shears can be used (see Unit 16).

To cut out holes or gaps in the centre of a piece of fabric, fold the fabric so that a cut can be made in the middle of the hole and, from the centre point, cut four lines to the edge of the hole. This makes access with scissors easier.

When all the pieces have been cut out with the templates still attached, tailor tacks should be put in where there are matching dots, darts or pocket joins. The tailor tacks should be pulled through the template. Then the fabric can be separated, cutting the tailor tacks so that each piece has a thread marker. Tailor tacks mark fabric exactly and can be removed easily after construction.

Cutting in industry

In industry, large-scale production means that it would simply be uneconomical to cut out one piece of fabric at a time. As a result, many layers of fabric are placed on a cutting table and a machine used to cut through all the layers at once (see Unit 17). Some machines cut using a blade, others use a laser. In industry, it is particularly important to keep waste to an absolute minimum. As a result, a great deal of time is spent working out how the various pieces needed for a textile item can be cut out using the smallest possible amount of fabric. Many cutting machines are computerised, with programmes which help to ensure that the cutting is as economical as possible.

Construction

Pieces of fabric are joined together. A number of SEAMS can be used, depending on the fabric, the item being made and the equipment being used. Seams must:
- hold the fabric together securely and be

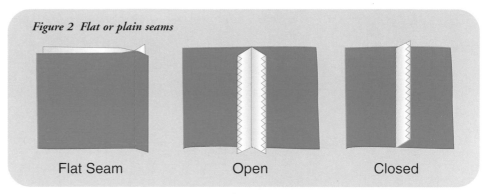

Figure 2 Flat or plain seams

Flat Seam   Open   Closed

able to withstand washing and wear and tear
- be neat and tidy on both the inside and the outside - no fraying edges
- be discreet and not noticeable (unless they form a design feature).

When making textile items at home or in the classroom, two operations must be performed before the fabric is joined permanently. First, the pieces of fabric should be pinned so that they are in the exact position for sewing together. And second, the fabric should be TACKED together to form a temporary join. Tacking is hand stitching using one thickness of thread and a running stitch of around 1 cm length. Tacking is used to hold the fabric in place. It should be done relatively quickly and should be easy to remove when the permanent seam is formed. Very often

thread of poorer quality is used.

Plain seam

A flat or plain seam (see Figure 2) is the most common and basic method used to join two pieces of fabric together. The RIGHT SIDES of the fabric are placed together so that the edge of each piece is on the inside of the item. After pinning and tacking, the fabric is joined together by a straight line of stitching 1.5cm from the raw edge of the fabric. Stitches should be 2-3mm in length or smaller for seams that will have to withstand a great deal of pressure. The beginning and end of the seam should be made secure by reversing a few stitches at the start and finish. The raw edges of the seam should be neatened on the inside to prevent fraying which would weaken the seam. This can be done in two

activities

1. a) Name TWO seams that would be used in the construction of the items pictured right.
   b) Draw sketches showing where the seams would be used in each item.
   c) Explain why different seams are used in different places.

2. Each of the items pictured right has a hem or an edge.
   a) Describe how the edges would be finished off.
   b) Explain why these edge finishes would be used.
   c) What are the advantages and disadvantages of using each edge finish?

Pair of jeans

A silk dress

Baby's vest

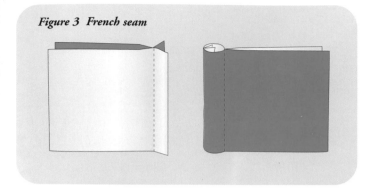

Figure 3 French seam

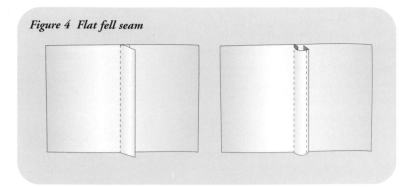

Figure 4 Flat fell seam

ways depending on the fabric:

● trim the SEAM ALLOWANCE (the fabric between the seam and the raw edge) to 0.75cm away from the stitching line and use a wide zig-zag stitch sewn at the very edge of the fabric. The seam turning is then pressed to one side. This is called a 'closed plain seam' and is used on less bulky fabric.

● neaten the edges of the fabric with a wide zig-zag stitch before the fabric is joined together. After the seam has been formed, the turning can be pressed open. This is called an 'open plain seam' and is used on bulky, thick fabric.

When joining knitted or stretch fabric 'stretch stitch' must be selected on the sewing machine or a narrow zig-zag stitch used to form the seam. This ensures that some 'give' is allowed in the line of stitching, making the thread less likely to break when the fabric is stretched.

It should also be noted that an overlocker (see Unit 16) can also be used to neaten a plain seam.

Plain seams are used to join fabrics which are not designed to be placed under a great deal of tension or subjected to a great deal of abrasion. The seam is discreet from the outside.

French seam

A French seam (see Figure 3) is used to join together fine, transparent fabric which is likely to fray badly and through which stitches are likely to be visible. The pieces of fabric are placed WRONG SIDES together, pinned and tacked and then stitched 1cm from the raw edge. The seam allowance is trimmed to 3-5mm from the stitching line. The fabric is then folded so that the right sides are together

and the seam 'rolled' to the edge. It is then necessary to pin, tack and sew 5mm from the stitched under edge, using straight stitch which is secured at the the beginning and end of the seam.

This seam is used on baby clothes (to prevent irritation of the skin), lingerie and some evening garments.

Flat fell seam

A flat fell seam (Figure 4) is very secure and will not allow the fabric to fray since, as with the French seam, no raw edges are visible. The pieces of fabric are placed wrong side together, pinned, tacked and sewn 1.5cm from the raw edge. One of the seam allowances is trimmed to 5mm. The wider seam allowance is then folded and pressed in half so that the two raw edges meet. The folded edge is pinned, tacked and sewn down near the fold using straight stitch.

This seam is used to join the inside leg of jeans as it is very secure and can withstand a great deal of abrasion, even though it is bulky. In outdoor wear, the seam is often painted on the inside with a waterproof resin to stop water penetrating.

Flat fell seams are often sewn using contrasting threads as two lines of stitching are visible on the right side.

Hems and edge finishes

There are very few textile items which have an unfinished raw edge. All woven items fray to some extent. Weft knitted fabric unravels and reduces in size. Warp knitted and bonded fabrics do not fray, but curl or lose shape.

At some stage in the construction of an item, it is therefore necessary to HEM the

edges which are not attached to another piece of fabric - to prevent fraying, warping and losing shape.

Textile items which do not need hemming are:

● items which have an intentionally frayed edge

● knitted items which have a finished edge as part of the item's construction.

A hem or an edge finish must be:

● strong and secure

● discreet

● not too heavy or it will distort drape.

There are a number of different ways of forming a hem on textile items either by hand or by machine.

Rolled hems

A rolled hem (see Figure 5) is formed by turning the raw edge of fabric over twice so that it is tucked in and not visible. It is important to ensure that the fold is parallel. The fold can be secured by sewing along the fold either by hand or by sewing machine.

For a discreet hem, thread of the same colour as the fabric should be used. For a decorative effect, different coloured threads

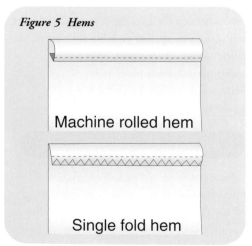

Figure 5 Hems

Machine rolled hem

Single fold hem

Figure 6 Hand stitching

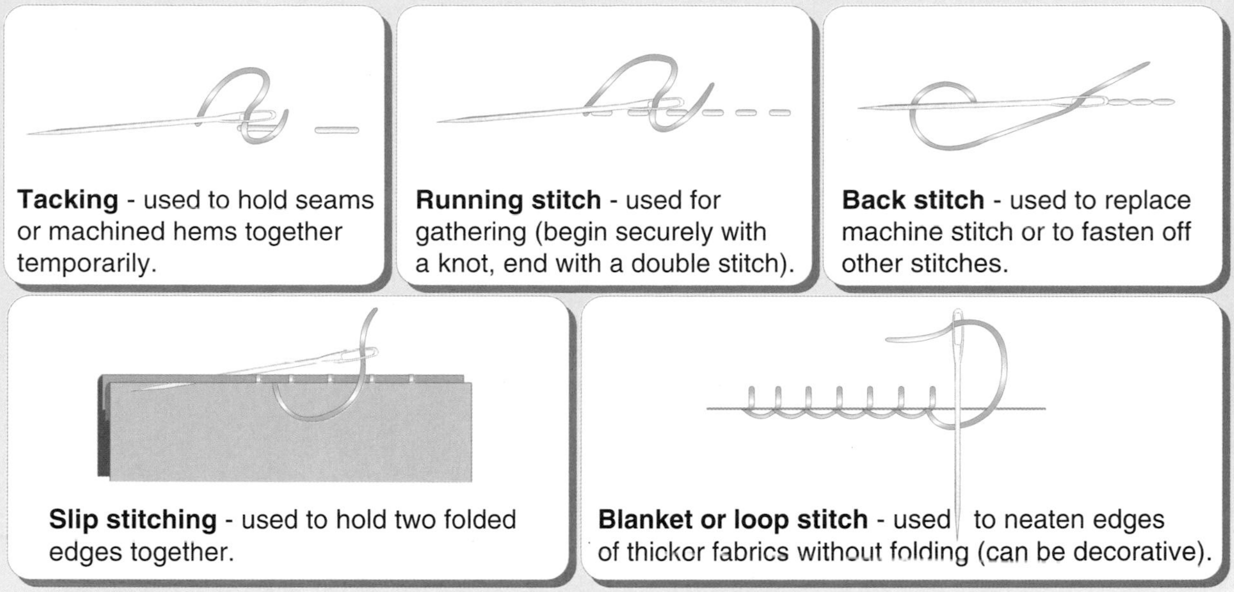

Tacking - used to hold seams or machined hems together temporarily.

Running stitch - used for gathering (begin securely with a knot, end with a double stitch).

Back stitch - used to replace machine stitch or to fasten off other stitches.

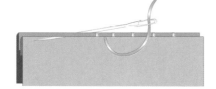

Slip stitching - used to hold two folded edges together.

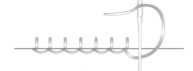

Blanket or loop stitch - used to neaten edges of thicker fabrics without folding (can be decorative).

can be used with decorative stitches.

Sewing hems by hand involves making small stitches that are invisible on the right side.

Single fold hem

For bulkier fabrics or items where there is tapered fullness (for example, a full skirt with fullness around the hem line) a single fold of fabric forms the hem (see Figure 5). Woven and weft knitted fabric must have the raw edge finished off by a zig-zag stitch or by overlocking to prevent the raw edge fraying or unravelling. The raw edge is then folded over once and sewn down either by hand or by sewing machine. It is important to ensure that the fold is parallel.

Figure 7 Top stitched pleats

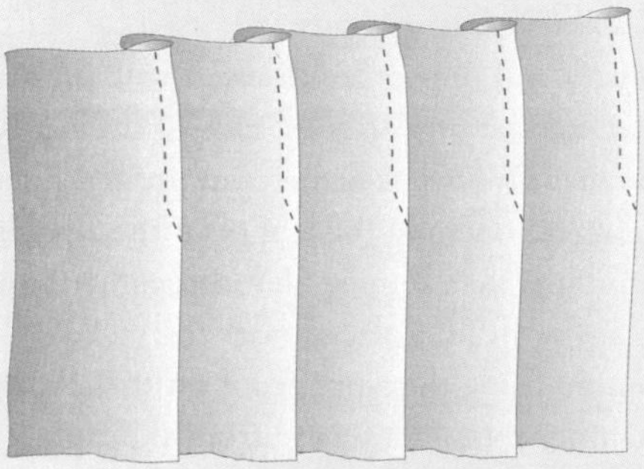

Warp knitted and bonded fabrics do not need the edge to be neatened as the hemming stitch keeps the hem stable.

Hand stitching

Most assembly techniques are carried out by sewing machines since sewing machines provide:

- speed
- accuracy
- a secure result.

There are, however, some processes which can effectively be carried out by hand. These are outlined in Figure 6.

Shaping and reducing fullness

When making textile items to fit irregular or curved shapes, it is necessary to take steps to make flat pieces of fabric fit. These steps can be taken either when planning or when making a template or during the construction of the item. There are three main ways of reducing fullness or altering the fit of textile items:

- TUCKS AND PLEATS
- gathering
- DARTS.

Tucks and pleats

Tucks and pleats are folds of fabric held in place by stitching. Larger pieces of fabric can be joined to narrower pieces. It is through tucks that a sleeve has room from shoulder to wrist to allow for comfort and body movement, for example. Similarly, with trousers and skirts, the fabric is tucked or pleated into a fitted waistband, allowing fullness over the hips.

Pleats can be stitched inside or partly top stitched (see Figure 7) to provide fullness at another place, or they can be left free and only secured along the seam line.

Tucks and pleats also add to the aesthetic appearance of the item.

Gathering

Gathering (see Figure 8) also gives fullness to one part of a garment. It is, in effect, lots of small tucks. Gathering is used on many different items - for example, curtains, smocked clothing, skirts and the sleeve heads of blouses. To gather a piece of fabric to fit into a band, yoke or sleeve head, two lines of parallel straight stitch are sewn across the length to be gathered - either by hand or by using a large stitch (4mm) on the sewing machine. The ends of each line of stitching do not need to be secured as the thread is pulled and the fabric gathered so that the gathered edge is shorter in length. The gathers are then evened out before being attached to the band, yoke or sleeve head.

Curtains are gathered using curtain tape which is sewn onto the folded top edge. The tape has two or three lengths of yarn running through it which are pulled to the required width of the curtain before it is secured.

Darts

Darts are used to make a garment fit more closely - for example, bodice darts are used to make a dress or blouse fit properly over the bust and into the waist and waist darts on trousers reduce fullness from the hips to the waist.

The principle is that a section of the fabric is removed, usually in a triangular shape, with the result that the fabric does not lie flat and so it can fit the body shape.

Darts usually start at the seam line and taper to nothing at their tip. Double-pointed darts found in one-piece dresses and closely fitted shirts are two darts combined into one, resulting in a long dart with the widest part over the waist tapering to nothing near the bust or shoulder blade and hips.

Attaching components

Components are an important part in the construction of textile items. A component must be attached so that it can perform its function securely.

Buttons

The size and shape of buttons should be

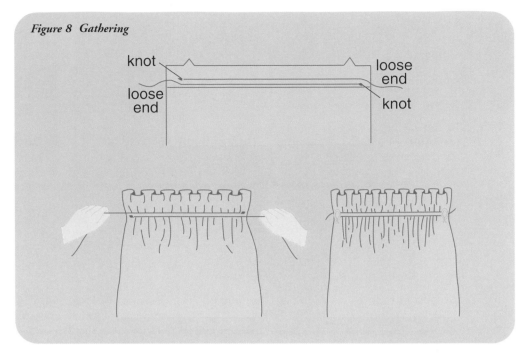

Figure 8 Gathering

chosen to match the colour and weight of the fabric to which they are being attached. Chalk, tailor tacks or pins should be used to mark the position where the button will be attached. Buttons with shanks are used on thick fabrics to give room for two thicknesses beneath the button when fastened. These can be sewn into position with a hand sewing needle and double thread. The end of the thread should be knotted and between four and six stitches made between the hole in the button shank and the fabric underneath. The job should be completed with a double stitch underneath the button.

Flat buttons with two or four holes should be sewn on using knotted double thread and with four stitches for each double set of

holes. Flat buttons can be sewn on using a sewing machine with a stationary zig-zag stitch. The exact width of the distance between the buttonholes is required. For flat buttons on bulkier or double fabric, a thread stem should be formed to lift the button off the fabric surface. Thread is wound around the stitches which hold the button in place (see Figure 9a).

Hooks and eyes

Hooks and eyes are sewn on at the hook end with buttonhole stitch for security. The hook is sewn down with several over stitches (see Figure 9b).

Zips

Zips can be attached to textile items in a number of ways. The method depends on the item. Normally, the raw edge of the fabric is turned under and sewn on top of the zip tape, close to the teeth.

Closed zips (see Figure 9c), used for skirts, trousers and dresses are inserted with an open seam at one or both ends of the zip. The seam is sewn together and pressed open, leaving an opening the length of the zip. The opening is then loosely tacked together and the zip sewn into place under the tacked opening using the zipper foot on the sewing machine, about 1cm away from the zip teeth. The tacking is removed from the front using a stitch cutter.

activities

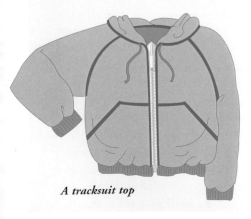

A tracksuit top

1. How many separate pieces of fabric are used to make the tracksuit top (left)? List them by name.

2. The tracksuit top is to be made from knitted fleecy cotton fabric with a dense, hardwearing construction. Describe what method of seam construction you would use to join the pieces together and why.

3. Make a plan of action for the construction of the tracksuit top. Include details about finishing off seams and attaching pockets, ribbing and fastenings.

Open zips, used for coats and cardigans, are sewn in so the fabric is separate until it is zipped together. Open zips are inserted by tacking the pieces together as if the item was fastened, pressing the temporary seam open and sewing the zip into place using the zipper foot on the sewing machine, about 1cm away from the zip teeth.

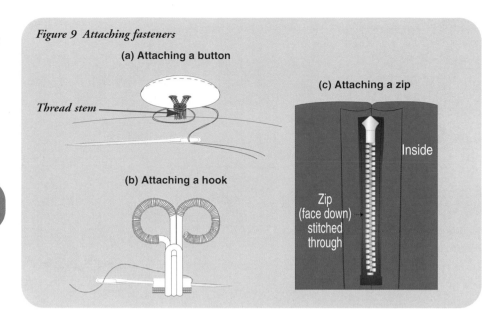

Figure 9 Attaching fasteners

(a) Attaching a button

Thread stem

(b) Attaching a hook

(c) Attaching a zip

Inside

Zip (face down) stitched through

Assembly and planning

In addition to using the correct method of construction, it is important to join together the fabric and components in the right order. Planning the construction of an item is a vital stage in the design process.

The order below provides general guidelines:

- prepare fabric pieces - make cutting edge even, zig-zag or overlock fraying edges and iron if necessary

- sew darts
- attach any pockets, motifs or construction details (eg zips) that cannot be added after construction
- stitch pieces together in a logical order (eg a sleeve can only be sewn onto a shirt after the back and front have been joined)
- trim any unfinished seams and loose threads and complete hand stitching of hems
- attach other fastenings.

A detailed plan of action should be written down and followed during the construction of a prototype.

Key Terms

Template - the shape of part of a textile item made in paper or card to allow the fabric to be cut out accurately.
Seam - stitching used to join two or more pieces of fabric together.
Right side - the outside of a textile item.
Tacking - running stitch sewn by hand to temporarily join fabric together.
Seam allowance - the extra fabric included at the edge of a fabric section to allow for the turning of seams.
Wrong side - the inside of a textile item.
Hem - the edge of textile item which is turned and joined to itself to make a straight edge.
Tucks and pleats - folds of fabric held in place by stitching.
Darts - triangular pieces of fabric designed to make a garment fit.

activities

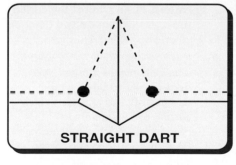

STRAIGHT DART

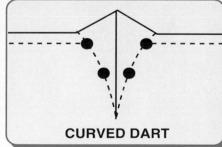

CURVED DART

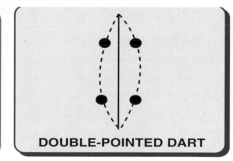

DOUBLE-POINTED DART

The darts (above) can all be used to reduce fullness in garments.

1. Using template paper or scrap fabric make an example of each dart. The dots are used for matching each side of the dart.

2. Using your worked example, explain how each dart changes the contours of the fabric.

3. Suggest TWO items or garments that might use each dart.

4. What other method of reducing fullness could be used instead of darts for each of the garments you have listed? What would be the advantage of using darts? Explain your answer.

Using equipment safely

Introduction

When designing and making textile items, a wide variety of tools and equipment need to be used. Knowledge about this equipment is necessary both to produce a high quality product and to ensure the user's safety.

Equipment can be divided into two main categories:

● hand-held equipment
● machines.

Units 16 and 17 examine the wide variety of tools and machines that are used, their functions and the safety requirements which need to be considered when using them.

Cutting tools

When cutting, suitable tools must be chosen to ensure that the pattern or fabric is cut accurately and efficiently, without damage. The main cutting tools used for making textile items are illustrated in Figure 1. They include the following.

Paper SHEARS - scissors used for the accurate cutting out of thin paper for pattern making.

Tailor's shears - large shears whose finger holes are shaped to make it easier to cut thick fabrics. One of the blades has serrations to prevent smooth fabric from slipping.

Fabric shears - large shears whose finger holes are shaped to enable accurate cutting. The blades have smooth cutting edges which blunt easily. It is important only to use them to cut fabric.

Pattern shears - shears used for cutting out pattern templates from cardboard or plastic. The blades are detachable.

Pinking shears - shears whose cutting edges have a zig-zag profile. This reduces the risk of fraying and creates an attractive, decorative edge.

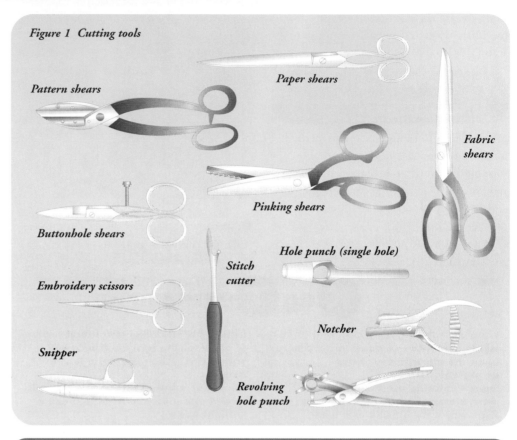

Figure 1 Cutting tools

Pattern shears

Paper shears

Fabric shears

Buttonhole shears

Pinking shears

Embroidery scissors

Stitch cutter

Hole punch (single hole)

Snipper

Notcher

Revolving hole punch

activities

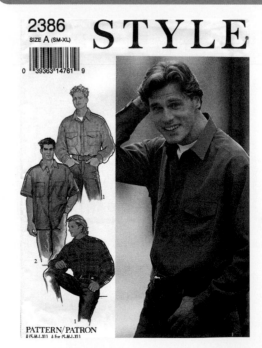

2386
SIZE A (SM-XL)

0 39363 14761 9

STYLE

PATTERN/PATRON

Look at the pattern (left)

1. Suppose you were going to make a shirt similar to that in the pattern. Make a list of the cutting tools you would use and describe when you would use them.

2. It is too expensive for someone who only makes clothes occasionally to buy a large number of cutting tools. Which cutting tools would you recommend such a person buys? Give reasons for your choice.

3. Safety is an important consideration when using cutting tools. Draw up a list of safety rules that must be obeyed when using cutting tools.

Buttonhole shears - shears designed to make a cut a short way into the fabric. The blades have a special gap and an adjustable screw which determines the length of the cut.

Embroidery scissors - small scissors used for catching and cutting fine short threads.

Snippers - a tool with spring-loaded blades which open automatically. These are used to snip and trim thread, remove tacking stitches and to open seams.

Stitch cutter - a tool designed to open machine-made buttonholes.

Hole punches - tools used to punch holes close to the edge of fabric (revolving punch) or into card or plastic (single punch).

Notcher - a tool which makes notches of various shapes. It is used to place position marks on cutting patterns (eg balance marks and seam allowances).

Needles

All sewing needles have an 'eye', a 'stem' and a 'point' (see Figure 2). They are made of nickel-plated steel. They must be flexible, smooth and sharp. A numbering system is used to distinguish them. The length and thickness of the needle needed for a particular job depends on:
● the fabric
● the thread
● the sewing techniques to be used.

Standard and long needles

Most needles are 'standard' or 'long'. Standard needles are also known as 'betweens'. Long needles are also known as 'sharps'. Standard needles are used for tailoring and fine work (shorter needles are easier to use on thicker fabrics). Long needles are used for general sewing and dress making.

Embroidery and darning needles

Embroidery and darning needles are particularly thick needles. The fabric to be used and the yarn thickness determines the length and thickness of the needle used for

a particular job. The eyes of these needles are longer and wider to enable embroidery yarns to be used. **Rounded** needles (or 'tapestry' needles) are used for coarse fabric and **pointed** needles (or 'crewel' needles) for finer materials.

Pins

Pins are made of steel and may have plastic heads. The length, thickness and type of pins chosen depends on the type of fabric and application. Pins may be used for:
● component assembly
● packaging.

Thimbles

A THIMBLE is a device for protecting the sewer's middle finger and to enable easier and quicker sewing. Thimbles are made from steel, brass or plastic. They have small depressions indented into them to prevent the needle slipping off. They are produced in a number of diameters to accommodate different finger sizes. It is essential to use the correct size to ensure comfort and safety.

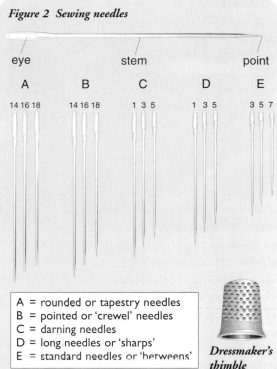

Figure 2 Sewing needles

A = rounded or tapestry needles
B = pointed or 'crewel' needles
C = darning needles
D = long needles or 'sharps'
E = standard needles or 'betweens'

Dressmaker's thimble

Sewing machine needles

Sewing machine needles can be divided into four main groups:
● set points
● round points (also called 'ball points')
● cutting points
● twin needles.

activities

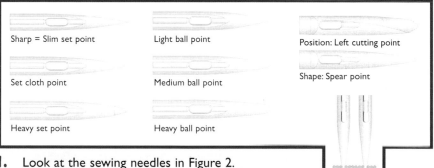

1. Look at the sewing needles in Figure 2.
   a) When choosing a sewing needle, what factors need to be taken into account?
   b) What would be the consequences of using the wrong size needle?
2. Look at the sewing machine needles (above). Which needle would you choose for the following jobs:
   a) repairing a seam on a jumper made of lamb's wool
   b) making a suede waistcoat
   c) adding a decorative pattern to a dress?
3. Give TWO examples of an occasion when you might use the following needles: a crewel needle, a long needle, a heavy set point and a spear point.

There are three types of set points. **Slim set points** can penetrate the yarns of the material being sewn. They are used for blind stitches and for fine, densely woven fabrics. They are not suitable for knitted fabrics. **Set cloth points** are the most versatile needles. They displace the yarns of the material without damaging them. **Heavy set points** have blunt ends and are used for button sewing machines.

There are also three types of round points. **Light round points** are used for sensitive fabrics like knitwear to prevent damage to the loops. **Medium** and **heavy round points** are used to sew elastic materials.

Cutting points are used to sew heavy-duty materials such as leather or coated textiles. They are classified according to the position or shape of the cutting edge (eg 'spear point' or 'right cutting point').

Twin needles are used for sewing raised seams and different decoration stitches with one- or two-coloured threads. Two ordinary needles are joined together with a set width between them. The set width determines the stitch width.

Knitting needles

Knitting needles are used for hand knitting. The needles come in various sizes and lengths and are sold in pairs. They used to be made from wood but are now more likely to be from lightweight materials such as coated metal or plastic. The needles are pointed at one end with a knob at the other end to prevent stitches coming off. The needle size is normally marked on the knob. Sizes vary, but they are becoming standardised as the metric system is adopted.

There are a number of different types of knitting needle:

Cable needles - short needles, pointed at both ends. Stitches which are held at the front or back of the work when cabling are slipped onto them.

Double pointed needles - needles with a point at both ends (and usually come in a set of four). They are used for knitting in rounds for a circular fabric.

Circular needles - two small needle sections pointed at both ends and joined together by a piece of flexible nylon. Circular needles are easier to handle than four needles, but can

only be used when the number of stitches being worked is sufficient to reach from one needle point to the other. They are available in various lengths and are useful when working straight knitting in rows with a large number of stitches.

Electric irons

The electric iron is used to create a smooth finish to fabrics. The heat is produced by an electric heating element and the temperature can be adjusted from 60°C to 220°C to accommodate the properties of the material being pressed. The thermostat in the iron keeps the temperature at the required setting by cutting off the current once the correct temperature has been reached. There is normally an indicator light which is illuminated as soon as the iron is turned on. When the iron reaches the correct

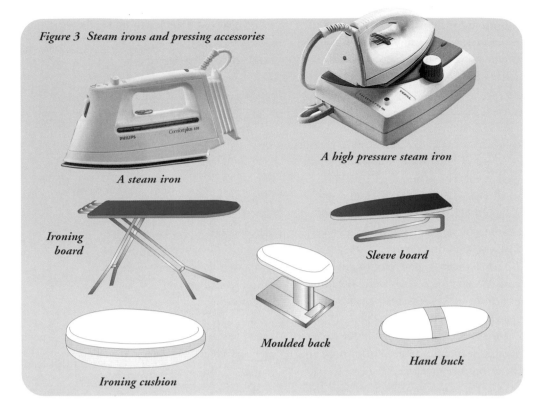

Figure 3 Steam irons and pressing accessories

A steam iron

A high pressure steam iron

Ironing board

Sleeve board

Moulded back

Ironing cushion

Hand buck

activities

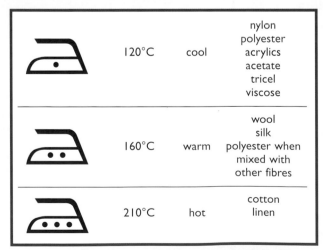

	120°C	cool	nylon polyester acrylics acetate tricel viscose
	160°C	warm	wool silk polyester when mixed with other fibres
	210°C	hot	cotton linen

Modern irons have three temperature settings indicated by one, two, or three dots.

1. When ironing and pressing different items, care should be taken to determine what fabric the item is made from. Explain why this is necessary.

2. What temperature and setting would you use for the following textile items: (i) a linen table cloth (ii) a cotton and polyester shirt (iii) a viscose football shirt.

3. What are the advantages of using a steam iron?

temperature this light is automatically switched off. It is vital to use the correct temperature setting for a particular fabric as damage may be caused if too high a temperature is used.

Steam irons

In domestic steam irons, steam is generated and utilised in one of two ways:

● at atmospheric pressure
● at high pressure.

In some steam irons, water is dripped onto the hot ironing plate where it evaporates. The escaping steam has a temperature of around 100°C. In other steam irons, a higher steam temperature is achieved because the water is heated in a pressure vessel. Electric heating elements evaporate the water and the steam escapes through perforations in the sole of the iron. As with dry irons, the temperature of the sole can be regulated.

Pressing accessories

Ironing boards are used to press large surfaces of fabric. The board usually has an adjustable height and a section for resting the iron. The board often has a felt or padded underlay to spread the pressure and absorb the heat.

A **sleeve board** is a smaller board used for pressing parts of textile items which are not flat (eg sleeves).

A **HAND BUCK** is a hand-held pad which is also useful in the pressing of parts of textile items which are not flat.

Ironing cushions and **moulded bucks** also serve the same purpose (see Figure 3).

Sewing machines

The simplest form of sewing machine is the flat bed sewing machine. Its basic components are shown in Figure 4.

Electric sewing machines may be semi-automatic, automatic or electronic.

Semi-automatic machines

Semi-automatic machines perform straight stitch and zig-zag using a swing needle. The stitch length and width can be adjusted to provide suitable stitches for a variety of

Figure 4 A semi-automatic sewing machine

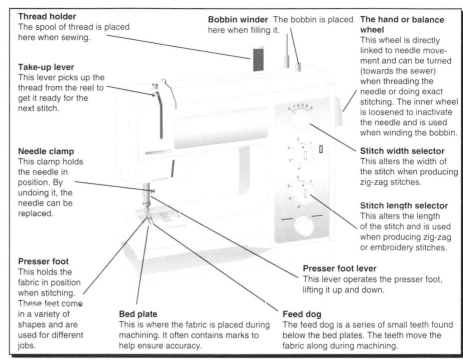

Thread holder
The spool of thread is placed here when sewing.

Take-up lever
This lever picks up the thread from the reel to get it ready for the next stitch.

Needle clamp
This clamp holds the needle in position. By undoing it, the needle can be replaced.

Presser foot
This holds the fabric in position when stitching. These feet come in a variety of shapes and are used for different jobs.

Bobbin winder The bobbin is placed here when filling it.

Bed plate
This is where the fabric is placed during machining. It often contains marks to help ensure accuracy.

The hand or balance wheel
This wheel is directly linked to needle movement and can be turned (towards the sewer) when threading the needle or doing exact stitching. The inner wheel is loosened to inactivate the needle and is used when winding the bobbin.

Stitch width selector
This alters the width of the stitch when producing zig-zag stitches.

Stitch length selector
This alters the length of the stitch and is used when producing zig-zag or embroidery stitches.

Presser foot lever
This lever operates the presser foot, lifting it up and down.

Feed dog
The feed dog is a series of small teeth found below the bed plates. The teeth move the fabric along during machining.

processes. Stitch lengths and stitch widths are measured in millimetres.

Automatic machines

Automatic machines are electrically operated either by foot or knee control. The machine can be set to do a particular job and it will then adjust its own needle position, speed and stitch sequence. The machine can also be set to allow for a variety of thicknesses of fabric.

Electronic machines

Electronic or computer-controlled sewing machines allow the user to programme in a process via a keyboard. When the relevant information has been keyed in, the machine produces the correct stitch in a suitable length and width. Individual models vary, but a wide variety of stitches, decorative details, numbers and letters can usually be preprogrammed into their memory. Computer disks or cartridges may be inserted to add to the variety of processes that the machine can complete.

Safe use of a sewing machine

Before using any sewing machine, it is important to read the instruction booklet that comes with that particular model. This will

provide information relating to:

● the machine's components
● threading instructions
● the bobbin winding method
● other operational instructions
● problem solving ideas.

Other safe working practices include the following:

● the flexes providing electricity to the sewing machine must be kept well clear of the needle
● only one person should operate a machine
● the foot control should be placed well under the table surface
● the needle should be held securely in the needle clamp
● the operator should make sure that long hair is tied back
● loose clothing - such as ties - should be tucked in
● full concentration is necessary at all times when operating a sewing machine
● the electric power should always be switched off when the machine is not in use.

Common faults

Many problems encountered when using a sewing machine are easily solved. Table 1 shows the sort of problems that often arise

Table 1 Sewing machines - common problems

Problem	Probable cause
Missed stitches	1. Blunt needle 2. Needle inserted wrongly
Upper thread breaks	1. Blunt needle 2. Bent needle 3. Needle inserted wrongly 4. Poor quality or knotted thread 5. Needle too fine or too coarse
Bottom thread breaks	1. Bottom thread tension is too tight 2. Bobbin is crushed or jammed
Needle breaks	1. Needle clamp not tight enough 2. Fabric pulled towards front 3. Too many thicknesses of fabric 4. Pin heads on stitching line
Puckered fabric	1. Blunt needle 2. Needle too large for fabric 3. Fabric being pulled through feed

and the usual causes.

Overlockers

An OVERLOCKER is a machine which combines the separate processes of:
- matching a seam
- neatening
- trimming.

As a result, an overlocker gives a professional finish to textile items. Overlocking is sometimes also known as 'overedging'.

An overlocker generally uses a variation of chain stitch, enabling it to seal the edge of the fabric and to prevent it from fraying. A four-thread overlocker has two needles. The seam is made with a double chain stitch, while a strong, long lasting finish is given to the turnings by the overlock stitch and, at the same time, the edges are trimmed off by a cutter. Overlockers may, however, have only two or three threads and one needle. Two threads simply overlock edges, making a very narrow seam. A three thread machine produces a more secure seam.

The cutting blade on an overlocker is very

Figure 5 An overlocker

activities

RICCAR 9200
- Eight stitches, two dials
- built-in motor with variable speed foot control
- convenient snap-on presser foot for quick, easy changing
- soft sewing light above the needle.

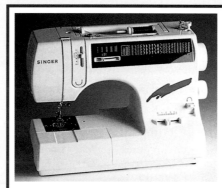

SINGER 6423
- 23 stitches built in - 12 decorative and 11 'flexi' stitches
- automatic one-step buttonhole built in
- sewing light and motor built in
- easy-to-follow path makes threading simple and quick.

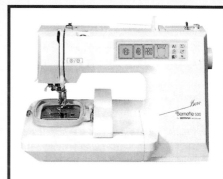

BERNETTE DECO 500
- will embroider 62 individual motifs
- colours and sizes can be mixed
- a variety of 88 borders can be sewn in 11 different stitch types
- the alphabet can be sewn in three sizes
- optional accessories available - eg memory cards and embroidery frames.

1. What are the main differences between the sewing machines featured above?

2. What factors, other than those mentioned, need to be taken into consideration when buying a sewing machine?

3. The following people want to buy a new sewing machine: (i) a student starting a two year GCSE Textiles course, (ii) a person who makes clothes for their children (iii) a person who makes clothes for a living and wants to include more decorative finishes such as smocking and embroidery. What machine would you recommend? Give reasons for your answer.

4. Write a set of safety rules to be followed by people using a sewing machine. Explain why you have included each rule.

sharp and care must be taken to keep fingers clear of this part of the machine when it is in use.

Knitting machines

There are three main types of knitting machine:

- plastic machines
- punch card machines
- electronic machines.

Plastic machines

Plastic machines are, in effect, one stage up from hand knitting, though they are considerably faster. The frame is lightweight, consisting of a single bed with 100-110 needles.

Plastic machines can knit a variety of yarns. Indeed, they can use the same yarn that is used for hand knitting. The patterning on plastic machines is manual.

It is easy to learn to use a plastic machine and the finish can be very close to that achieved when hand knitting.

Punch card machines

Punch card knitting machines are either single bed or double bed metal machines that have plastic punch cards for automatic patterning. The patterns repeat over 12, 18, 24, 36 or 40 needles depending on the model. Most commonly, patterns repeat over 24 stitches.

The single bed machines have just one row of needles (200 needles on a standard gauge model) and a knitting carriage which slides across the bed. One row is knitted each time

Figure 6 Knitting machines

plastic

punch card

electronic

the carriage is passed across the bed. Using the basic stitch, a single-faced stocking stitch is produced with the wrong side facing the knitter. Textured stitch can be produced by using different pattern cards and different coloured yarns.

Double bed machines have two rows of needles facing each other at an angle with a connecting arm between the two carriages.

Electronic machines

With the advances in information technology, electronic knitting machines have been designed. These use MYLAR SHEETS instead of a mechanical punch card pattern selection. Each Mylar sheet has the pattern marked out on it. The machine scans the sheet and transfers the information to electronic circuits which control the needle selection. A maximum 200 stitch pattern repeat is available on some machines.

With added connections to computers, graphics packages can be used. These help to create designs for knitted fabric.

activities

Sue is a designer of jumpers in western Ireland. She employs eight knitters and aims to expand her business to cater for the tourists visiting the area. She wants to invest in a number of machines that will increase production as well as helping her develop her design ideas.

Mike has recently learned to hand knit. He would now like a machine so that he can produce plain knit jumpers for his friends and family as Christmas presents.

1. Describe the main differences between the three main types of knitting machine.

2. What type of knitting machine would you recommend for the people featured above? Give reasons for your answer.

3. Devise a set of safety instructions which should be followed when using a knitting machine.

 WHICH STEAM IRON?

BEFORE investing in a product or service, consumers need to investigate a wide range of products to ensure that they buy the product or service which is most suitable for their requirements. Information about products and services can be gathered in a number of ways. Consumers might choose a particular product because a friend recommended it, for example, or they might compare the features and prices of different models by examining the information provided by the manufacturer. The trouble with information provided by the manufacturer, however, is that it is unlikely to highlight any drawbacks or shortcomings. Faced with similar information from three different companies, it is often difficult to be sure which is most suitable. One solution is to seek an independent opinion. For this, the magazine *Which?* is particularly useful. *Which?* is an independent magazine produced for consumers specifically to help them to decide which products are most suitable for them. Each month a team of researchers tests several products and gives an independent and extensive breakdown of them. In April 1996, for example, a team of researchers examined and tested 15 steam irons. As well as testing the irons in the laboratory, the irons were assessed both by professional ironers and by ordinary users. The results of the tests were then compiled in a table and each iron was given a mark out of ten. On the strength of the research, a number of irons were picked out as 'best buys'. As well as reporting on the tests, the article also gave information on special features and tips on maintenance.

This brochure provides detailed information on one type of steam iron. It was produced by the manufacturer.

	Hinari Lifestyle IR 462	Kenwood ST450	Morphy Richards Profile 42810	Moulinex Ultimate 200 V56	Phillips Mistral 20 HI 220	Rowenta Trio DE-19	Salton Harmony 5021	Tefal Ultraglide 1606	Ufesa Styrium PV-153
Price (£)	15	22	30	40	19	25	18	35	25
Weight (kg)	0.8	1.1	0.9	1.4	1	1	1	1.0	1
Flex length (m)	1.9	2.4	2	2	1.9	1.9	1.9	1.8	2.1
Extra boost of steam	✓	✓	✓	✓	✓	✓	✓	✓	✓
Self-cleaning system			✓	✓	✓			✓	✓
Quality of end results	◑	○	○	☆	☆	○	○	○	○
Ease of use	○	○		☆	☆		☆	☆	☆
Durability against scale	◑	●	◑	★	○	☆	●	★	☆
Cooling time	○	○		○	○	○	○	☆	○
Temperature accuracy	★	★	○	★	○		★	◑	★
Easy to fill and empty		✗	✓	✓	✓		✓	✓	✓
Cord easy to store		✓	✓	✓	✓		✓	✓	✓
Easy-to-use controls		✓	✓	✓	✓		✓	✓	✓
Clear heating settings	✓	✓		✓	✓				
Total test score	**5**	**6**	**5**	**8**	**7**	**7**	**6**	**7**	**7**

★ best ← ☆ ○ ◑ ● → worst ✓ has this feature ✗ has this drawback

This table was adapted from Which? magazine, April 1996.

Activities

1. Why are the reports published in *Which?* magazine particularly useful to consumers?
2. Using the table above write a report on TWO of the steam irons explaining their benefits and drawbacks.
3. Judging from the results of the tests, which steam irons would you recommend as 'best buys'? Explain why.
4. Suppose you wanted to buy a sewing machine and you were able to test a number of models beforehand. Draw up a table which could be used to compare the features and performance of each model.

ASSEMBLING A BRA

PHOTO I shows all the different pieces and components needed to assemble a bra. Photo 4 shows the bra when it has been assembled. The bra was assembled in Chris Dee's workshop (see p.105) using equipment which was specially designed to do this work. The bra was assembled in the following way:

1. The basic components were cut out using a hand-held electric knife.
2. An overlocker was used to sew up the edges of the main pieces.
3. The cups were top stitched (see photo 2).
4. The padding was assembled.
5. The padding was presewn into the cups.
6. The voile backing was presewn onto the lace band.
7. The cups were placed into the cradle of the overlocker and sewn with a wide stitch to accommodate the bone casing (see photo 3).
8. The back band was sewn into place using the overlocker.
9. A three point zig-zag stitch was used to place elastic around the edges of the bra.
10. A twin needle machine (specially adapted) was used to feed the bone casing through.
11. The bra wires were pushed through the bone casing and bar tacked.
12. The straps and bows were sewn on using the bar tacker.
13. All ends were finished using the bar tacker.

The pieces of fabric and components needed to make a bra

Overlocking the cup seams

Top stitching the cup seams to flatten them

The finished product

Activities

1. Bras are assembled following a set number of steps. Explain why the steps have to be completed in order and what would happen if the order changed.
2. What sort of seams are likely to be used on a bra? Give reasons for your answer.
3. Draw your own design for a piece of clothing. Make a list of the fabric pieces and components you would need and describe
   (i) the order in which the pieces would be assembled and
   (ii) the methods used to assemble the garment.

Industrial production techniques

Making yarns and fabrics

Unit 7 looks at how fibres are made into yarns and fabrics. For reasons of economic efficiency, yarns and fabrics are manufactured on a very large scale, using large machines (see Figure 1). The manufacture of yarns and fabrics is now highly automated. Most machines used to make yarns or fabrics are controlled by computers.

Spinning

Different systems are used for different types or mixes of fibres. The techniques used to make yarns vary according to the length and properties of the fibres. There are,

therefore, a number of different spinning systems, designed for:

● wool (including worsted) - where the length of fibres can vary depending on the source.
● cotton - where the fibres vary according to the source.
● flax, hemp and jute (the 'bast fibre system') - where fibres can be up to 1,000mm in length.
● silk - where fibres of predetermined lengths are spun
● regenerated and synthetic fibres - where continuous filaments are spun.

The system used depends on the length of the fibres and the tightness of the yarn being produced. Some systems are interchangeable -

Figure 1 Industrial spinning

for example, the woollen system can be used to spin some synthetic fibres of similar lengths to wool fibres.

Weaving

Today it is unusual for fabric to be woven on a hand loom (see the Case Study on Harris

activities

The Camber desinit jacquard loom is designed to weave complex patterns. The warp yarns are suspended from the wheel at the top of the machine and controlled by a computer. The pattern is programmed into the computer. As the loom runs, the computer automatically selects each warp yarn in the right order to make the pattern. This new generation of jacquard looms has a simplified design which enables the machine to operate at higher speeds and with greater reliability.
Source: Camber, 1997

1. How does the way in which the Camber desinit jacquard loom works differ from the way in which the handloom on p.40 works?
2. What advantages does this machine bring to the manufacturer?
3. Draw a design that might be woven using this machine. What processes would the fabric you have designed go through after being woven?

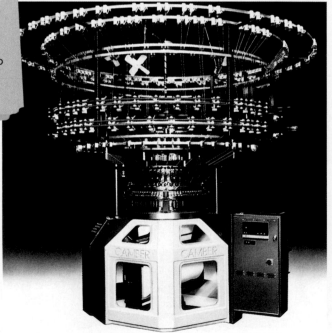

The Camber desinit jacquard loom.

Tweed, p.50, for a notable exception). Most woven fabric is produced on large high speed looms powered by electricity and controlled by electronic sensors and computer systems. A major advantage of machines like this is that they provide closed loop feedback (see Unit 18). If, for example, the tension of a warp thread is wrong, sensors in the machine automatically register this and the machine stops, allowing the fault to be fixed.

There are two main types of weaving:
● shaft weaving
● jacquard weaving.

Shaft weaving is performed on looms where the warp and weft yarns are held in a frame. Shaft weaving produces uniform weaves - such as plain, twill and sateen. Jacquard weaving, on the other hand, produces fabric with complex designs and patterns. This is achieved by controlling each warp yarn individually. Older jacquard looms control warp yarns with punch cards. Newer jacquard looms control warp yarns by means of a computer programme.

Knitting

Knitted fabrics are made from interlocking loops formed from a single yarn or from many yarns. All knitted fabric made on an industrial scale is made using a machine. Flat bed machines produce sheets of knitted fabric. Circular machines produce fabric in tubes (see Figure 2).

Industrial equipment

Unit 16 looked at the types of equipment used to measure, mark, cut and join fabric to make textile items on a small scale. Making textile items on a large scale requires quite different equipment. In the textile manufacturing industry, careful management and organisation is required to maximise efficiency and maintain profits. The equipment used must be appropriate for the business.

Choosing equipment

A textile manufacturer must take into account a number of factors when planning the purchase of new equipment:
● the equipment must complete the task safely and efficiently
● size and weight are important - can the floor support the load? Is there room?

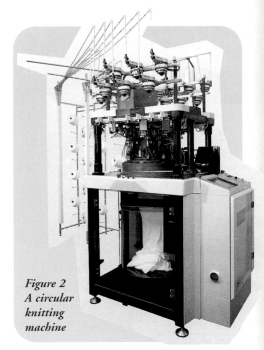

Figure 2
A circular
knitting
machine

● is there an appropriate power source?
● what other functions or processes is the equipment capable of?
● is a great deal of technical expertise needed to be able to adjust the equipment?
● does the equipment make a level of noise that might adversely affect the workforce?
● are spare parts and servicing readily available?

activities

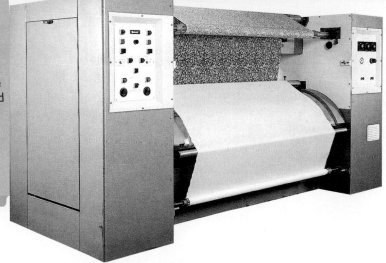

The Monk Cotton Group's CFP700 Continuous Fabric Printer produces a pattern which has photographic clarity. The machine can be used to print patterns on a wide range of fabrics and cloths including wool and cotton mixes and pile fabrics. The machine works by transferring the dye embedded in special paper onto the fabric by means of heat. The heat is provided by a heated cylinder. The transfer printing paper is wrapped around the cylinder and then the fabric is wrapped on top of that. Special temperature sensors at different points on the cylinder ensure that the heat is uniform to within 1°C. One customer uses the same roll of paper three times and then sells it to florists (to be used as wrapping) for the same price it cost to buy.
Source: Woodcocks, Scotland, 1997

1. What is meant by 'photographic clarity'. Why is that a good selling point?

2. Draw a diagram to show how this machine works.

3. Suggest THREE reasons why a curtain manufacturer might invest in this machine.

4. Describe THREE other ways of applying colour to large quantities of fabric.

Equipment for finishing and colouring

When the fabric has been woven or knitted, it needs to be finished and coloured (see Units 11 and 13). Sometimes dyeing and finishing is undertaken by one company (see, for example, the Case Study on The Standish Company, p.111).

Equipment for measuring

A PATTERN DRAFT is a diagrammatic representation of the way in which an item is to be constructed. It forms a working plan for the item's manufacture. The pattern draft is developed by calculation, taking account of the following measurements:

- actual body size measurements
- size charts related to the end use and derived from studies made of measurements of human bodies (anthropometric data - see Unit 20)
- specifications dictated by the designer for non-clothing items.

The development of a new collection is done by modifying existing designs or block patterns (see Unit 14). This time-consuming work is done more easily and faster using a CAD system. Basic patterns are first digitised (information is converted into series of numbers for the computer). Any designs can then be stored, retrieved and adapted at any time.

Grading

. Grading is the stepped increase or decrease of a master pattern piece to create larger or smaller sizes (see also Unit 3). Grading can be done manually using a grading machine which grips the master pattern and moves it precise distances horizontally and vertically so each edge can be traced. Alternatively, grading can be done using a computer. This system operates in two ways:

- the grading increments (steps) are fed into the computer and different sizes are generated automatically
- the pattern for each individual size is calculated separately using the data from the size charts.

Once the pattern has been generated on the computer, it can be used in two ways, depending on the level of automation in the factory. In a fully automated system, the pieces are sorted automatically and arranged in a LAY PLAN which is transmitted to the automatic laying and cutting system. Alternatively, the patterns are plotted (drawn) and then used as

Figure 3 A pattern design, preparation and programming system

This system allows the user to design and prepare patterns for jacquard fabrics.

activities

The new Trumeter Super 2000 Series measuring machines include new exclusive components to ensure reliability and continuing accuracy even when operated under the most robust conditions. The length of many types of material can be measured. Operation is by the material passing between a measuring roller and an adjustable spring-loaded pressure roller. This means the machine is activated by the movement of the material. The machines have a brake to prevent overspin at the end of a piece. If a material has pile, it is essential that the measuring wheel runs on the side of the material opposite the pile. Models can be fitted with mechanical or electronic counters.
Source: Trumeter, 1997

1. a) What task does the Trumeter Super 2000 Series perform?
   b) How do the machines work?
2. Why do you think large-scale fabric or clothing manufacturers might want to purchase one of these machines?
3. What other measuring devices might a large-scale clothing manufacturer need?

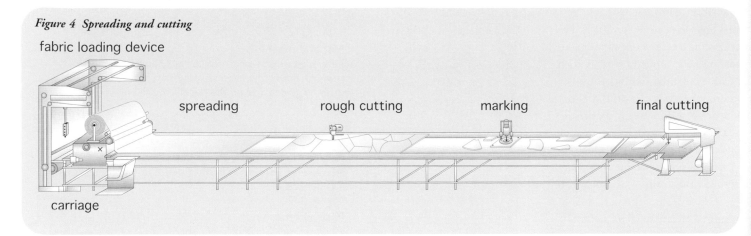

Figure 4 Spreading and cutting

fabric loading device

spreading   rough cutting   marking   final cutting

carriage

paper patterns for manual cutting.

A lay plan is made by positioning all the individual pattern pieces of a textile item on the fabric in such a way that they fit as closely and efficiently as possible to minimise waste. As with items made on a small scale (see Unit 14), pattern pieces are laid in a way that takes account of the directional properties of the fabric (weave direction, grain, nap or pile). It may be necessary to allow for matching checks, stripes or other designs. Lay plans can be made in two ways.

1. **The manual method.** This is the simplest method. The templates are placed manually onto the fabric and their outline is then traced either onto the fabric or onto special marker paper. The arrangement of the templates is decided by experience and know-how or by following a small-scale printed diagram.

2. **Computer generation.** After grading, a computer can be used to produce the lay plan and CUTTING MARKER (the sheet with the position of each template marked on it). A light pen is used to move individual pieces around the screen so that the best layout is achieved. More advanced systems calculate the materials needed. The finished lay plan is stored on the computer. It can be recalled and printed as a miniature plan at any time.

Spreading

Spreading is the smooth laying out of fabrics in layers of specified lengths with the cutting marker laid on the top layer so that a large number of fabric thicknesses can be cut together.

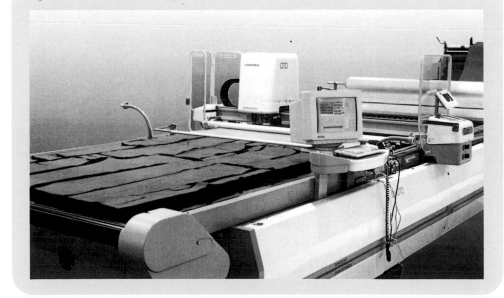

Figure 5 An electronic cutting bed

Cutting

Cutting is performed in two stages. First rough cutting separates the individual pieces of fabric. And second, final cutting cuts out each piece accurately. A range of cutting tools are used with different degrees of precision:

● **circular cutters** are used to divide a LAY (multiple layers of fabric) into sections. They can only cut in straight lines or gradual curves.

● **straight knives** have a vertical blade which works like a saw. They are used for both coarse and precise cutting.

● **band knives** have an endless steel blade that moves vertically through layers of fabric for precise cutting.

● **die cutters** cut fabric shapes out in the same way that a pastry cutter cuts out pastry. They are mainly used for leather and coated or laminated fabrics.

● **computer controlled cutting machines** are fully automated and they cut fabric using sharp, vertical knives.

Laser beams, high energy plasma (ionised gas) beams and high pressure water jets can be used to cut fabric very accurately.

Marking the pieces of fabric

Before the fabric is joined together to make an item, special marks or 'notches' have to be made as accurate guides for assembly. Like tailor tacks when making items on a small scale, these marks must not be visible on the finished item.

Drill markers are used to puncture a small

hole in the fabric. This hole is visible for some time, but wears away eventually. **Hot drill markers** use a heated needle to make the holes more durable. Drilled holes are then marked with a coloured fluid which is delivered down flutes in the drill. A clear liquid containing a **fluorescent marker** is often used. This makes a dot which is only visible under an ultraviolet light which is placed near the sewing machine. This method is used to mark the position of notches and dart lengths. Hot drill markers are mainly used for knitted fabrics made of natural fibres. Synthetic fibres would melt and fuse together.

Joining fabric together

Sewing machines used in the mass production of textile items vary considerably depending on the type of stitch they can do and the shape and position of the bed plate (see Figure 6).

Stitches

Sewing machines are capable of sewing a variety of stitches. Domestic sewing machines form lock-stitch. This is formed by two

Figure 6 Types of sewing machine

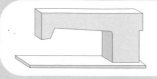

Flat bed machine
This type of machine is used for all kinds of flat sewing work. Owing to the large working area, the material can easily be guided around the needle and the presser foot.

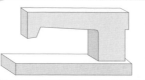

Raised bed machine
This type of machine is used for the assembly of presewn parts and for the fitting of components and special attachments. Specialised machines such as buttonholers have a raised bed.

Post bed machine
The increased working height and the post on this machine make it easier to work on tight curves and corners, to sew in sleeves and to complete large items.

Cylinder bed machine
This type of machine has an increased working height and a bed in the shape of a horizontal arm. It is used for tubular parts - for example cuffs, sleeves and trouser legs. It is also used for button sewing and bar tacking.

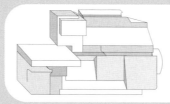

Side bed machine
This type of machine is used for sewing edges. As a result, only a small working area is needed.

Figure 7 Stitch types - their features and uses

Chain stitch
Each loop is connected with the following loop of the same thread. The seam looks different on each side. The stitches can easily be unpicked. This stitch is often used for temporary stitching.

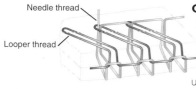

Overedge chain stitch
Loops from the needle thread go right through the material and are interconnected on the underside with themselves or with another thread. At least one thread passes round the edge of the material. This stitch is used to neaten and to bind edges.

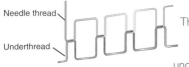

Lock-stitch
This stitch is formed when a needle thread from one side of the material is interlaced with an underthread supplied from a spool on the other side. It is difficult to unpick. and both sides of the seam look the same.

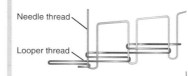

Multi-thread chain stitch
Loops from the needle thread go right through the material and are interconnected on the underside by thread from a looper. Each side looks different and the stitch can easily be unpicked. it is used for seams that need to be flat.

Hand stitch
Single threads are passed from one side of the material to the other so that the thread is held by the material. This stitch is suitable for sewing edges.

Covering chain stitch
This stitch is formed from three threads. The cover thread lies on the top surface. It is held in place by the needle thread. The needle thread is interlaced on the underside by a looper thread. This stitch is used to make flat seams in knitted fabrics.

threads - a needle thread interlaced with an under thread from a bobbin. Both sides have the same appearance. The stitches are difficult to unpick and are not as extensible (stretchy) as other stitches. The features and uses of lock-stitch and the other stitches formed by sewing machines are summarised in Figure 7.

Pressing

Pressing means shaping a textile item. It is an important technique in the manufacture of textile items. Pressing is the result of the application of heat and pressure. Steam, compressed air and suction assist the process. Steam is an efficient medium for heating and it provides the moisture needed for setting materials such as wool. Steam also relaxes fabrics and helps them to avoid shrinkage during later pressing. In industry, there are three general pressing operations:

- **underpressing** - this is a technique used to press open seams to prepare them for the next stage of manufacture
- **moulding** - this is a means of providing a three-dimensional shape without using darts. Sections of an item are pressed over a shaped surface (a buck)
- **top pressing** - this is the final finishing operation on the fully assembled item.

Equipment used in industry to press textile items works on similar principles to the domestic iron (see Unit 16). The temperature of the sole plate is controlled by a thermostat which can usually be adjusted from 60°C to 220°C to suit the characteristics of the fabric being pressed. Steam is generated either in the iron itself from water heated up in a chamber or it is generated in a separate station and fed

Figure 8 Industrial production techniques

Spinning → Weaving → Finishing → Measuring
Spinning → Knitting → Colouring
Cutting ← Spreading ← Grading
Marking ← Preparation ← Joining ← Pressing

through the holes in the iron sole plate. A separate generator is more commonly used in industry since the reservoir is larger and does not need filling up so often.

Mechanical presses are used for pressing flat sections and for moulding shapes. Pressing is done between a stationary buck and a movable head. After the head has been lowered, steam is supplied from above or from below. Pressure, temperature and pressing time are adjustable.

Whole garments can be finished with 'steam dollies'. The garment is placed on a stand and inflated by blowing steam and air onto it. This method is only suitable for items made of dimensionally stable fabric. Garments can also be placed on hangers or frames which are conveyed through a chamber or tunnel finisher where they are steamed and dried. Time, the temperature and the amount of steam can be adjusted according to the fabric being processed.

activities

The Autoten Fabric Examination Machine manufactured by James Bailey (Engineers) Ltd is a versatile fabric examination machine for all types of fabric up to 5 metres wide. It allows any form of inspection area from horizontal to vertical, with or without operator walk-through platform. The machine has a variable speed drive with adjustable tension control and a piece end detector. Optional extras include overhead lighting, an automatic width detector and a fault analysis system.
Source: James Bailey (Engineers) Ltd, 1997

1. a) Suggest points at which fabric might need to be examined during the production process (use Figure 8 to help you).
   b) What would an examination of the fabric at these points hope to reveal?
2. What are the advantages of an examination machine with this particular design?
3. Look back through the unit and make a list of ways in which large-scale production of textile items differs from small-scale production.

What are systems?

A SYSTEM can be defined as a set of objects or activities which together perform a structured task. A system can be mechanical, electrical or electronic, or it can be an activity to produce a product. An example of a mechanical system is a hand loom which converts thread into woven cloth. An example of an electronic system is an electronic knitting machine which converts yarn into knitted fabric. An example of a manufacturing system is a dyeline in a textiles factory which converts white fabric into blue fabric.

For something to be described as a system, the following points must apply:
- the system must be made up of parts or activities which do something
- the parts or activities must be connected in an organised way
- the parts or activities must affect what is going through the system so that there is some change to it by the time it leaves the system.

A successful system may be a combination

Figure 1

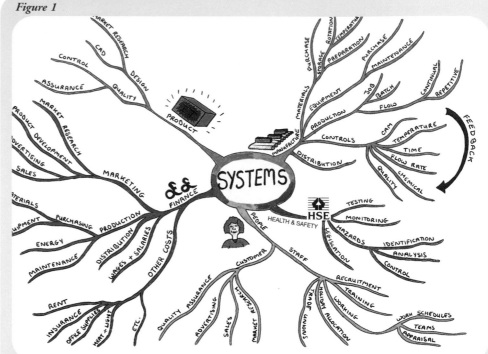

This diagram shows some of the systems operating in a large company. The five main 'branches' show systems involving: products, people, finance, health and safety, and manufacture. Each branch divides into smaller branches showing some of the sub-systems that make up the larger systems. For example in the manufacture of a product, the production system could be flow production, which in turn could be continual.

of several smaller 'sub-systems' which all rely on each other. If one of the sub-systems breaks down, the whole process may be affected. For example, large-scale production of denim jeans relies on the regular delivery of component parts. If the zips or buttons are not delivered on time, the jeans cannot be made, production ceases and profits are lost. Figure 1 shows how a company relies on many systems in order to operate effectively. These systems all interact with each other.

Why do we use systems?

The purpose of a system is to change the nature of a task. Systems may improve or maintain standards of quality, efficiency and cost effectiveness. In short, they may do one of the following:
- make a task easier
- make a process more efficient
- slow down or speed up a process
- help to analyse an activity.

When designing systems it is important to ask:
- what do I want the system to do (eg convert fibres into threads or assemble a product)?
- what will be transferred through the

Figure 2 Input, process and output

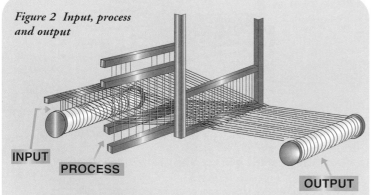

This diagram shows a production system in which threads (the input) are woven on a hand loom (the process) to produce woven fabric (the output).

Input/process/ output

At its very simplest, every system is made up of three parts: INPUT, PROCESS and OUTPUT (see Figure 2).

Input - information, materials or energy which is put into the system. In the textiles industry this is likely to be the raw materials or component parts.

Process - what happens to the information, materials or energy. In the textiles industry, this may be the making of the textiles product.

Output - the outcome of the system (ie what is produced). For example, this might be a pair of jeans and its distribution for sale to the consumer.

The input, process and output varies according to the type of system. Take an industrial system for producing woven material for example. The input might be the threads fed into an electronic loom. The process might be the weaving done by the loom. And, the output might be the woven fabric. But within that production system, the loom itself can be described as a system - an electronic system. The input

system (eg materials, energy, movement)?

● how will the system operate (eg manually, mechanically or electrically)?

of this system is the on-off button which starts the loom. The process is the series of operations which changes electrical energy into the movement of the moving parts. And the output is the weaving motion which joins threads together to make a woven fabric.

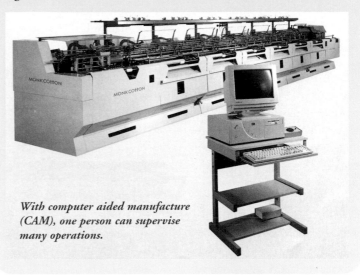

Figure 3 CAM

With computer aided manufacture (CAM), one person can supervise many operations.

The system boundary

When designing a system, the first thing to establish is the SYSTEM BOUNDARY. Everything inside the system boundary belongs to the system. By deciding where the system boundary is, it is easier to understand how the system works. For example, if you were asked to design a system appropriate for producing denim jeans, the system boundary would not include:

● primary production (eg harvesting and processing cotton)

● the production of fibres
● the production of yarns
● the production of fabric.
It would, however, include:
● design of the jeans
● manufacture of the jeans
● selling the manufactured jeans.

Controlling systems

It is necessary to CONTROL the information, materials or energy as they move through a system.

The advantage of being able to control a system is that work can be done more efficiently, more accurately, faster or slower.

activities

1. Look at the photographs (right) and in each case:
   a) describe what sort of system is shown.
   b) identify the input, process and output.
   c) suggest how the system might be controlled.
2. a) Draw a flow chart for a production system designed for the manufacture of household carpets.
   b) Describe the system boundary for this system.

A washing machine

A workshop manufacturing lingerie

An eyelet maker

For example, the speed of an assembly line needs to be controlled. Too fast and workers may not be able to complete tasks. Too slow and workers may waste time.

Many companies use computers to control the production system. For example, computer aided design (CAD) might be used in the design stage (see Unit 3). In large companies the manufacturing process is also often controlled by computers. For example, industrial knitting machines are often linked to a computer. The computer is programmed to ensure that a particular pattern or shape is knitted. This is an example of COMPUTER AIDED MANUFACTURE (CAM - see Figure 3).

The advantages of CAM are as follows:
- a computer programme can ensure that a task is performed in exactly the same way every time
- a single person can control many operations at the same time
- human error is reduced
- fewer people need to be employed and so labour costs are low
- dangerous jobs can be performed without people being involved.

The disadvantages are:
- there are fewer jobs
- if the computer crashes, the whole system comes to a standstill
- computer programmes are unable to cope with problems not foreseen by the programmers.

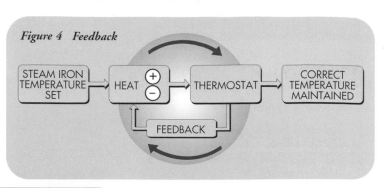

Figure 4 Feedback

STEAM IRON TEMPERATURE SET → HEAT (+ −) → THERMOSTAT → CORRECT TEMPERATURE MAINTAINED

FEEDBACK

Feedback

FEEDBACK is information that is passed back from a later stage in a system to an earlier stage (see Figure 4). Feedback is important because it alerts the system to any changes that may need to be made in order for the system to be run more efficiently.

Feedback can be used to control parts of a system. If the layers of fabric are not all being cut by an electric knife, for example, this information can be fed back to the operator who can then make the necessary adjustments. Similarly, a quality check at key stages of production may indicate that something has gone wrong. Feedback systems which involve people are called **open feedback systems**.

Sensors can be used to monitor levels in a system. If, for example, the temperature level in an electric iron rises too high (or too low), a sensor detects this and sends back the information so that the temperature can be lowered (or raised). Thermostats in washing machines are another example. The temperature is set and the heater in the washing machine continues to work until the temperature of the water reaches the desired value. The sensor detects this value and acts to switch the heater off. When the temperature falls below the set value, the sensor sends information back along the system and the heater is turned on again. A system like this which works automatically is called a **closed loop feedback system** and results in a circular pattern on the flow chart (see Figure 4).

Sometimes there is a time delay between the system being triggered in some way and the system responding. This is known as 'lag'. For example, there is often a time delay between turning down the switch which controls the temperature of an iron and the iron itself cooling.

Feedback in a system can be either positive or negative. Positive feedback occurs when the information fed back acts to increase the signal (ie to step up production). Negative feedback occurs when information is fed back to reduce the output. Negative feedback tends to produce stability.

activities

The Memory Craft 8000 is a computerised sewing machine. It has a visual touch screen which is linked to a series of sensors. For example, there is a contact pad on the feed dog which senses if the presser foot is up or down. The machine will not run until the presser foot is down. When producing preprogrammed embroidery, the machine guides the operator by providing a set of options displayed on the in-built screen. The operator then chooses the type of stitch or design by pressing the appropriate picture on the touch screen and following the instructions. The machine only allows the operator to take a new step once the previous step has been completed.
Source: Memory Craft 8000

1. Explain why the Memory Craft 8000 is a system.
2. Suggest how an operator could control the system.
3. Identify TWO methods of feedback in the system and the uses to which each is put.

Key Terms

System - a set of smaller tasks that combine to carry out a larger task.
Input - information, materials or energy which enter or activate a system.
Process - operations which affect the inputs into the system.
Output - the outcomes of the system.
System boundary - the extent to which something should be treated as part of a system.
Control - the setting of standards for the system and maintaining them.
Computer aided manufacture - the use of computers to help control the production system.
Feedback - information which is passed from one part of a system to another.

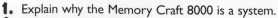

case study CHRIS DEE'S LINGERIE

BETWEEN 1976 and 1984 Chris Dee worked on her own making underskirts and basic lingerie at home. What she made during the week, she sold at a local market each Saturday. In 1984, her husband Dave joined her and they decided to expand the business. By 1997, Chris and Dave were able to employ four full-time and five part-time members of staff. Dave is responsible for buying the raw materials and for general organisation and book-keeping. Chris decides what should be made, comes up with new designs and helps with assembly. The goods that are made are now sold in four local markets.

On average, each week Chris' workshop is able to produce the following items:

- 100 underskirts
- 30 cami tops
- 200 bras
- 200 briefs
- 30 specialist briefs
- 10 suspenders
- 25 nightdresses
- 10 'bodies'
- 15 silk dresses.

Chris Dee's workshop

The way in which Chris organises production is as follows. The working week is usually divided into two. In the first half of the week, everybody in the workshop makes garments in one colour (white, for example). In the second half of the week, everybody makes garments in another colour (black, for example). For the first half of the week, the machines might be used to make white bras, briefs, undershirts and bodies. Whilst bras are being made, everybody in the workshop is involved in assembling bras, though each person has a different job to do. One person might overlock the seams, for example, while another sews on the straps, a third secures the wire and so on. Bras come in many different sizes and several designs are made. On average, 12 bras of a particular design and of a popular size are assembled at one time. For less popular sizes, as few as four are assembled. The aim is to ensure that there are enough bras to sell on the market stalls and, if possible, to have a few left over to keep in stock for sale in the following weeks. When sufficient bras have been made, the workshop then begins work on other garments - cami tops, for example, or briefs.

Chris Dee's market stall

Activities

1.a) Do you think that the method of production used by Chris Dee to produce lingerie is job, batch or flow? Explain your answer.

b) Identify an input, process and output in the system used by Chris Dee.

2. Draw a flow chart showing the stages in the design, production and selling of Chris Dee's lingerie.

3. What are the advantages of using the production system that has been set up by Chris Dee?

4. Describe THREE problems that might cause the production system to malfunction. How could these problems be overcome?

What are production systems?

Production systems are the different methods of production which can be used to manufacture designs. Like other systems they have input, processes and outputs (see Unit 18).

The processes used in production systems fall into three main categories depending on how many products are to be manufactured. These categories are:

● job production
● batch production
● flow production.

The system used to manufacture the product will depend on:

● the quantity of products to be made
● the nature and quality of the products required
● the selling price of the products.

The output from a production system is the product itself. This might be a finished item like a rucksack or a pair of pyjamas or it might be a part or a component used to make the product like thread, buttons, zips and interfacing. Another output from a system could be wastage. This may be left over from cutting or trimming or it may be faulty goods that do not meet the required standard. This wastage might be recycled and fed back into a different system or it might be discarded.

Figure 1
Job production

The hat above was specially commissioned for a wedding. The jumper was specially hand knitted for the baby. Both are examples of job production

activities

The family business Cobra, based in Telford in Shropshire, is Britain's biggest supplier of replacement car seats. Since 1978 the company has multiplied sales five times. It has grown from producing 10 car seats a day to 160. Last year, it sold more than 24,000 seats. Cobra makes three basic designs - recliners, bucket seats and professional competition seats - in 15 versions. Unlike the original seats fitted by car makers in their factories, Cobra can make a seat to exact measurements with a personal choice of foam density, fabric, colour and, to finish it off, a monogram logo embroidered onto the cover. Angela Dunsford, who set up the company with husband Geoff, said: 'We advise on fabrics, colours and embroidery. We can trim the interior with the back seats to match and it's all made to measure.'
Source: The Times, 18 November 1995

1. Do you think the method of production used to manufacture Cobra replacement seats is job, batch or flow? Explain your answer.
2. How does a customer buying a Cobra replacement seat benefit from this type of production?
3. What are the advantages and disadvantages of this type of production system?

Job production

JOB PRODUCTION is a production system where a one-off item is made. The product is made from start to finish either by one person or by a number of people working on separate parts of the same item. The finished product is unique, though it might look similar to other items, perhaps differing slightly in style, shape or the type of fabric used.

An example of job production is the designing and making of a one-off wedding dress for a particular woman. A larger-scale example might be the production of carpets specially woven to fit a particular building. The political lobbying company Ian Greer Associates (IGA), for example, commissioned special carpets (with the letters 'IGA' incorporated into the design) for their offices in London.

Products made by job production methods are usually of high quality and require a great deal of workers' time to complete. This means that the production system is very labour intensive. The people who make these items need to be skilled. Job production items are likely to be more expensive than items produced in batches or items which are mass produced. For example, haute couture designer clothing is more expensive to buy than the equivalent mass produced chain store clothing.

Batch production

In BATCH PRODUCTION, relatively small numbers of identical or similar products are made and then equipment and labour are switched to another product. Batch production is useful where the product may have to change depending on the orders coming in. For example, a company which manufactures protective clothing might make a batch of blue overalls with no pockets for one customer and a batch of blue overalls with pockets for another customer. Batch products are cheaper than equivalent job produced items because production costs are lower. The problem with batch production is that if production is switched from one product to another then time may be lost in resetting equipment to make a new batch. Increasing the number of products made means that stock is often created. This may cause storage problems and wastage if some of the products are left unsold.

Making more than one item means that staff may specialise in one aspect of the work. However, the work may be repetitive and boring.

Flow production

REPETITIVE FLOW PRODUCTION is a system where large quantities of the same product - for example, tights or disposable dish cloths - are manufactured. Flow production usually requires very high investment to buy the complicated machinery needed to carry out precise repetitive work. The machinery often runs for 24 hours a day, seven days a week. The

*Figure 2
Batch production*

The dress above was designed by Jasper Conran and made in batches for sale in selected Debenhams stores. It comes in three colours (black, red and white) and sizes 8-16.

mass production of items leads to lower unit costs because:

● materials can be bought in bulk
● semi-skilled or unskilled labour can be used
● the initial high cost of the machinery is

activities

Dawna Henson was dissatisfied with modern foam-filled plastic cot mattresses. She felt that wool was the ideal material and invented a way of making wool-filled mattresses. Because of the price of the raw materials, wool-filled mattresses are considerably more expensive than foam-filled mattresses. A wool mattress costs £200, compared to £50 for a foam one. Nevertheless, Dawna's company - The Fairchild Company - is expanding. At present, the company produces 3,000 mattresses per year, but Dawna reckons they could push the total up to 12,000. The Rural Development Commission helped Dawna to automate her loom and to build three more. Thick continuous rolls of wool are fed into the machines. They come off as blocks and a cover is sewn on. The company buys wool through the Wool Marketing Board. It is tested rigorously to ensure an absence of chemicals. Some mattresses are ordered by people suffering from allergies. Often, customers place specific orders - such as requiring unbleached wool.
Source: The Times, 28 March 1995

A mattress produced by the Fairchild Company

1. Do you think the method of production used to manufacture wool-filled mattresses is job, batch or flow? Explain your answer.

2. What are the advantages and disadvantages of buying a mattress from The Fairchild Company?

3. In what ways are the mattresses customised?

spread over a large output.

The unit cost of a product tends to fall as more are produced. If the flow production is partially or fully automated, then costs can be further reduced because there are fewer workers to pay.

Jeans being made on an assembly line is an example of CONTINUAL FLOW PRODUCTION. As the jeans move along the assembly line, machinists work on a specific stage of production - such as sewing on the label, inserting zips or attaching waistbands. When the jeans have passed through all the stages, they are complete.

Work on an assembly line can be monotonous for workers. If there is a breakdown on one part of the assembly line then the whole production line grinds to a halt. Simple manufacturing tasks like attaching rivets and finishing off seams are performed in flow production systems.

Production control

At a basic level, control in production systems may be exercised by operatives

controlling equipment. Each stage in the production process - for example, measuring, cutting and assembling - might be carried out manually by skilled craftspeople. Alternatively, parts of the production process might be automated.

The design of a product can be carried out by computer aided design (see Unit 3). Computer-controlled machines can then be used to manufacture the products. These machines use specially designed computer software. The double jersey circular knitting machine in Figure 3 is an example. A manufacturing process controlled by computer software is known as computer aided manufacture (CAM - see Figure 3 and p.104). CAM can be used for single products, batches or mass production. Advances in computer technology are such that, in many production systems, few people are employed. An order might be sent by electronic mail. The manufacturing machines can then be programmed to fulfil the particular specification required by the order. Computers operate the machinery and make the product. The finished product can be checked using a computer-controlled coordinate measuring machine. Once passed, the product can be

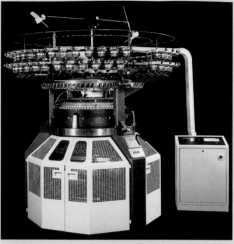

Figure 3 Computer aided manufacture

This double jersey circular knitting machine produced by Camber has an integrated management control system which allows the operator to control machine speed and roll size and to stop motion faults. This system can be linked to a central computer for remote monitoring of all machines. It also has a computerised pattern selector.

stored automatically and the bill sent to the customer along with the product. If the product does not meet the specification, the information can be fed back into the system and the programmes adjusted accordingly. This is an example of **computer integrated manufacture** (CIM - see Figure 4).

The advantages of using computers in production are:
● the speed of the process
● the accuracy of the process
● the reduced costs.

However, the machines must be maintained to avoid failure - which can be costly.

Stock control

An important part of controlling a production system is STOCK CONTROL. Stocks are the materials and components which are used in the manufacture and assembly of textile items. It is important to ensure that there are enough materials and components to make the product and that they are the correct materials to carry out the work. Stocks may be kept in a warehouse and held in reserve until they are needed. A stock controller checks the stocks going in and out so that a flow is maintained. As the stock of

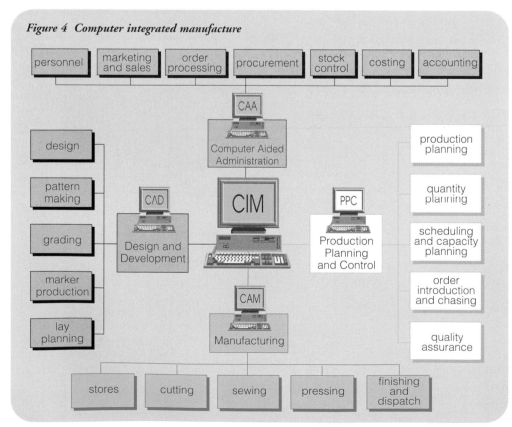

Figure 4 Computer integrated manufacture

personnel | marketing and sales | order processing | procurement | stock control | costing | accounting

CAA — Computer Aided Administration

design, pattern making, grading, marker production, lay planning

CAD — Design and Development

CIM

CAM — Manufacturing

stores | cutting | sewing | pressing | finishing and dispatch

PPC — Production Planning and Control

production planning, quantity planning, scheduling and capacity planning, order introduction and chasing, quality assurance

A stock room

materials falls, new stocks are ordered so that they do not run out. If stocks were to run out, production would be halted. This would be very costly for a business.

Some businesses operate a system known as JUST-IN-TIME PRODUCTION. The amount of stock held (if any) is very low. Instead, the manufacturer asks its suppliers for regular deliveries which are used immediately in production. This has the following advantages:

● warehouse costs are reduced
● the cost of stocks being held is reduced
● a business must insist that materials or components are delivered free of faults
● quality (see Unit 22) is improved
● production is speeded up.

Speed and quality considerations

The speed of production affects the quality and eventual cost of a product. Quality, accuracy and precision are key elements in production. To achieve these by hand takes a great deal of time and patience. In some automated batch and flow systems, precision can be ensured by programming computers to make items of a high quality. Computer-controlled machines are also able to make some products more quickly than it is possible to make the same items by hand.

For single, unique products, automated batch and flow systems are inappropriate because tools and equipment would have to be reset for each job, wasting valuable time and slowing down the whole production process. However, some diversity can be achieved by mixing and matching. For example, a company making men's and women's slippers may make the same design using different fabrics or colours, with varying trims or embellishments. This goes some way to increasing choice and providing customers with a limited range of models which appear to be different from the standard range. CUSTOMISED PRODUCTS, on the other hand, are products which are changed in some way to meet a specific customer's request. For example, a customer might order 50 pairs of blue overalls from a manufacturer and request that a company name is stitched on each pair. Although the overalls would be made using the same basic design, stitching on the company logo would mean producing a customised product.

activities

The Bonas electronic jacquard networking system provides a direct two-way communication link between Bonas electronic jacquard machines and a central computer (the File Server) located anywhere in the mill. Designs can be stored on the File Server hard disk. Pattern data can be sent from the File Server to any jacquard loom in the weaving shed. Production data can be sent to the File Server from each loom. The weaver is able to load in a whole week's jobs, reschedule (for example, if an urgent order comes in), transmit a complete fabric specification and weaving specification and add in any special customer requirements.

Source: Bonas, 1997

CAD System

Weaving Shed

File Server

Data Monitoring System

1. What is meant by (i) CAD and (ii) CAM?
2. How does the Bonas electronic jacquard networking system work?
3. Suggest THREE advantages that a company might gain by introducing this system.

Key Terms

Job production - a production system where a one-off item is made.
Batch production - a production system where small numbers of identical or similar products are made.
Repetitive flow production - a system where large quantities of the same product are manufactured.
Continual flow production - a system where a product passes through a number of stages during manufacture.
Stock control - the ordering and issuing of materials or components used in production or finished products waiting for customers.
Just-in-time production - a production system which requires few, if any, stocks to be held.
Customised products - products specially designed to meet a customer's requirements.

DESIGNING and making costumes to be worn by actors on stage or in films requires a different approach to designing and making clothes to be sold in shops. One of the main requirements of a costume that is worn on stage is that it must be right for the character and for the play. If the play is set in the 19th century and the director wants the costumes to look authentic, for example, it is no good designing a costume which has Velcro fastenings that can be seen by the audience. In addition, most plays (and films) are produced on tight budgets. As a result, the costumes have to be produced as cheaply as possible. At the same time, they must be durable enough to last for the run of the play (or the duration of the shoot). The costume featured on this page was designed for a children's show called 'Why do bees buzz?' performed in the Dukes Theatre, Lancaster in February and March 1997. The wardrobe supervisor at the Dukes Theatre, Debbie Knight, explained the processes that are undertaken in the production of costumes: 'The style of the set and costumes is decided by the designer in association with the director. The production manager considers whether the designs are practical and affordable and, if they are, produces working drawings for the technical department. If a costume is to be made rather than bought or hired, decisions regarding fabrics and methods of construction will be made with the wardrobe supervisor and cutter. Practical considerations have to be taken into account. For example, an actor might have to do something particularly physical or it might be necessary to change costumes very quickly.' Calico is frequently used for period underwear and as a backing fabric (because it is cheap). The dyeing and printing of fabrics is avoided as this increases the cost and time involved producing a costume. Dye, bleach and French enamel varnish are used, however, to 'break down' costumes (to make them look worn and distressed). Debbie Knight adds: 'Costumes have to be strong. They will be treated roughly and worn hard but must still look wonderful and be practical.'

Our third show for children under six and their families
Written and Directed by Chris Speyer
Music by Ieuan Goch ab Einion
Designed by Jill Amos

Why do bees BUZZ?

THE **DUKES** LANCASTER

Thursday 27 February - Saturday 22 March 1997
BOX OFFICE 01524 66645
The Dukes, Moor Lane, Lancaster LA1 1QE

Mr Bumble, a character in 'Why do bees buzz?'

Activities

1. Is the information on this page an example of job, batch or flow production? Explain your answer.
2. Name some inputs into the costume production system.
3. Draw a flow chart showing the stages in the design and production of costumes.
4. Why is Mr Bumble's costume particularly suitable for the purpose for which it was designed?
5. Design a costume for a character in a play or film and explain what considerations have to be taken into account when deciding on the design.

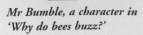

THE STANDISH COMPANY

THE Standish Company, based near Wigan, dyes and finishes fabric. Since May 1996, the company has been dyeing and finishing fabric for a single customer - Carrington Career and Workwear Fabrics. Between May 1996 and May 1997, The Standish Company dyed and finished around 10 million metres of fabric for Carrington Career and Workwear Fabrics. Most of this fabric was then used to make overalls, boiler suits, lab coats and other garments used at work. The Standish Company employs around 100 people.

An external view of The Standish Company

The fabric to be dyed and finished arrives at Standish as loomstate fabric (normally a polyester/cotton mix) and then undergoes three main processes:

- preparation
- dyeing
- finishing.

The fabric is then inspected, stored at Standish and transported to Carrington Career and Workwear Fabrics as requested. The diagram below shows the processes that fabric undergoes when it arrives at Standish.

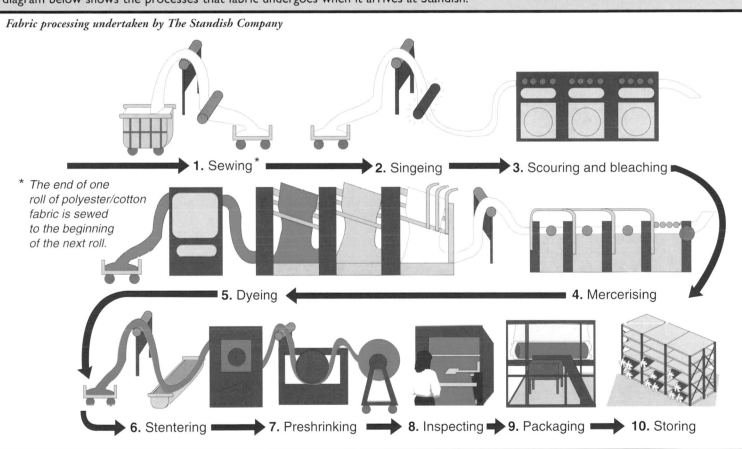

Fabric processing undertaken by The Standish Company

1. Sewing*   2. Singeing   3. Scouring and bleaching

* The end of one roll of polyester/cotton fabric is sewed to the beginning of the next roll.

5. Dyeing   4. Mercerising

6. Stentering   7. Preshrinking   8. Inspecting   9. Packaging   10. Storing

Activities

1. Do you think that the method of production used by The Standish Company to dye and finish fabric is job, batch or flow? Explain your answer.
2. Draw a flow chart showing the various processes which fabric passes through as it is prepared, dyed and finished.
3. What are the advantages of using the production system that has been set up by The Standish Company?
4. Describe THREE problems that might cause the production system to malfunction. How could these problems be overcome?
5. The Standish Company has set up a Total Quality Management scheme (see Unit 22). Explain how this might work.

What are aesthetics?

What often first attracts people to a product is its appearance. It might be the shape of a 'futuristic' iron or the bright colours of a fabric. It might be a new and different design which moves away from the 'normal' appearance of a product - for example, an unusual hat design or a swimming costume that incorporates floats.

What a person likes or dislikes about the appearance of a product is related to the product's AESTHETICS. What attracts them may be one or more of the following:

● colour (see also Unit 13)
● lines and patterns
● shape and form
● fashion and style
● texture and finish.

These criteria can be used to evaluate whether or not a product is aesthetically pleasing. They may also be used as a starting point to help design an aesthetically pleasing product.

Aesthetics is not just about the visual. It is also about the other senses. When an item has a good feel or a pleasant ambience, this is because it is aesthetically pleasing. For example, a woolly jumper might give the feeling of warmth and comfort and a product made of silk might create a feeling of wealth and sensuality. These feelings help to determine whether the products are aesthetically pleasing or not.

Colour

We see objects because they reflect light which is detected by our eyes. We see colours for the same reason. Natural light (white light) is made up of a range of colours which

are collectively known as the SPECTRUM. Natural light also contains colours that humans cannot see but other animals can see (eg infrared and ultraviolet). When white light hits the surface of a material, pigments on the surface absorb some of the colours in the spectrum and reflect others. The surface of a red dress absorbs all colours except red, for example. As a result, the dress has a red appearance. Similarly, a yellow shirt absorbs all colours except yellow and has a yellow appearance.

The appeal of colour has already been touched upon in Unit 13. Colour plays an important part in determining whether or not a textile item has an aesthetic appeal. There are a number of ways in which colours might be used. First, people often have strong feelings about colours and colours are often associated with particular experiences. For example, later in life many people do not like to wear the colour of their school uniform or they may favour a colour because it suits their

Figure 1 Some people might find the design of this bedroom aesthetically pleasing. Others might not.

skin tone. Second, colour has different associations in different cultures. For example, white wedding dresses are common in the West because white symbolises purity. In the

activities

Lands' End Direct Merchants UK is a company which produces a relatively small range of clothing in a large variety of colours. The Drifter Crew Neck pictured below is available in nine different colours.

1. Which colours do you think would be most popular in each season?

2. What factors should a customer take into consideration when choosing the colour of their chosen sweater?

3. Suppose that Lands' End wanted to expand the number of colours for this type of sweater. Suggest THREE colours that you would add to the range and explain why you think they would be appropriate additions.

East, however, red wedding dresses are common because red is regarded as the colour of celebration. Third, colours may reflect the time of year. Textile designers tend to produce dark and rich coloured items in the winter to create a warm feeling. Lighter and brighter colours tend to be used in the spring and summer to reflect the brighter light and warmer temperatures. Fourth, colours can be used to identify groups of people. Football teams, for example, can be identified by their colours. The colour of a school uniform makes it easy to identify pupils from a particular school. A country can be identified by the colours on its flag. Sixth, colour can be used for camouflage or to make things blend in. For example, the armed forces use printed fabric for their combat uniforms. And seventh, colour can be used to create visual effects. For example, in clothing dark colours are generally slimming and light colours tend to exaggerate size.

activities

1. Look at the picture above. Are the clothes aesthetically pleasing or not? Give reasons for your answer.
2. Describe an article of clothing which you find aesthetically pleasing. Explain why you find it aesthetically pleasing.
3. You have been asked to design a pair of running shorts which are both functional and aesthetically pleasing. Write a specification and produce a working drawing of the shorts.

Lines and patterns

Line is a basic design element which is used to create style, shape, pattern, form and texture. Different lines have different effects on the aesthetics of a textile item.

Vertical lines appear to add height and make a product appear narrow. They lead the observer's eyes up and down the item. Clothing is sometimes designed with vertical stripes. This elongates and visually 'slims' a fuller figure.

Horizontal lines appear to shorten a shape or a figure. They emphasise and create a feeling of solidity.

Diagonal lines can add a sense of movement to an item. They create a feeling of instability.

Curved lines create a softened effect.

A pattern is a group of lines or shapes. Patterns may be simple or complex, regular or irregular. The intended use or application of the item is the major influence on the effect of a pattern.

Shape and form

To a designer, SHAPE generally refers to something that is two-dimensional and FORM to something that is three-dimensional. Everything has shape or form.

In textile designs, basic blocks (see Unit 14) are shapes that fabric is cut into before construction. When these shapes are sewn together, they produce a three-dimensional item which has form.

The shape and form of a product is not necessarily purely aesthetic. A swimming costume may look good, for example, but it is also functional. Improving the aerodynamics of the costume will help the swimmer to move easily through the water, reducing friction and the amount of energy required to swim fast. The skill of the designer is in improving performance and yet keeping the item attractive.

Regular shapes have SYMMETRY. Imagine an invisible line through the middle of the design. A symmetrical design would look the same on each side. Most clothing designs are symmetrical because

Figure 2 This outfit was shown at the 1997 British Fashion Show. Colour, shape and form are particularly important.

the human body is symmetrical.

The shape or form usually has its parts constructed in PROPORTION with each other. This means that each part is compared to another. Parts of an item do not end up in proportion by chance. Natural laws like gravity and evolution dictate how long or large something will be. For example, the brim of a hat cannot extend too far without losing its rigidity and flopping down. Quite often it is easy to see if part of an item is out of proportion or not simply by looking at it. Disproportion can also be used as a design feature in textile items. For example shoulder pads and bustles dramatically change the proportions of clothing.

Fashion and style

Designs which are popular at a particular time are said to be fashionable. Fashions do not last. People's opinions change and new designs take the place of older ones. Within fashions, there are many different styles. Fashions may be tied to a time period.

Fashions can be very short-lived. Some popular designs stay in fashion for a a few months or even weeks. These are called 'fads'.

In clothing, many fashions are repeated over time. For example, pencil skirts were in fashion just after the Second World War and then, again, in the 1970s. Flared trousers were fashionable in the 1960s and have re-emerged in the mid-1990s.

Texture and finish

It is not just the colour of a material which appears on its surface. The surface also has a TEXTURE and a finish. Texture is usually gauged by touch. A surface may range from rough to smooth. A knitted fabric made from staple fibres, for example, is likely to have a rough texture whilst a sateen woven fabric made from filament fibres is likely to have a smooth texture. The type of fibres used and methods of processing both affect the texture of a fabric.

Texture can also be visual as well as tactile. In other words, the item might have the look of a particular texture. Some designers are particularly fascinated by texture.

Ergonomics

ERGONOMICS is the study of the interaction of people with the equipment they operate and the environment in which they work. Studying ergonomics should help to improve an environment so that people can work in comfort using the smallest amount of energy. Unsuitable machinery and poor conditions in a workplace might result in inaccurate work and an unsatisfactory product being produced by an employee.

Two important aspects of ergonomics are anthropometrics and, anatomy and movement. Taking these into account when designing should help to produce items which are:

- easy to use
- difficult to operate incorrectly
- able to be operated correctly every time
- efficient.

Anthropometrics

ANTHROPOMETRICS is the scientific study of body sizes. It can be used to produce a range of approximate sizes, identifying maximum and minimum limits, that a product can be designed for.

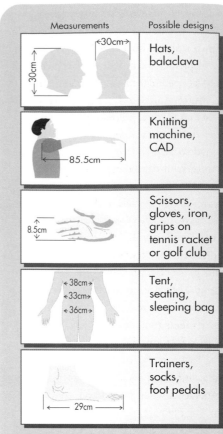

Figure 3 Anthropometric measurements of an average male adult and designs for which they could be used.

Any part of the human anatomy can be studied to produce anthropometric data. For example, the hand might be studied to obtain data for the manufacture of driving gloves. To be efficient, a range of people using the gloves need to be able to grip the steering wheel without straining. Similarly, the back might be studied to obtain data for the manufacture of rucksacks. To be efficient, a rucksack needs to allow a person to carry a load in comfort without overbalancing.

Data can be found by measuring different people, taking averages and setting maximum and minimum limits.

Anthropometrics have to be given special attention for arthritis sufferers, wheelchair users and children.

Anatomy and movement

There are many situations where frequent movement is required. Designs must take this

activities

1. a) Using the diagram (right), choose THREE areas where measurements are important.

   b) Suggest what parts of the body are likely to be measured and why.

2. Explain what ergonomic problems might occur if the guidelines in the diagram (right) are not met.

3. Why might the wearing of inappropriate clothing cause ergonomic problems in a factory?

4. How might the study of ergonomics help a sportswear company to design clothes for athletes?

Guidelines for seating and posture in a typical ofice

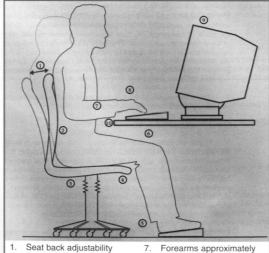

1. Seat back adjustability
2. Good lumbar support
3. Seat height adjustability
4. No excess pressure on underside of thighs and backs of knees
5. Foot support if needed
6. Space for postural change. No obstacles under desk
7. Forearms approximately horizontal
8. Minimal extension, flexion or deviation of wrists
9. Screen height and angle should allow comfortable position
10. Space in front of keyboard to support hands/wrists during pauses in keying

Source: Display Screen Equipment at Work, HSE, 1996

into account. For example, mountaineers need to carry their equipment with them, but they also need as much freedom for their limbs as possible. As a result, mountaineering rucksacks need to be designed so that the mountaineer has ease of access but is not impeded in any way. Similarly, protective clothing needs to be designed so that, as well as being fully protected from danger, a person is able both to move around easily and safely and to perform the necessary tasks. It is not normally commercially viable to make a mountaineering rucksack or protective clothing to suit each individual's anthropometric needs. Instead, these products are made in a range of styles and sizes. The measurements used to decide which sizes to make can be found by gathering anthropometric data.

In addition to movement, space can be a consideration when designing. For a small room, for example, a fold away bed which doubles as a settee might be the perfect solution since it makes the best use of the available space (see Figure 4). Designs like this are called 'space saving designs'.

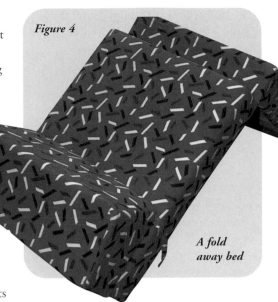
Figure 4

A fold away bed

Function and

The FUNCTION of a product is what a product does. For example, the function of a pair of woollen gloves is to protect a person's hands against the cold.

It is important for designers to consider both function and form when designing textile items. There may be a conflict between function and form which successful designs will solve. For example, a mountaineer's rucksack might look interesting if it was shaped like a guitar, but it would be unable to hold as much equipment as a standard rucksack and it would not provide the balance that a standard rucksack provides. Similarly, a triangular duvet and duvet cover might look interesting, but they would not provide as much warmth and cover as a rectangular duvet and duvet cover.

Age, gender and special needs

Designs and the functions of products are different if aimed at different groups.

Age differences - products differ in size, shape and function depending on the target age group.

Gender differences - the anatomy of men and women is different and this can sometimes influence a design.

Special needs - designs might be adapted to take into account the special needs of people who are disabled or ill or people who work in special conditions.

activities

A heavy rucksack is most efficiently carried when the load is supported primarily by the hips. This avoids strain on the spine and back muscles without impeding or restricting breathing. However, to maintain stability some of the weight must also be carried on the shoulders. As the distance between shoulders and hips varies from person to person, it is important that the rucksack fits the wearer's back. For this reason the Cyclops system is available in four back sizes. All Berghaus load carrying rucksacks are anatomical - ie they are designed to fit the body shape, enabling the spine to function effectively and safely by allowing the vertebrae to maintain their natural curve. Some models have an aluminium internal frame which can be bent to the shape of the body yet supports the load.
Source: Berghaus, August 1995

1. How have Berghaus attempted to produce rucksacks which suit people's anthropometric needs?

2. a) What measurements did Berghaus need to take to gather anthropometric data for their rucksacks?
   b) Draw one or more diagrams showing the key measurements that would need to be taken.

3. How might the design of a rucksack differ if it was intended for use by a child?

This anatomical frame distributes load onto hips.

Key Terms

Aesthetics - what a person likes or dislikes about the appearance of a product.
Spectrum - the range of colours which makes up white light.
Shape - the shape of something two-dimensional.
Form - the shape of something three-dimensional.
Symmetry - a property of a shape which means that it is identical on either side of an imaginary line placed down the middle.
Proportion - the relation of one part to another so that they are in harmony or balance.
Texture - how rough or smooth the surface of a product is.
Ergonomics - the interaction of people with their environment.
Anthropometrics - the science of body sizes.
Function - what a product does.

Evaluation methods

Evaluation methods

EVALUATION is a process used by manufacturers to make sure their products meet certain targets. Products are evaluated at every stage of designing and making. To be effective, this is done by testing and trialling. It may also be less obvious. For example, evaluation takes place when people make superficial 'value judgements' about what they like or dislike. Evaluation that takes place at key stages along the design and making process is called **continuous evaluation**.

Evaluation may be selective, where one aspect of a product is studied in detail. It may also be **comprehensive**, taking in the whole product or a much wider range of aspects. Comprehensive evaluation is likely to throw up conflicts. Decisions will have to be made about which aspects are most important. The manufacturer will have to **prioritise** each aspect.

Value judgement guidelines, such as basic opinions on whether somebody likes or dislikes a product, may not provide enough detail for evaluation purposes. For a more thorough and accurate set of targets, standards have to be set by which products can be evaluated. These standards are called CRITERIA. Each criterion needs a gauge or a scale by which a product can be measured. The scale might be physical. An 'ideal' template might be created and the product measured against this template or a scientific investigation might be undertaken. On the other hand, the criterion might be a way of gauging opinion such as a piece of market research or a test in which the product is compared and contrasted with other similar products.

Figure 1 A quality check

Table 1 Evaluation criteria

- **Fitness for purpose**
- **Cost** - raw materials and production
- **Environmental effects** - resources, waste
- **Function** - does it work properly?
- **Aesthetics** - colour, shape and form
- **Ergonomics** - is it the right size? Will it fit where it is meant to fit?
- **Anthropometrics** - does it fit human measurements and sizes?
- **Health and safety** - strength, flexibility, grip, resistance to heat
- **Needs of different cultures**
- **Suitability for age range, social group or special needs**
- **Quality** - how well has it been made?
- **Process** - is the best process used for making the product?
- **Value for money**.

activities

Hotpoint Aquarius 1200

Wash size - 4.5kg
Spin speed - 400-1200
Dry size -2.3kg
Features - variable spin and no spin; auto half load; quick, economy and gentle wash facilities; super rinse; pulse spin; auto crease care; full or low heat drying.

Zanussi WDJI094

Wash size - 4.5kg
Spin speed - 1000/650
Dry size - 2.25kg
Features - variable water level; quick wash; super economy button reduces hot cotton wash temperature; rinse sensor; door locked light.

Creda 1200 Cascade

Wash size - 4.5kg
Spin speed - 1200/700
Dry size -2.3kg
Features - automatic water level senses load size; fast, energy save and special woollens wash; crease care option; 'Deep Wash' increases water levels; auto energy save on drier - heat reduces if timer overset.

1. Suggest FOUR criteria that might be used to compare the washer driers.

2. Explain how a manufacturer might:
   a) test the products
   b) gauge consumer reaction to the products.

3. Explain why the production of a prototype might be important before manufacturing electrical equipment.

Whichever scale or criterion is used, data can be gathered, analysed (looked at in some detail) and conclusions can be drawn. The more information that is gathered, the more reliable the information is likely to be.

Meeting original needs

Perhaps the main criterion of any product manufacture is whether it meets the needs of the people it was designed for. The starting point for evaluating any finished product or its prototype has to be the product's specification (see Unit 2). This lays down the guidelines and details required by the consumer. It also sets the TOLERANCE LEVELS that the manufacturer has to work within. To check a prototype or finished product against a specification, it is necessary to convert each criterion into a question. An affirmative answer indicates that the criterion has been met. Product specifications and tolerances are examples of CONSTRAINTS. Constraints are limitations placed on a design. These might be measurable limits like tolerances. They might also be other specific criteria such as colour, the type of material to be used or some physical property like being waterproof.

Comparing and contrasting

A manufactured product may be compared with or contrasted to other similar products on the market. This type of evaluation is often carried out as part of information gathering before a specification is written. However, it can also be used to judge a completed procedure or prototype. For example, the handle on fabric shears made be made from styrofoam as a prototype and then compared with existing handles to find out whether the grip is better or worse. The criteria used for the comparison could be any of those mentioned in Table 1. For example:

- **safety** - one soft toy may be more suitable than another for very young children because it is larger and has detachable parts
- **suitability for different cultures** - a unisex uniform may not be suitable for a particular culture which has strict rules about what men and women may be allowed to wear
- **value for money** - one sewing machine may be more expensive than another, but it may be better value for money as it has a greater range of functions
- **function** - a swimsuit made from a knitted fabric may be more suitable than one made from a woven fabric because it can stretch and hug the body's contours more effectively.

Testing and trialling

A product or prototype might be tested scientifically. This is usually to test the working properties of the materials it is made from (see Figure 2). TESTING can be destructive, where the material is tested until it breaks or is destroyed (see Figure 3), or it can be non-destructive, where it

Figure 2 A Testrite piling tester. This machine carries out standard tests for determining the piling tendencies of knitted and woven fabrics. The two boxes are tumbled a set number of revolutions recorded on a counter.

leaves the materials intact. TRIALLING is a non-destructive form of testing.

The aim of scientific testing is to generate reliable information. This is done by fair-testing. In any scientific investigation a number of factors might affect the working properties of the materials a product or prototype is made from. These factors are called '**variables**'. Each of the possible variables has to be identified. All of the variables are then kept the same except for the variable which is to be tested. This variable may then be compared with a 'control'. For example,

activities

Fibre	Burning	Smell	Residue
Cotton	rapid, bright flame	like burning paper	pale grey powder
Wool	slow, sputtering flame	burning hair	friable cinder
Silk	slow, sputtering flame	burning hair	friable cinder
Viscose	rapid, bright flame	like burning paper	pale grey powder
Acetate	melts, burns, drips	pungent, vinegar	sets hard
Polyester	shrinks, melts, burns, drips in filaments		sets hard
Acrylic	shrinks, melts, burns, with a sooty flame		sets hard

A manufacturer has been asked to produce a new uniform for firefighters. Different fabrics have been tested to see the effects of flames on them. The results of the tests are shown in the table (left).

1. What form of testing could this be described as? Explain your answer.

2. Describe how the tests may have been carried out to produce reliable information.

3. What other textile products might be subjected to this particular test? Give reasons for your answer.

suppose that a company aimed to produce sails for yachts. Different types of fabrics might be tested to assess their strength. But it is not only the type of fibre used which determines the strength of a sail. The fabric construction, the thickness of the yarns and the length and width of the fabric are also important. In order to test types of fabric for strength, therefore, it is necessary to test all the variables one by one. This helps the designer produce a more accurate evaluation of what fabric is best for the job. To increase accuracy still further, the same test might be repeated many times and an average strength calculated for each type of fabric. Trialling involves trying out a design or a product in the same or a similar environment to that in which it will be used. Prototyping is a type of trialling. If a product has been made with a person or a group of people in mind, it can be trialled by inviting the person or some of the

Figure 3 A flammability test

group to actually use it. For example, if a bag has been made for a paramedic to carry emergency medical supplies to the scene of an accident, the designer might give a prototype of the bag to a small number of paramedics to see how useful they find it. The designer may have designed the bag to be easy to carry and to have a number of specific compartments

for different supplies and equipment. But if, for example, the paramedics who trialled the bag complained that it was too big and too heavy to carry or if they found it difficult to get equipment out of the compartments quickly, the designer would need to modify the design. Often, it is not until the product is trialled that problems such as this become clear.

Market research

Information, observation and comments about a product can be gathered and assessed. This is called MARKET RESEARCH. Usually, a range of people likely to use the product is identified and invited to test the product, perhaps using a questionnaire or an interview (see Figure 4). Specific groups of people are often targeted for specific products. For example, if a raincoat has been designed for disabled people who use wheelchairs, it would make sense to target disabled people who use wheelchairs when doing market research. Targeting non-wheelchair users would not be as useful. The aim of the interview or questionnaire is to find out what the respondents think about the product. If a large number of people are questioned, to produce a cross-section of opinion, then it is likely that the results of the market research will be more reliable than if only one or two people are questioned. The

activities

In February 1997, Jonathan Pratt (right) one of the world's leading mountaineers, signed a two year sponsorship deal with the outdoor clothing company Craghoppers. In return for the sponsorship, one of his jobs is to test prototypes of clothing manufactured by Craghoppers. To do this, he uses the clothing on expeditions. Any problems with the clothing are then rectified before it is mass produced. Pratt's current goal is to be part of the team which completes the first alpine-style ascent of Kangchenjunga's North Face. Kangchenjunga is the third highest peak in the world.
Source: Craghoppers, 1997

1. What is a prototype?
2. What benefits does a prototype give to designers prior to manufacturing the product?
3. Suggest TWO ways in which the design of the mountain gear produced by Craghoppers might have to be altered following Jonathan Pratt's attempt to climb Kangchenjunga.

4. Make TWO concept drawings for the prototype of either:
   (i) a portable carrier for computer disks
   (ii) a bag which could be used by a mother with a new baby
   (iii) a swimming costume which keeps the wearer afloat.
   Annotate your drawings to show the differences between each design and how they would affect its use.

Figure 4 Market research can be used to evaluate consumers' reactions to designs.

information from market research can be collated and analysed using a database or spreadsheet.

Reviewing

It is not just the product which might be evaluated. The process of designing and making may also be evaluated in order to highlight problems or to emphasise good working practice. This type of evaluation is usually called REVIEWING.

Before a manufacturer makes a product, a schedule or plan for making will have been designed. This might be done by a single person who works out an order for making. It might be carried out as a pen and paper exercise. Alternatively, it might mean writing a computer programme for use in computer aided manufacture.

First, the product will be made on a 'dry run'. This will highlight any problems in the process. A number of dry runs might have to be carried out to test different parts of the process. For example, a new machine for weaving fabric might be checked out and the speed of manufacture altered. It is only by trying out the process that a manufacturer will find out how reliable it is. On the evidence gathered, problem areas can be highlighted and adjustments made in order to improve the process. This is called REFINING. For example, the time taken to

produce a batch of socks might be speeded up to see if more can be made in less time. Alternatively, the process might be slowed down in order to reduce wastage caused by damage to the products during production. The aim of many reviews of industrial manufacturing processes is to improve the efficiency of a system. If a system is not working as expected then alternative ways of making might be suggested. This may involve changing all or part of the process.

Some large companies have a whole department dedicated to product modification. Practical work in class, by necessity, is usually limited to prototyping work - with little opportunity to refine or start again. If the work was carried out again, however, valuable suggestions could be made

Figure 5 A calico prototype of the bodice for a wedding dress

as to how the process of making could be improved. This is called SYSTEM EVALUATION and can be carried out as follows:

1. Identify all stages in manufacturing (including design work).
2. Highlight problem areas (eg accuracy of making, available equipment, time taken for dyes to dry).
3. Explore how problems were resolved.
4. Suggest possible future improvements to the process.
5. Propose alternative ways of making the product with respect to certain criteria such as:
- using a different system (eg batch production or flow production)
- reducing cost
- improving quality
- improving health and safety.

Key Terms

Evaluation - a process used to make sure products match the targets set.
Criteria - value judgements by which products are evaluated.
Tolerance levels - maximum and minimum levels for each criterion set.
Constraints - limitations placed on a design by a customer.
Testing - investigations to discover the working properties of materials.
Trialling - trying out possible designs before making.
Market research - gathering information about products by asking for people's opinions.
Reviewing - evaluating the designing and making process.
Refining - making adjustments based on evaluation evidence.
System evaluation - finding ways of improving a production system.

activities

Safety Zone is a new company producing beachwear for young children. The main aim of the company is to produce fun clothing which children will wear to protect them from the sun's harmful rays. Before producing a catalogue, the company undertook some market research. Ann Falvey, the company's managing director, felt that this was vital to ensure that the items they were producing would sell.

1. What is market research?
2. Why did Safety Zone decide to do market research before producing their catalogue?
3. Who do you think the market research would be aimed at? Why?
4. Produce a set of questions the market researcher might have asked.

The sort of products that Safety Zone hope to sell.

What is quality?

A product may be said to have QUALITY when it has achieved a degree of excellence or a 'high grade'. To be of quality, a product must meet customers' expectations and specifications. Quality can also be seen in standards of customer care.

It is not only the quality of a finished item which is important. It is also necessary to consider:

● **the quality of design** - the ideas, drawings and plans for the product
● **the quality of a production process** - the methods used to manufacture and assemble the product.

By aiming for quality a company can hope to achieve a good reputation, good sales and customer loyalty. Quality can also save the company money by reducing waste and increasing efficiency during the production of goods. Further, it can increase profits. When judging the quality of a textile item, the following criteria might be used:

● the look of the item
● the fabric, yarns and components
● assembly
● fitness for purpose

Figure 1 High quality textile items

activities

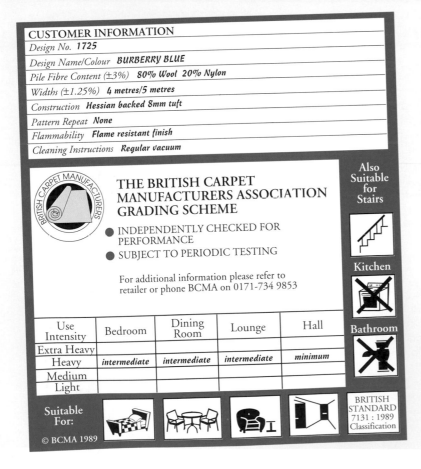

CUSTOMER INFORMATION

Design No.	1725
Design Name/Colour	BURBERRY BLUE
Pile Fibre Content (±3%)	80% Wool 20% Nylon
Widths (±1.25%)	4 metres/5 metres
Construction	Hessian backed 8mm tuft
Pattern Repeat	None
Flammability	Flame resistant finish
Cleaning Instructions	Regular vacuum

THE BRITISH CARPET MANUFACTURERS ASSOCIATION GRADING SCHEME

● INDEPENDENTLY CHECKED FOR PERFORMANCE
● SUBJECT TO PERIODIC TESTING

For additional information please refer to retailer or phone BCMA on 0171-734 9853

Also Suitable for Stairs

Kitchen

Bathroom

Use Intensity	Bedroom	Dining Room	Lounge	Hall
Extra Heavy				
Heavy	intermediate	intermediate	intermediate	minimum
Medium				
Light				

Suitable For:

BRITISH STANDARD 7131 : 1989 Classification

© BCMA 1989

The British Carpet Manufacturers' Association (BCMA) has produced a scheme for grading pile carpets according to quality and durability. In 1988 the British Standards Institution adopted this scheme and a British Standard (BS7131) was introduced. BS7131 has three domestic grades (grades 1-3) and three non-domestic grades (grades 2-4), making four grades in all - light, medium, heavy and extra heavy. The BCMA scheme allows customers to see whether a carpet meets the minimum, an intermediate or a higher rating within each of the four grades.
Source: BCMA, 1996

1. a) How do you judge the quality of a product? Brainstorm a list of at least SIX questions you might ask.

b) Choose a textile item you like and check it against the quality criteria you have drawn up. How does it perform?

2. Using the information above explain what it means if a carpet has BS7131 grade 4 on its label.

3. Explain how the BCMA scheme helps customers choose an appropriate carpet. Use examples to help explain your answer.

4. How does the BCMA scheme help carpet manufacturers to maintain quality?

- size
- value for money
- consistency
- safety
- energy efficiency
- packaging.

Measuring quality

When setting criteria to measure quality it is important to set a realistic standard. If a company sets a standard it cannot achieve, this could be counter-productive, producing more defects and taking up more time. The standard set should be the **optimum** (the best possible) for the skills of the workforce, the equipment and materials available.

Some small defects may not affect the smooth running of a production process. These minor faults can be taken into account by setting maximum and minimum levels (tolerance levels) for a product or its component parts. Tolerance levels are best established after the testing and trialling of an item. The more data available, the more reliable the limits will be.

A quality product is one which achieves the stated requirements, specification and set tolerances in areas such as:
- reliability
- durability
- safety
- strength
- size and shape
- appearance
- cost.

A quality product will be 'fit for the purpose' for which it was intended. When comparing two similar products, one may be said to be of higher quality if, for example, it lasts longer, has a better finish, has more useful components or is a better fit.

Methods used to evaluate quality include:
- quality control
- attribute analysis
- quality assurance.

Quality control

QUALITY CONTROL is a way of checking the quality of a product during or at the end of the production system. Raw materials, intermediate products and final products might all be tested and inspected to ensure that the production system is working correctly and efficiently and that the product itself is of a high enough standard.

During the production process procedures are set in place to check that the specifications are being met. For example, when items are being sewed together checks might be carried out to make sure that work of a consistent quality is being produced. Operators are helped to work to the required standards by clearly defined working methods and appropriate training. Quality control checks in the sewing department (stitching and seam allowances might be checked as might the density, length and tension of stitches for example) are an example of intermediate inspection. The final inspection would be concerned with the size, fit and overall

Figure 2 A quality control check in a factory producing nylon yarn

impression of the finished textile item.

In companies with a quality control department, specifications are set and used by the quality controller to make sure that the product is within the required tolerances. If, at any stage, the product is not within these limits, extra work may be necessary or the product or part of a product might be discarded and replaced. Extra work and replacing a product or

activities

1. Draw a flow chart showing the different stages in Classic Lace's production process and the points at which quality control checks are made.

2. What is the purpose of each of these checks?

3. Suppose you were responsible for quality control at a factory which received undyed cotton fabric and produced ready-to-wear shirts for large retailers. Describe the quality control checks that you would make at each stage of the production process.

Classic Lace is a manufacturer of lace edgings based in Nottingham. The factory converts nylon yarns into lace edgings used by manufacturers of lingerie, underwear and outerwear. Most patterns are designed by Classic Lace in conjunction with the customer. The output from the 24 knitting machines is roughly 3,100 kg per week. The yarn is brought in on cones in a natural colour. It is checked on delivery and then fed into the knitting machines. After being knitted, it is examined and either sent for dyeing and finishing or is sold in its undyed form. When the lace is dyed, it is checked to make sure that the shade meets customer requirements and then reeled onto cones. Quality control is the responsibility of the factory manager.
Source: Neville Shulton, Classic Lace, 1997

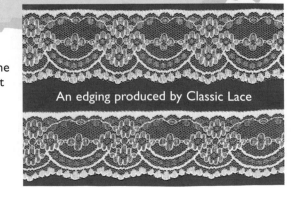

An edging produced by Classic Lace

part of a product cost a business both time and money.

Attribute analysis

Evaluation of quality need not be measured using quality control inspection or testing. It can be judged simply by the presence or absence of defects. This is called ATTRIBUTE ANALYSIS. For example, during manufacture:

- parts may be left off by accident or damaged
- parts may be assembled incorrectly
- features may not meet the required standard (for example, the colour of the dye might not be uniform or the seams might not be straight).

In batch or large volume manufacture, the quality of production can be calculated by working out the percentage of faulty goods. This is not possible with one-off products because unique goods are produced.

Quality assurance

When goods are sent out to customers the company gives its assurance that certain standards have been met in the following areas:

- the **product** meets its labelling and advertising claims, it is the correct size and it is safe to use
- **quality control** has been maintained throughout the manufacturing process
- **legal requirements** have been met.

QUALITY ASSURANCE is a way of working that involves a customer either directly or indirectly in the manufacturing process. During the design process, a detailed specification is produced using information from market research (see Unit 21). During the designing stage and sometimes during the manufacture, the customer might also be involved directly.

In addition to legislation and the guarantees offered by manufacturers, a number of CODES OF PRACTICE have been drawn up. These tell the customer that work has

been carried out to a certain standard and to the required specifications. Many countries have their own codes of practice and there are European and International codes as well.

Companies that carry a code of practice standard are checked regularly by external assessors. If procedures and instructions are not being followed then the company risks losing its code of practice.

Total quality management

Quality assurance is not just about inspection and testing. It is a way of working that requires everybody in a business to take responsibility for ensuring quality work. This is known as TOTAL QUALITY MANAGEMENT. Rather than waiting for somebody else to inspect or test that a job is being done correctly, the person doing the job carries out their own inspections. This leads to a more efficient business operation because people take pride in what they do and so defects and wastage are reduced.

activities

Jane French (right) set up Sure Foot Socks, a company which produces high quality socks of various designs. She employs 50 people. The design team devises the pattern, using their own ideas and market research. Each worker is given a pattern for the style and design of the sock and asked to produce a certain number of pairs in a given time. Each worker checks their own supplies (for example, of wool or wool/cotton yarn) and checks the finished product for loose threads or discrepancies in the pattern. Every pair is labelled with the individual's marker code so that customers can return faulty products to the actual makers of the socks.

1. What is the evidence that Sure Foot Socks operates a total quality management scheme?
2. Suggest THREE benefits to the company which result from this approach to quality.
3. a) What is the difference between quality control and quality assurance?
   b) Describe how Sure Foot Socks (i) controls and (ii) assures quality.

Quality symbols

There are a number of signs and symbols that are used by manufacturers to tell customers about product standards (see Table 1 and Figure 3). The British Standards Institution (BSI) is an independent organisation which operates in the field of standards, standardisation and quality assurance. The kitemark that accompanies some BSI products (see Table 1) tells the customer that the product has been tested to destruction, to ensure that it meets certain safety standards.

The CE mark is a European Union standard. Products with the mark have to have a technical file which tells how production standards have been maintained. This file can be checked at any time. Products with the mark are allowed to pass freely within the European Union. The CE mark is not, however, a measure of quality, safety or environmental protection.

Figure 3 Quality symbols used on textile items

Table 1 Examples of product standards		
Product	**Quality sign**	**Quality features**
Soft furnishings eg curtains, duvet covers, sofa covers	BSI Kitemark	Companies must ensure that their products are durable and can suffer a reasonable degree of surface abrasion before piling occurs.
Electronic sewing machines	BEAB approved	The product has been tested by BEAB (the British Electro-technical Approvals Board). It complies with UK legal requirements and meets an acceptable level of compliance with appropriate standards eg it is fitted with a moulded, fused plug.
Safety harnesses for yachts	BSI 4224	Shows that the BSI has checked the manufacturers', claims and the product complies with the standards used in yachting harnesses and ensures the tensile strength of the yarns used.
Flame retardant clothing	CEN	The fabric is produced using a process which gives fire retardant properties which meet the specifications set by the European Union.

The Lion Mark is a symbol of toy safety and quality. This symbol was developed by the British Toy and Hobby Association (BTHA) as a badge of membership for toy manufacturers (who must take out a licence with the BTHA). A manufacturer must sign a code of practice which includes toy safety matters, advertising standards and other matters (such as counterfeiting). Displaying the Lion Mark shows customers that products are up to the standard laid down by British Standard BSEN 71.

Other symbols of quality used in the textile industry include the Woolmark and Woolblendmark (awarded by the International Wool Secretariat), the Irish linen trademark, the silk seal and the International Cotton Emblem (see Figure 3).

Product safety

One of the criteria used when evaluating the quality of a product is whether it achieves safety requirements. It is important that every product is safe to use, but safety is particularly important for products to be used by young children. Ensuring that products are safe can be achieved in a number of ways:

- making sure that products do not contain toxic dyes or other dangerous chemicals or materials
- creating a design which does not incorporate components that could catch on something (for example, cords and toggles which could accidentally be pulled around the wearer's neck)
- testing designs to ensure that they are durable (for example, testing climbing rope to ensure it is strong and does not wear easily when rubbed against a rock face)
- ensuring that the size and shape of a design is safe (for example, make sure a toy is not too small to be swallowed)
- designing products with safety features (such as fastenings on parachutes).

The cost of quality

The cost of quality is made up of two parts - the cost of 'conformance' and the cost of 'non-conformance'. The cost of conformance is the cost of procedures which are necessary to run the quality assurance system and to ensure that faulty goods are never or seldom made. The cost of non-conformance is the cost which results from errors, faults, additional inspection, testing or repairing, unnecessary waste, the downgrading of faulty products, the return of faulty products, loss of good will and loss of a market opportunity.

The British Association of Toy Retailers (BATR) joined with the British Toy and Hobby Association (BTHA) in adapting the Lion Mark for use by retailers. The symbol displayed in the shop, in catalogues and in retailer advertising indicates that the retailer has agreed to the Code of Practice and, as such, is prepared to make strenuous efforts not only to offer safe toys for sale, but to ensure that management and staff are briefed on toy safety matters such as age warnings. Some, though not all, toys sold in these shops will carry the Lion Mark.
Source: Toy Safety Information Booklet for BATR Lion Mark Approved Retailers and their Staff, BATR, 1996

APPROVED LION MARK RETAILER

activities

1. What is meant by the Lion Mark?
2. What does the BATR sign (below left) tell customers about a toy shop?
3. British Standard BS5665 relates to safety standards for toys. Suggest THREE aspects of safety that manufacturers of toys made of textiles need to take into account.

Key Terms

Quality - a high grade or level of excellence.
Quality control - a way of checking the quality of a product during or at the end of the production system.
Attribute analysis - a way of evaluating quality by measuring the presence or absence of defects.
Quality assurance - guarantees made to the customer about the quality standards of a company.
Codes of practice - standards which indicate that the quality of production meets a certain level.
Total quality management - making quality the responsibility of everybody in the business.

case study THE WOOLMARK

PRODUCTION of wool is a large and very important industry. In 1995, total world wool production stood at 2,614 million kg of which 65 million kg was produced in Britain. British wool is exported to more than 50 countries. Items made of wool can carry two special labels which are issued by the International Wool Secretariat (IWS) - the Woolmark and the Woolblendmark. The Woolmark scheme covers a very wide range of products including clothing, carpets, home furnishings, blankets and hand knitting yarns. The Woolmark is recognised by more than 400 million consumers worldwide.

Before a manufacturer is allowed to use the Woolmark on their product, they must become a licensee - they must sign a licence agreement which covers all aspects of the Woolmark scheme and they must agree to apply the Woolmark only to those products which meet the performance requirements laid down in the specification.

The IWS judges whether Woolmark licensees are meeting standards. The IWS offers practical assistance to manufacturers. Product technologists visit licensees to check raw materials and factory records. IWS technologists take samples of products from the factory for testing and they purchase Woolmark products from retail outlets to make spot checks. The aim is to ensure that products are of sufficient quality to provide consumer satisfaction.

Quality of wool is determined mainly by fineness. Other considerations are staple lengths and colour. The most expensive wool is usually 15 microns or less and of extremely good colour (white), like the Merino sheep above. One micron is the equivalent of 0.001mm. This wool should have a long staple fibre and a high 'quality number'. The quality number is the buyer's estimate of fineness. Larger quality numbers indicate finer and therefore better quality wool. In wool processing, the diameter of fibres is the most important characteristic and so quality numbers are gradually being replaced by the measurement of the mean fibre diameter in microns.

The Woolmark is given to items made from Pure New Wool. These items must meet certain quality standards laid down by the IWS. The IWS's quality specifications cover not only fibre content but also other factors that affect the performance of products including the change of appearance in wear, durability and stability when the product is cleaned. The IWS introduced the Woolmark scheme in 1964. The symbol was designed by an Italian, Francesco Saroglia. The symbol had to be designed to be artistically acceptable as well as meeting the complex legal and technical requirements that would enable it to be used all over the world.

CERTIFICATION TRADE MARK
PURE NEW WOOL

Activities

CERTIFICATION TRADE MARK
WOOL RICH BLEND

The Woolblendmark was introduced in 1971. It is given to quality-tested goods that are rich in wool. This mark may be applied to clothing, carpets (but not rugs), upholstery, curtains and blankets. Woolblend products must have at least 60% new wool content except in the case of wool/cotton blends where the wool content may be 50%. All Woolblendmark products must meet quality specifications similar to those that apply to Woolmark products.

1. a) List FOUR products which might carry the Woolmark.
    b) What advantages does the Woolmark bring to consumers who purchase these products.
2. Describe the difference between items which carry the Woolmark and those which carry the Woolblendmark.
3. Explain how a manufacturer would qualify for a licence to use the Woolmark and explain the steps that the IWS would take to ensure the quality of the manufacturer's product.
4. a) When designing an international symbol a number of considerations need to be taken into account. Describe them.
    b) Produce designs for international symbols which show that: (i) a product has been hand made, (ii) a product has been made from recycled materials, and (iii) a product is safe for children.

This information is provided courtesy of the International Wool Secretariat (IWS). ® Woolmark and Woolblendmark symbols are IWS registered trademarks © IWS 1997

PROBAN AND QUALITY CONTROL

The NAMAS mark

PROBAN is a chemical which was first developed by Albright and Wilson Ltd in the 1950s. It is applied to fabric to provide it with a durable flame retardant finish. It can be used on cotton and other cotton blend fabrics and provides protection against injury from spark, flash, flame and molten metal splash. The earliest application of Proban-treated cotton was in children's nightwear. Today, Proban is used for protective clothing in a wide range of industries such as welding, metal cutting, foundries and electrical, oil and gas exploration and supply. Proban garments are also used in branches of the military, police and rescue services.

The Proban chemical is sold only to textile finishers who have entered into a Licence Agreement with Albright and Wilson Ltd, the owners of the Proban Trademark. This Licence Agreement requires that the licensee sends samples from each production run to the Proban quality control team. New licensees send one sample from every 500 metres of production. Once it is established that the licensee is proficient in Proban processing a set number of samples have to be submitted (see Table1). Samples must not be taken from the extreme ends of production runs or from within one metre from sewings. When submitted, all samples must be numbered so that the position within the production run is known. On reaching the Proban quality control team, the submitted samples are cut in half and both halves are coded. One half is stored for reference and the other is washed a set number of times prior to flame retardant testing (see Table 2). The tests for flammability depend on the final use of the fabric. For example, the general test (BS5483) examines the effect of a naked flame on the fabric. If samples fail to meet the required performance standard, the licensee has to reprocess the fabric. If the samples pass the set requirements, a Proban Test Certtificate is issued. After receiving a Proban Test Certificate, the licensee can apply for Proban labels which can then be sewn onto each garment made with that batch of fabric. The number of labels issued is limited to the number appropriate to the meterage of fabric used for the batch. If a fabric is given a treatment after the Proban treatment that may affect the flame retardant performance of the fabric (eg pigment printing), an Intermediate Test Certificate is issued. On completion of the additional treatment, samples of the fabric are resubmitted. If these samples pass, a Test Certificate is issued and labels can be supplied. The Proban quality control scheme is accredited (officially recognised) by the National Measurement Accreditation Service (NAMAS), ensuring that testing is carried out under strictly controlled conditions.

Clothing treated wtih Proban

Table 1 Number of samples required

Total fabric in run	Samples required
0-2,000 metres	One every 500 metres
2,000-10,000 metres	One every 1,000 metres
10,000+ metres	One every 2,000 metres

A sample from each dyed shade or print colourway forming part of the run must be submitted for a separate testing.

A Proban label

Table 2 Number of washes

Sample	Washes
UK protective clothing	50 at 93˚C
UK knitted articles	50 at 74˚C
Sheeting and blankets	200 at 74˚C
Curtains	50 at 74˚C
Mattresses	3 at 74˚C

This table shows the number of washes performed by Proban's quality control team before flammability tests are performed.

Activities

1. What is Proban? Why is it important to have strictly monitored quality control tests?

2. Why is it important that the Proban quality control scheme is accredited by NAMAS?

3 Draw a flow chart showing how the manufacturers of Proban ensure that products which use their treatment meet the required standards.

4. How can customers be sure that garments with the Proban label are of a consistent quality?

What is marketing?

When textile items have been designed and produced, the goods have to be sold. There is a great deal of competition between manufacturers and retailers to persuade consumers to buy their products. The way in which a manufacturer or retailer promotes their products is called MARKETING. Marketing can be defined as satisfying people's needs profitably. Marketing is not just about selling. It is about finding out what people want, producing products that people want, charging a suitable price, promoting products and selling them in a convenient place. The main ways of marketing a product are as follows:

- advertising
- packaging
- display
- research.

Advertising

Businesses need to communicate with their customers. PROMOTION is about:

- making customers aware that a product is for sale
- telling or explaining to customers what the product is
- making the customers aware of how the product will serve their needs
- persuading customers to buy a product for a first time or again.

Businesses have to decide how best to promote the products they make and sell.

Figure 1 This advert appeared in a company's annual report. One of the aims of the annual report is to attract new shareholders.

Should they advertise, for example, or should they use point of sale promotion? This decision involves weighing up the relative cost of each form of promotion and how best to target their potential customers. They also need to decide whether to organise the promotion themselves or to use an outside organisation like an advertising agency. Advertising agencies are businesses which specialise in organising the advertising of other businesses. J. Barbour & Sons Ltd, a company which produces high quality jackets, for example, uses the advertising agency Morris, Nicholson and Cartwright Ltd to organise its advertising campaigns.

Goods are advertised through the media. This includes:

- television, radio and cinema
- magazines
- national and local newspapers
- trade newspapers and journals (specialist publications aimed at businesses or

activities

Chicco Romantica. Stylish design and simplicity for ease of use.

Style on the outside, comfort and practicality for baby on the inside

CROMBIE

For further details please call: 0171 409 0220 or 0115

1. What image is the advertiser trying to create in the adverts above?

2. What sort of people is each advert designed to appeal to?

3. How might each advert encourage consumers to buy the product?

4. Choose a textile item and design an advert for it. Explain under the advert who it was targeted at and why.

workers in a particular industry)

- directories (including Yellow Pages and The Thomson Directory)
- posters and transport (eg billboards on the side of the road and adverts on buses and vans).

Different parts of the media are used to attract different groups of people. For example, a product aimed at young children might be advertised on television when children's programmes are being screened rather than late at night. In addition, the part of the media targeted determines the size of audience. For example, an advert seen at peak time on the television will be seen by millions of people. An advert placed in a specialist trade journal, on the other hand, might only be seen by a few thousand people.

As well as advertising new products, advertising companies also relaunch existing products - products that have been available for some time and, because they have been available, have become 'part of the furniture'. The image of a product may be changed to give it a new lease of life. For example, Brintons have been making and selling carpets for many years, but they have only recently started advertising. This has given their carpets a new lease of life (see Case Study on pp. 130-131).

All adverts are controlled and monitored by the Advertising Standards Authority (ASA). The ASA ensures that adverts comply with the rules laid down in the strict Code of Advertising Practice. This code is designed to make sure that adverts are not misleading or making false claims about the product.

Advertising is an essential but costly process. The high costs of promotion may mean that a new product does not make much of a profit initially. If, however, the product meets customers' needs and the advertising is effective, this will ensure that profits are made.

Packaging

Most goods are packaged. Packaging serves a variety of functions:
- protection
- providing information

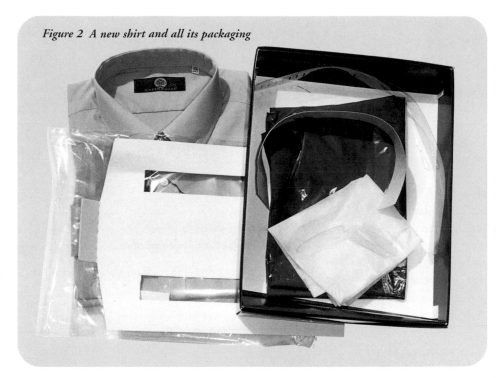

Figure 2 A new shirt and all its packaging

- promotion.

Often packaging serves more than one of these functions at the same time. For example, the polythene bag in which a sweater is wrapped protects the sweater from damage and, usually, information about the product (including the name of the manufacturer or retailer) is printed on it. The colour and design of the packaging need to reflect the image of the product. The packaging also needs to provide any information required by law.

The type of packaging used depends on the product, the use it is put to and the cost. Expensive textile items usually have more expensive packaging than cheap items.

Unlike food products, most textile items do not require very specialised forms of packaging. Usually, the main function of the packaging is to protect the item when it is being moved around. Many textile items are not packaged until they are bought and taken out of the shop. This is the case with fabrics bought off the roll and most clothing which is displayed in shops. When the item has been paid for, it is packaged in special wrapping if the fabric is delicate. Normally the item is then placed in a bag which displays the name of the retailer prominently.

Primary and secondary packaging

PRIMARY PACKAGING is the wrapper, box or bag in which the item is sold. There may be several layers of primary packaging (see Figure 2 above). SECONDARY PACKAGING is the extra packaging required for distribution, storage and movement - for example, a large number of textile items might be packed together in boxes while being transported from the factory to the warehouse and from the warehouse to the point of sale.

When assessing what type of packaging is most appropriate, several factors should be taken into account:
- the fragility of the product
- whether the product itself needs to be visible
- cost
- recyclability

Environmental issues

Many people are concerned about the environment. Consumers can help to protect the environment by choosing to buy products produced in an environmentally friendly way - for example, choosing to buy an unbleached cotton shirt. Manufacturers respond to consumer pressure and government pressure to produce products which are less harmful to the environment.

Manufacturers may be contributing to environmental problems by using products and processes which create pollution or use up more energy than is necessary. They may also use too much packaging on their products. This causes the following environmental problems:

● increased fuel costs in distribution
● extra domestic waste
● problems of collection, disposal and pollution.

With packaging, environmental groups say that the first concern should be to reduce the amount of waste created. This can be done by:

● using reusable shopping bags
● reusing plastic carrier bags rather than taking a new bag in each shop
● refusing extra unnecessary layers of packaging
● writing to manufacturers who have over-packaged their goods.

The second priority should be to reuse as much as possible and the third priority should be to recycle as much as possible. In addition, we can choose to buy recyclable goods or products in recycled packaging.

Displaying goods

The amount of goods sold can be greatly affected by the way in which they are displayed or shown to the public. If customers cannot see products properly, they are less likely to buy them. Retailers spend a great deal of time and money ensuring that their merchandise is displayed in a way which is appealing to the customer (see Figure 3). Depending on the type and size of the shop, textile items

Figure 3 Displaying textile items in a department store

activities

All shops display the products they are selling to encourage customers to buy them. Often shops use special lighting effects and the use of colour to create a mood or feeling. In-store music adds to the atmosphere. Research has shown that when customers are encouraged to stay in the shop for a longer time, sales increase because people make purchases they had not previously considered or planned ('impulse buying'). A relaxed atmosphere encourages customers to linger.

1. What techniques do retailers use to encourage people to enter their shop?

2. Once in the shop, what factors may make customers stay longer than they had intended?

3. What sort of atmosphere is created in the shop shown in the photos, right? Describe the factors which might lead to impulse buying in this shop.

Two views of the Oasis store in Birmingham

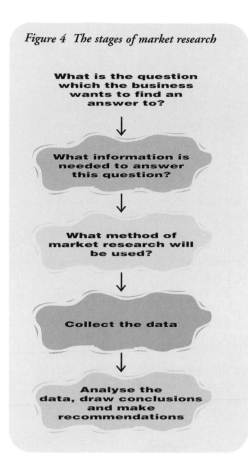

Figure 4 The stages of market research

What is the question which the business wants to find an answer to?

↓

What information is needed to answer this question?

↓

What method of market research will be used?

↓

Collect the data

↓

Analyse the data, draw conclusions and make recommendations

are displayed in windows or inside the shop near to where the stock is held. Window displays encourage customers to go into the shop. Once inside, goods which are well displayed encourage the customer to buy them. Often goods are grouped together by design or colour, aiming to tempt a customer to buy more than one item at a time. For example, a shirt and matching pair of trousers displayed together is likely to be purchased as a set.

Textile items, particularly clothes, are displayed with particular attention to the environment in the shop. Mannequins are often dressed in clothes and accessories to show how a whole outfit might look. Rooms are set up to display soft furnishings as they might look in a room at home. Lighting effects are utilised to show off a fabric's colour and texture.

Clothing is advertised and displayed by live models in fashion shows. When a fashion designer launches a new collection, models wear the clothes for the press, customers and other designers. This is a very exclusive way of advertising and displaying goods. A less exclusive way of displaying goods is to produce a catalogue. Catalogues are a very important means of selling textile items, especially clothes. Some companies have few or even no shops and sell most or all of their products by mail order direct to the customer.

Market research (see also Unit 21)

Each year thousands of new textile items are launched worldwide. Many are unsuccessful and production of them stops after a short while. A failed product means little profit or even losses for the company which produced it because the company has spent money developing the product, launching it and perhaps investing in new production facilities. Market research can help to minimise the risks when launching a new product. Figure 4 shows the process or stages of market research. Market research attempts to find the answers to questions a business might have about its market. For example, a company might want to find out if launching a new product would increase total sales of its products. The market researcher must then decide what information would help to answer this question. For example there might be a need for DESK RESEARCH (collecting existing information from other companies and from non-business sources such as newspapers, the government, trade associations and research organisations) as well as a need for FIELD RESEARCH (collecting information which nobody has collected before by undertaking direct investigation - for example asking potential customers about their needs and desires and finding out whether the new product fulfilled them). Once the information is collected, it is then analysed. The company then has to make a decision about what to do in light of the information thrown up by the market research. It might decide to launch the new product, for example, or to shelve it and invest in another project.

activities

Market research was carried out on a sample of 100 men aged 30-55. Each man was asked about buying and wearing ties. The results of the questionnaire are shown right.

37%
bought their own ties most of the time

27%
never buy ties

17%
bought ties for special occasions

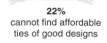
22%
cannot find affordable ties of good designs

6%
never wear ties

1. What conclusions can be drawn from the survey?

2. To make a good profit what sort of people should a shop selling ties aim to attract into the shop? How might it do this?

3. What use would the results of this survey be to somebody about to open a menswear shop? What other information might they need?

Key Terms

Marketing - the way in which a manufacturer or retailer promotes their products.
Promotion - communication between business and consumer.
Primary packaging - the wrapper, box or bag in which an item is sold.
Secondary packaging - extra packaging required for distribution, storage and movement.
Desk research - collecting existing information.
Field research - collecting information which nobody has collected before.

BRINTONS CARPETS

BRINTONS Limited was established in 1783 and today is one of Britain's largest privately owned companies. Brintons manufactures high quality woven Axminster and Wilton carpets for the UK residential market and for the UK and international contract markets.

For over 200 years, Brintons made no real effort to communicate with consumers. This was typical of the carpet industry. Little advertising was being used and most of what there was comprised of unimaginative room set photography. Brintons realised that an innovative advertising campaign would set the company apart from the crowd and make an impact on the public. As a result, the decision was made to launch a campaign. Initially, 17 advertising agencies were contacted. Six were selected for further discussion and then four were invited to produce detailed proposals. Cowan Kemsley Taylor (CKT), a London-based advertising agency, produced what Brintons later described as a 'breathtakingly innovative concept'. Through careful strategic planning and research, CKT identified that women are generally the decision makers when it comes to purchasing carpets. They decided that the campaign needed to generate feelings of style, elegance and beauty. A casual remark that Brintons carpets were 'good enough to wear' led to the idea of making elegant clothes out of carpet. CKT produced a rough cut, using students from the Royal College of Art to help with designs. The result was the production of simple garments from carpet samples. Although basic, the samples had a stunning impact and CKT were awarded the contract for the campaign in July 1993.

The first deadline for the campaign was the October issues of selected home interest magazines. To give Brintons added credibility, the company decided to use a top fashion designer. Vivienne Westwood is one of the UK's leading fashion gurus and winner of the British Designer of the Year award. She is also somebody known for her wit, style and commitment to quality. As such, Vivienne Westwood seemed the ideal choice.

Since July 1993, the Brintons advertising campaign has gone through three phases. The aims of the first phase were to:

- build Brintons as a brand name with UK retail consumers
- raise the profile of carpets as an interior design
- direct carpet purchasers to Brintons carpets
- make Brintons advertising stand out from the crowd
- target those who make the decisions when it comes to buying carpets
- promote style and elegance in carpets.

Five outfits and a pair of shoes were chosen from Vivienne Westwood's designs. Simonetta Gianflici was the model considered right for the target audience of ABC1 females aged 35 to 55. The adverts were placed in selected consumer magazines such as *Good Housekeeping, Homes and Gardens* and *Ideal Home*. A number of posters were also produced. An analysis of the campaign showed that it was reaching the target audience. Consumers were found to ask specifically for Brintons carpets. Unprompted brand recognition trebled during the campaign and prompted awareness increased by 100%.

Phase Two of the campaign began at the end of 1994 and aimed to build on the success of the first phase of the brand recognition

Phase I

Phase I

building exercise in the UK retail market. Vivienne Westwood was retained to design the new collection. This new collection had an 18th century theme, reflecting Westwood's major interest as well as coinciding with the era in which Brintons was established. Six garments were made to create the '1783 collection' which was launched in January 1995.

Phase Three was launched in 1996. The aim of this phase of the campaign was to keep the award-wining fashion campaign, but to combine it with carpet in a practical setting. The images created were those of carpet clothing which flows out into a room setting. The overall impression of the campaign is theatrical, sophisticated and witty. The campaign used four images - evening wear, outdoor wear, children's wear and leisure wear. Once again, the adverts were shown in selected home interest magazines (*Good Housekeeping*, *Homes & Gardens*, *House Beautiful*, *Ideal Home* and *World of Interiors*). The readership of these magazines is around seven million people. The adverts were also shown in major weekend titles (*Sunday Times magazine*, *Sunday Telegraph magazine*, *Radio Times*, *M&S magazine*, *Mail on Sunday* and *Expresso*). This raised the readership exposed to the campaign from seven to 24 million people.

Phase 2

Phase 3

Evening Wear
by **Brintons**

FOR CARPET DESIGNS
TO DELIGHT YOUR
FRIENDS WITH CALL

0800 505055

FOR A BROCHURE.

Activities

1. a) Why did Brintons decide to launch an advertising campaign?
   b) Describe the main aims of each phase of the campaign.
2. a) Where did Brintons decide to place their adverts?
   b) Why do you think these were considered to be the best places?
   c) What other media might have also been suitable for this product?
3. Why do you think the campaign went through three phases?
4. Draw a concept sketch for one of the adverts in the Brintons campaign. Explain what phase of the campaign it is best suited to.
5. What problems did those involved in the campaign have to overcome in order to produce the images seen on these two pages?

Units 20, 21 and 22 show that aesthetics, evaluation and quality are all factors which must be taken into account by a manufacturer of textile items. There is also a whole range of other factors that manufacturers must consider.

Environmental effects

The processes used to produce a design can affect the environment. It is possible to assess how environmentally friendly a product is by carrying out a 'cradle to the grave' analysis. This examines the effects of the extraction and processing of the raw materials, the production process itself and the disposal of the product when its useful life comes to an end.

Raw materials

It is not possible to extract raw materials without causing some damage to the environment. The destruction of the rainforests, for example, is important environmentally because rainforests help to remove carbon dioxide from the atmosphere and because they produce oxygen. Deforestation is thought to be contributing to global warming.

Careful management can limit the damage done to the environment when extracting raw materials. SUSTAINABLE FORESTRY, for example, can help minimise damage. Trees are grown from saplings, allowed to mature and then cut down. New trees are then planted

Figure 1 Drilling for oil

immediately to replace those felled. Since one new tree is planted for every tree felled and the young trees are left to mature, the forest is not destroyed. Another solution is selective felling where only certain trees are felled in an area.

Sustainable forestry and selective felling are of particular relevance to the production of regenerated fibres (see Unit 6). These fibres are derived from wood pulp. As a result, environmentalists have put pressure on manufacturers to ensure that the wood pulp they use comes from areas practising sustainable forestry or selective felling.

Natural fibres, on the other hand, are derived from plants and animals and are, therefore, replaceable and recyclable. So long as the crops and animals are managed carefully in an environmentally friendly way, the production of natural fibres should result in minimal damage to the environment.

All fabrics from natural sources (natural and regenerated fibres) are also biodegradable - when they have reached the end of their useful life, they decompose. This means that waste disposal is not a problem.

Synthetic fibres, on the other hand, are made from coal or oil. These are non-renewable resources and their extraction can cause significant environmental damage. Most synthetic fibres are not biodegradable and so

activities

Cotton is grown on more than 5% of the world's arable land and it accounts for 41.6% of all retail clothing sales. Nine developing countries rely on it for more than 25% of their foreign currency. Cotton growing uses a great deal of water and 60% of the world crop requires irrigation. Unless it is rotated, it will exhaust the soil and pollute ground water. Cotton accounts for around 25% of world sales of pesticides. The World Health Organisation estimates that cotton growing causes one million cases of acute pesticide poisoning each year and up to 20,000 deaths. Organic cotton is produced without chemicals. It is hand-picked, removing the need for chemical defoliants (which aid machine harvesting), and it is not treated with chemicals during spinning, weaving or knitting. In 1993, organic cotton in the USA accounted for 0.4% of the total crop.
Source: The Ethical Consumer, Issue 33 1994

1. How does large-scale production of cotton affect the environment?
2. a) What are the benefits and drawbacks of producing organic cotton?
   b) Why do you think so little organic cotton is produced?
3. a) Why do you think cotton is such a popular fibre?
   b) What steps could be taken to improve the environmental impact of large-scale cotton production?

Spraying pesticide onto cotton plants.

waste disposal is a problem. It should be noted, however, that new fibres have been developed in recent years which are made from recycled plastic (plastic is made from oil). Using recycled materials reduces the demand for the use of new raw materials.

Production problems

Raw materials have to be taken to mills where they are manufactured into yarns, fabrics and textile products. They may be carried by road, rail or ship. These methods of transport use fuel which adds to global pollution as exhaust fumes are emitted. Transportation can be kept to a minimum by producing goods near to raw material sites. Modern vehicles with efficient and clean-burning engines also help keep pollution to a minimum. Recycling may reduce the need for transportation, though the materials to be recycled themselves have to be transported.

Once at the mill, the production of textile items requires energy and may involve the use of toxic chemicals. Waste energy (usually heat) and waste products (such as chemical effluents) are produced and need to be disposed of. If wastes are discharged straight into the atmosphere, they may contribute to global warming.

Efficient production processes which use as little energy as possible are most environmentally friendly. Mass producers can reduce energy consumption by insulating buildings to reduce heating costs and by using microelectronic circuitry and operations which lower electrical energy demands. Recycling materials used in a production process (such as water or chemicals used in the manufacture of fibres or the application of finishes) can reduce costs and reduce the environmental impact of the process.

The life of a product

Some textile products are made to last while others are designed to survive only for a short period (see Figure 2). Tights and stockings may only be worn a few times before they ladder and have to be disposed of. Socks may be worn many times and

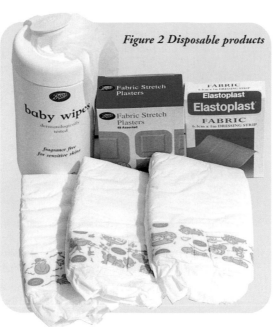

Figure 2 Disposable products

last for several years before wearing out. The longer a product lasts, the fewer new products that have to be made. Designing products to be long lasting reduces the amount of environmental damage caused by repetitive production.

When a product is designed deliberately to be used only once or a few times or is designed to wear out, this is known as PLANNED OBSOLESCENCE. By encouraging people to keep up to date with current trends, the fashion industry encourages people to change their clothing

Figure 3 A clothes bank

or household items before the end of their useful life.

Disposal

All textile products wear out over time. Many products are discarded as refuse and left to rot away naturally if they are biodegradable. The recycling of textile items, however, is becoming increasingly important. Worn-out clothes are collected by charities, shredded and used to make materials such as mattress fillings, insulation materials, carpet underfelt and washcloths. Most recycling points include clothes banks (see Figure 3).

Legal factors

As a product is designed and made, a number of legal considerations must be taken into account. These protect both the manufacturer and the consumer.

Patents

A manufacturer may have developed a totally new product. To prevent this being copied, it is possible to obtain a PATENT from the patent office in the UK. A patent prevents other companies from copying the invention for a period from the date of application. International patents which cover all countries can also be obtained A patent is only granted if the invention does exactly what the manufacturer claims it does. Patents are usually sought for new fibres or machinery and equipment used to process fibres and fabrics.

Logos

Many businesses have their own logos. These are emblems which may contain letters or the company name. They allow customers to distinguish one company and its products from another. Many companies register their logos and products as trademarks. This means patenting the logo or the name of the product so that others cannot copy it without permission.

Consumer legislation

A number of pieces of legislation exist to protect the consumer when buying textile items.

The **Trade Descriptions Act** makes it illegal to make false or misleading claims about products. It covers statements, adverts and labels that make false claims.

The **Weights and Measures Act** makes it illegal to sell goods which are underweight or short-measured.

The **Consumer Protection Act** aims to prevent the sale of harmful or defective goods. Injured people can sue the supplier.

The **Consumer Safety Act** provides government with the power to ban or regulate the sale of dangerous goods - for example, electrical equipment.

The **Sale of Goods Act** and the **Supply of Goods and Services Act** state that goods, when sold, must be of satisfactory quality and fit for the purpose as described.

Social, cultural and moral factors

To create a successful product, designers and manufacturers must take into account the fact that different people have different needs and different cultures have different values. It is important, therefore, to evaluate whether, and to what extent, a product will be accepted by a particular culture. For example, women in some Muslim countries wear clothing that is designed to cover their bodies. It would, therefore, be insulting (and impractical) to try to sell bikinis or mini skirts to such countries. Designers and manufacturers who wanted to sell women's clothing in such countries would need to design clothing which met the demands of this particular culture.

Different social groupings or age ranges also have different needs and values. For example, an elderly person with arthritic hands needs clothing that is easy to put on and take off. Most clothing is designed with a particular social group and age range in mind.

Sometimes it may be necessary to consider whether it is moral or ethical to produce a certain product. For example, in order to maximise profits and to keep labour costs to a minimum, clothing retailers buy clothes that have been assembled all over the world. This may include buying clothes that have been produced in sweatshops. Sweatshops are poorly equipped and unsafe working environments where workers are poorly paid and have no job security. Some retailers have a policy of refusing to trade with manufacturers who do not meet certain standards or who treat their workers badly.

Economic considerations

Businesses want to be successful. They want to provide people with the things they require. They want people to buy the products they manufacture. They want to make enough money to make a profit or at least to stay in business. To do this, businesses use several techniques.

Satisfying people's needs profitably is called 'marketing' (see Unit 23). Marketing is not just about selling. It is about finding out what people want, producing products that people

Figure 4 Trademarks

Tactel®

LYCRA® ONLY BY DUPONT

Scotchgard

B.S. 3120
PROBAN®
DURABLE FLAME-RETARDANT FINISH
HOT WASH WITH DETERGENT
DO NOT BOIL
NO SOAP OR SOAP POWDERS
NO HYPOCHLORITE BLEACH
DRY CLEANABLE

activities

Many workers in the clothing industry (especially in developing countries) are children or people forced to work in sweatshop working conditions. As part of its campaign against this, Oxfam's Clothes Code is challenging the top five UK clothing retailers to ensure that their sourcing guidelines are based on a code of conduct. The code of conduct calls for:

- freedom of association - eg being allowed to join a trade union
- equality of treatment
- wages that exceed or match the industry or legal minimum and which are paid in full on time
- working hours which do not exceed 48 hours per week
- acceptable health and safety standards
- security of employment
- social security provisions to cover sickness, injury and old age
- a ban on the employment of children under 14
- a ban on forced labour.

Oxfam encourages supporters to write to one of the top five retailers.

Source: Oxfam Clothes Code Campaign, 1997

Employees in this workshop in the Dominican Republic have no rights. They can be fired for being ill or not reaching their daily quota.

1. Why do you think Oxfam launched its Clothes Code Campaign?

2. How might the lives of workers in the clothing industry change if the Clothes Code Campaign is successful?

3. How might the Clothes Code affect the retailer?

4. What does the passage (above) tell us about the considerations that need to be taken into account when mass producing textile items?

want, charging a suitable price, promoting products and selling them in a convenient place (see Figure 5 and Unit 23).

To be COMMERCIALLY VIABLE over time, the costs of production need to be lower than the price charged for the product. The costs of production might include:

- the cost of raw materials or components
- the cost of mills, offices, machinery and equipment
- the salaries and pay of workers and management
- energy and transport costs.

A business can reduce costs in a number of ways. It can try to reduce the amount of waste material in production, for example, or it can organise the production process more efficiently.

It is possible to reduce the unit cost or AVERAGE COST of a product by increasing output. For example, a business might buy new equipment to make a product. If only one order is placed, the cost per unit of making one batch is much higher than the cost per unit of making many batches. This is because the cost of the machinery can be spread over a greater output. This is one reason why one-off products tend to be more expensive to produce than products made in batches. Mass producers have very high costs of equipment but can spread these costs over enormous production runs.

There may be a conflict between economic considerations and other factors. For example, it may be possible to reduce the costs of production by using cheaper fabrics or components, but this might affect the overall

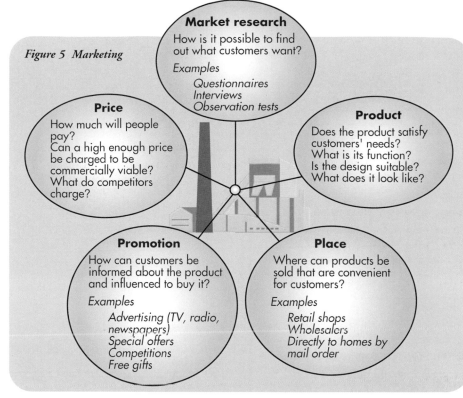

Figure 5 Marketing

Market research
How is it possible to find out what customers want?
Examples
Questionnaires
Interviews
Observation tests

Price
How much will people pay?
Can a high enough price be charged to be commercially viable?
What do competitors charge?

Product
Does the product satisfy customers' needs?
What is its function?
Is the design suitable?
What does it look like?

Promotion
How can customers be informed about the product and influenced to buy it?
Examples
Advertising (TV, radio, newspapers)
Special offers
Competitions
Free gifts

Place
Where can products be sold that are convenient for customers?
Examples
Retail shops
Wholesalers
Directly to homes by mail order

quality of the product. Production may be cheaper if a business can dump its waste products into rivers or the air, but this causes environmental damage. It may be cheaper to produce a single, standard product, but this does not take into account different tastes and the needs of different cultures and different social groups.

Key Terms

Sustainable forestry - continuous replacement of trees cut down for timber.
Planned obsolescence - designing products which will wear out.
Patent - a licence which prevents an invention being copied.
Commercially viable - where, over time, revenue from sales is greater than cost so that a profit is made.
Average cost - total production costs divided by the number of products made.

activities

McColl & Dawson are bespoke tailors who make suits for men. A personal template is made by the pattern cutter for each customer. This is done by hand and takes one day. The making of the suit, including fittings and adjustments, takes up to two days. The cost of a suit is £250, excluding fabric (which is an extra charge or is provided by the customer). In May 1997, McColl & Dawson received an order for five suits for the same person, to the same design and measurements. The master tailor estimated that the suits could be made in less time due to multiple cutting, fitting and the need to draft only one template. As a result the cost was reduced:
First suit = £250
Each subsequent suit = £175
Total price = £950
Cost of each suit = £195

1. Suggest FIVE costs McColl & Dawson will incur when making suits.
2. Suggest TWO reasons why the cost of producing suits has fallen with a multiple order.
3. Explain how the passage above provides an example of both job production and batch production.
4. Why is it more expensive to buy a suit from a bespoke tailor than one 'off the peg'?

unit

25 Health and safety

Importance of health and safety

Accidents that take place in a work environment not only cause discomfort, they can also lead to temporary or permanent injury and absence from work. In extreme cases, a person might be disabled or even killed. The prevention of injury in the workplace is therefore of paramount importance because it concerns people's wellbeing and health. It is also important to employers because:

● production suffers if somebody is sick or injured
● the temporary replacement of injured staff is an extra cost
● equipment repairs may have to be carried out
● equipment may be out of use until it has been checked and repaired
● an employer may have to pay legal costs and compensation.

Protection at work

The **Health and Safety at Work Act**, passed in 1974, has four main effects on health and safety in the workplace:

1. It imposes criminal liability on employers for failing to meet regulations.
2. It set up the Health and Safety Executive (HSE) to be responsible for checking that the Act is being followed. HSE and local authority inspectors visit work places to check that health and safety regulations are being met.
3. It gives employees the right to be represented on health and safety matters.
4. It places an obligation on workers to use safety equipment.

Figure 1 Part of a health and safety notice
Your employer has a duty under the law to ensure so far as is reasonably practicable, your health, safety and welfare at work.
In general, your employer's duties include:
• making your workplace safe and without risks to health;
• keeping dust, fume and noise under control;
• ensuring plant and machinery are safe and that safe systems of work are set and followed;
• ensuring articles and substances are moved, stored and used safely;
• providing adequate welfare facilities;
• giving you the information, instruction, training and supervision necessary for your health and safety.
Your employer must also:
• draw up a health and safety policy statement if there are five or more employees;
• provide free any protective clothing or equipment specifically required by health and safety law;
• report certain injuries, diseases and dangerous occurrences;
• provide adequate first aid facilities;
 As an employee, you have legal duties too - for example, taking reasonable care for your own health and safety and that of others who may be affected by what you do or do not do.

HSE
Health & Safety Executive

The **Workplace (Health, Safety and Welfare) Regulations**, which became law in 1992, conform with European Union regulations regarding health and safety. They also set out an Approved Code of Practice for employers.

The other main regulations that relate to health and safety in the workplace are as follows:

The **Management of Health and Safety at Work Regulations**, 1992, which relate to the implementation of health and safety arrangements.

The **Provision and Use of Work Equipment** Regulations, 1992, which relate to the safe use of equipment and machinery.

The **Personal Protective Equipment at Work Regulations**,1992, which relate to

activities

The Provision and Use of Work Equipment Regulations 1992 contain regulations applying to the safe use of work equipment. The term 'equipment' is used to cover:
• single machines - such as sewing machines
• tools - such as power shears
• any equipment assembled to work together - such as an assembly line to manufacture finished woven cloth from wool yarn.
 The regulations also state that equipment must only be used for operations for which they are suitable. This takes into account the internal integrity of the equipment, the place where it is being used and the purpose for which it is being used.

1. Suggest THREE examples of: (i) single machines, (ii) tools, (iii) equipment assembled to work together.
2. Choose TWO tools and suggest one task that might be suitable for using the tool and one task that would be unsuitable. Explain your answers.
3. What benefits does health and safety legislation bring employees?

protective clothing and equipment.

The **Health and Safety (Display Screen) Regulations**, 1992, which relate to workers using computer screens and the technical requirements of workstations.

The **Manual Handling Operations Regulations**, 1992, which relate to the transport and handling of loads by hand.

Risk assessment

The Health and Safety at Work Act requires businesses to make a RISK ASSESSMENT of their activities. The assessment should point out what must be done to ensure that all aspects of the working environment comply with health and safety legislation. An employer or person delegated by the employer (the health and safety officer) checks the working environment for possible risks and then puts into action procedures and/or equipment that will reduce risks for employees.

Risk assessment covers:
● the layout of the workshop or work area
● dust and fume extraction
● the use and storage of chemicals
● safety procedures for operating machinery.

The employer is also responsible for regular checks to ensure that standards are

Figure 2 Protection at work

Plastic/rubber gloves
(Sometimes disposable. Used for handling chemicals such as acids and alkalis)

Visor
(Eye and face protection)

Gauntlets
(Chainmail gauntlets can be used when cutting. Plastic gauntlets can be used when handling chemicals. Cloth gauntlets can be used for handling hot materials)

Steel capped shoes
(For general heavy work in workshops to protect toes)

Ear defenders
(Used when operating noisy machinery)

Overalls
(Increased protection for clothing)

Respirators and face masks
(Used with machinery and dyes that generate dust)

Hard Hat
(Used for head protection)

Safety wellingtons
(Used in slippery conditions and when handling chemicals)

Goggles
(Eye protection)

Apron
(General purpose protection of clothing. Leather aprons give heat protection)

Chemical suit and hood

maintained. The results of these checks must be displayed.

The work environment

The layout of the work area, whether it is the whole building, a room or a work station, needs to be organised to minimise risks. Areas should be designed for certain tasks and clearly identified as such. Storage sites, gangways (walkways) and traffic routes should also be clearly marked. Traffic routes should be kept clean and free from blockages. There are recognised colour codes for all these areas. Most factories place the markings as indelible lines on the floor.

Work areas should be big enough to accommodate comfortably the number of employees working there. They should have suitable lighting (natural, if possible), emergency lighting and ventilation. Temperatures should be reasonable inside buildings (at least 13°C where strenuous activity is carried out and at least 16°C where the majority of the work requires sitting or non-strenuous activity). Generally, the temperature should be warm or cool enough to provide comfort without the need for special clothing.

Safe working practices must be observed when using hand-held equipment. For example, internal injury from temporarily storing pins and needles in the mouth is

activities

Flat bed screen printing

Finishing dyed fabric - tentering cotton fabric (see also Unit 11)

1. Identify the possible health and safety hazards that might occur with the activities illustrated left.

2. Suggest what protection might be used to ensure that the task is carried out as safely as possible.

3. Which of the Health and Safety regulations relate to equipment and clothing? Why are these regulations necessary?

a hazard which can easily be avoided by providing the correct containers at the work station.

Dust and fume extraction

When working with dyestuffs and powdered chemicals used in finishing fabrics, dust and fumes are generated. These airborne dangers need to be removed from the atmosphere so that they are not inhaled. People who are responsible for mixing dyes or chemicals used to finish fabrics must take the following precautions:

- protective clothing should be worn - including goggles to cover the eyes and a filter mask over the mouth and nose
- work should be carried out in a well-ventilated environment
- any accidental exposure should be treated immediately
- instructions for mixing or reconstituting dyes and chemical finishes should always be followed.

Chemicals

Virtually all chemicals in a work environment provide some sort of danger.

Some are toxic (poisonous) if inhaled or swallowed. Others may be damaging to the eyes or they may burn skin or cause irritation. For example, sodium hydroxide, used to mercerise cotton fibres, will burn the skin if it splashes onto it.

The **Control of Substances Hazardous to Health (COSHH) Regulations**, 1994, form part of risk assessment. They require employers to assess risks arising from substances hazardous to health. They set out:

- the likely hazards of toxic, harmful, irritant and corrosive substances (for example, dyes, mordants, finishes and detergents)
- how these substances can be safely stored and handled
- how these substances are to be dealt with in the case of accidents.

Specific guidelines are set out by the HSE. These guidelines were written with the assistance of the Textiles Industry Advisory Committee (TEXIAC). The aim of TEXIAC is to help protect employees and others from hazards to their health and safety arising from work activity. Some dyes and chemicals are recognised as hazardous to health. Others are not. It is advised that all chemicals are used only when the following precautions are followed:

Figure 3 Safety signs

- work as cleanly as possible to protect everybody in the work area
- always read the label
- ask for information from the employer about exactly what chemicals are being used and how they should be handled safely (hazardous substances have a safety data sheet with them)
- wash hands thoroughly before eating or drinking
- wear the protective equipment provided and report any defects
- inform a GP if ill health is suffered as a result of working from dyes or chemicals.

Machinery

Instructions for the safe use of machinery should be clearly displayed beside the machine. They should be clear and precise to help the machinist operate the machine safely and efficiently. Warnings should be displayed to show the potential hazards of machines and any essential protective clothing to be worn. All machines should have an emergency shut-off button that operates properly and is clearly

marked. When not in use, machinery should be switched off, isolated and secured to avoid accidents. Employers must provide adequate health and safety training and retraining in the correct use of equipment.

Clothing that is worn while using equipment depends on the specifics of the machine. Usually, properly secured overalls should be worn since these have no loose ends which might become caught in the machine whilst it is operating. Loose clothing should be removed and long hair tied back. Goggles should be worn to protect eyes and ear defenders should be worn if the machinery is particularly loud or is used for any length of time. Any items to be used on a piece of machinery should be held securely using clamps or fixing bolts. Most machines have protective guards which should be in place prior to operation.

Machinery should be serviced regularly to make sure that it is working efficiently. Cutting blades and machine needles need to be sharp. A blunt blade may jam and cause serious problems for the operator. A service record should be kept for each piece of machinery. Faulty or broken machinery should be clearly labelled as such and put out of use.

Procedures

All working environments should have clearly displayed procedures for a number of eventualities. These are:
- fire drill - which includes orderly evacuation and the closing down of workshops
- guidelines for conduct in the work area - such as safe and proper behaviour and legal responsibilities
- general instructions in case of accidents - such as first aid procedures for limb injuries.

It is important that people in a work area are well acquainted with these procedures and have practice carrying them out.

First aid

All work areas should appoint a person to be in charge of first aid. Businesses with more than 50 employees must have somebody qualified in first aid. Workplaces should have a clearly marked and well stocked first aid box. Essential items are:
- a printed card listing contents and a leaflet providing advice
- individually wrapped sterile dressings
- sterile eye pads with attachments
- triangular bandages
- safety pins
- a selection of sterile, unmedicated wound dressings.

Some people are allergic to certain medicines (eg aspirin). In a business, medicines, tablets and creams should not be administered by the person in charge of first aid.

Cleanliness and waste

Work areas, rooms and equipment should be kept clean and tidy. Waste materials should not be allowed to accumulate and should be placed in appropriate waste disposal units.

All workplaces should appoint a person to be in charge of first aid and they should possess a clearly marked and well stocked first aid kit.

Floors and doorways should be cleaned regularly. Care must be taken that materials used for cleaning do not cause a hazard themselves - for example, if they are flammable, slippery or toxic. Cleaning materials are subject to COSHH Regulations 1994.

Waste should be disposed of in a suitable manner. Waste fabric and chemicals can sometimes be recycled. Otherwise, a supplier or waste disposal company should be contacted so that they can be disposed of legally.

activities

A worker employed by a company which manufactures children's clothing suffered a severe injury when her hand was cut by a band knife. The injury needed micro-surgery and the she was out of work for eight months. The accident occurred as the worker was cutting out pieces of fabric. An air cushion made the fabric move easily. The worker was not expecting the fabric to move so quickly and ran her hand into the blade. She had been employed by the company for about five weeks and had received virtually no instruction on how to use the band knife safely. She had only seen how to turn the knife on and off. She was asked to operate it because the normal operator was absent. The machine was in a poor state of repair and did not have a safety guard properly attached - as a result, the blade was completely exposed. The company was fined £6,000 for failing to train the operator and for inadequately guarding and maintaining the machine.
Source: Adapted from the HSE Newsletter, August 1994

1. What, according to the article, were the TWO main reasons for the accident?
2. Suggest ways in which the company might prevent a similar accident happening in the future.
3. A workshop producing children's clothes has four electric sewing machines. Fabric is cut by hand and then assembled by machine. Draw up a list of procedures that would need to be followed to ensure that the risk of injuries was minimised.

HALF of all fibres produced today are synthetic fibres manufactured from oil. Not only is oil a non-renewable resource, it is necessary to burn oil to produce synthetic fibres and this produces large quantities of carbon dioxide and other by-products which are harmful to the environment. Fibre manufacturers are aware of the environmental impact of the production of synthetic fibres and are constantly searching for environmentally-friendly alternatives. That is why Lyocell fibre was developed. Lyocell is a new type of solvent-spun cellulosic fibre produced by Courtaulds Fibres, one of the biggest fibre manufacturers in the world. Lyocell is used for technical textiles, non-wovens and special papers. When it is used in fashion garments, Lyocell is known as 'Tencel'. The first Tencel range of fashion garments was launched in 1992.

Lyocell has a number of advantages environmentally. First, the solvent spinning process is clean and simple. The only major raw materials are wood cellulose and water. Lyocell is spun using wood pulp from managed forests where replanting rates exceed usage. Second, the chemicals used in the spinning process are recycled. Wood pulp and amine oxide solution are mixed and heated until the cellulose dissolves. The clear solution that results is then extruded into a dilute solution of the amine oxide. This produces the fibre. The dilute amine oxide is purified and recycled simply by evaporating the excess water. Third, Lyocell production uses a non-toxic solvent which is recovered, purified and recycled as an integral part of the

manufacturing process. Fourth, waste products from the production process are minimal and not classified as harmful. Fifth, the process uses less energy, less water and less non-renewable resources than other processes. And sixth, products made from Lyocell can be recycled, incinerated, landfilled or digested in sewage. Indeed, in anaerobic digestion (digestion without oxygen) in a sewage farm, the fibre degrades completely in just eight days. In aerobic digestion (digestion with oxygen), in a landfill site, Lyocell is substantially broken down after four weeks.

Part of the Tencel range of fashion fabrics. Tencel is the name used for Lyocell in the fashion industry.

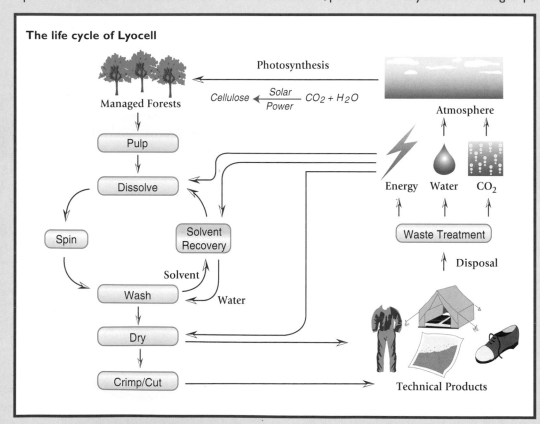

The life cycle of Lyocell

Managed Forests → Pulp → Dissolve → Spin → Wash → Dry → Crimp/Cut

Photosynthesis

Cellulose ← $\dfrac{Solar}{Power}$ ← $CO_2 + H_2O$

Atmosphere

Energy Water CO_2

Solvent Recovery

Solvent

Water

Waste Treatment

Disposal

Technical Products

Activities

1. Is Lyocell a natural, regenerated or synthetic fibre? Explain your answer.
2. Make a list of the factors which make Lyocell an environmentally-friendly fibre.
3. 'With Lyocell, pollution is minimised'. Using the information above, explain this statement.
4. Judging from the information on this page, what problems are caused by the production of fibres which are not environmentally friendly?
5. Write a newspaper article which considers the environmental problems caused by the textiles industry and how they might be overcome.

THE RUGMARK

This photo shows Paltan Ram and his son Madan Ram in the courtyard of their house in Kharondi village in India. Madan was rescued after two years of bonded labour in a carpet factory. He was kidnapped when he was eight and put to work without pay for 12 hours a day, seven days a week. His workplace was a dingy carpet shed with little ventilation and poor lighting. He was rescued by Mukti Pratishthan who had been asked by his father to look for him.

UNTIL recently there was no way of knowing whether or not carpets and rugs produced in South East Asia had been made by illegal child labour. The charity Christian Aid estimated that in 1994 the carpet industry employed 300,000 children in India, 200,000 in Nepal and 500,000 in Pakistan. Boys as young as six are known to have been bought or kidnapped and then forced to work long hours for little or no pay. Often their working conditions are appalling with little ventilation and poor lighting. By the time many child workers become adults, they suffer from poor eyesight and lung diseases (as a result of breathing in dust and fluff). A common tactic is for the loom-owner to give a cash advance to the parents and later to tell them that the cash was in fact a loan. They then claim that the cost of keeping the child has increased the debt. As a result, the child becomes 'debt-bonded' and tied to the loom indefinitely.

In September 1994, Indian and European campaign groups introduced a child-friendly labelling scheme called the 'Rugmark' which would ensure that child labour had not been used in the rug or carpet's manufacture. The aim of the scheme was to preserve the carpet industry in India but to force it to employ adults rather than children.

Indian carpet exporters wishing to use the Rugmark have to register their looms. The label carries a code enabling the carpet to be traced both to the exporter and to the specific loom. Spot checks are carried out on all registered looms. The scheme has been very successful. By March 1996, 10,000 out of the 90,000 looms in India with export licences had been registered. In July 1996, a similar scheme was set up in Nepal. By April 1997, more than 500,000 carpets labelled with the Rugmark had been exported to Germany. Both exporters and importers pay a fee for the Rugmark label. This fee is used to finance the scheme and to provide education and training facilities for children. In 1996, the Rugmark opened its first primary school/rehabilitation centre for children removed from carpet weaving.

Source: Ethical Consumer March/April 1996 and Anti-Slavery International, April 1997

RUGMARK

The Rugmark

How Rugmark monitoring works:
- Exporters in India or Nepal provide the Rugmark Foundation (RMF) with a list of their looms.
- Inspection begins on a random selection of the exporter's looms. Once 35% have been inspected without problems, the exporter is approved.
- Licensees with an order for Rugmarked carpets send a copy to RMF with a list of selected looms.
- RMF issues the labels.
- Inspection continues until 100% have been checked. Then random spot checks are made.

To guard against corruption:
- Inspectors work in pairs which are changed daily.
- Inspectors only find out which site they will visit when they receive their daily rota from Delhi.
- Inspectors are well paid.

Activities

1 Why was the Rugmark scheme introduced?
2. How does the Rugmark scheme work?
3. What effect do you think the use of child labour in South East Asia has on the British carpet industry? Explain your answer.
4. The UK is the third largest importer of Indian carpets but the Rugmark scheme has not been adopted in the UK. What could supporters of the Rugmark scheme do to encourage it to be adopted in the UK?
5. 'What counts is the price of a textile item in the shops not how and where it was produced.' Give arguments for and against this view.